BRADDOCK'S COMPLETE GUIDE TO
HORSE-RACE SELECTION AND BETTING

BRADDOCK'S COMPLETE GUIDE TO HORSE-RACE SELECTION AND BETTING

WITH STATISTICAL INFORMATION BY 'RACING POST'

Third Edition

PETER BRADDOCK

Longman Group UK Ltd
Longman Group UK Limited,
Longman House, Burnt Mill, Harlow,
Essex CM20 2JE, England
and Associated Companies throughout the world

© Longman Group 1983
© Longman Group UK Limited 1987, 1990

First published 1983
Second edition 1987
Third edition 1990

British Library Cataloguing in Publication Data
Braddock, Peter, *1930–*
    Braddock's complete guide to horse race selection and
    betting. – 3rd ed.
    1. Great Britain. Racehorses. Racing. Horse racing
    I. Title
    798.4′01′0941
    ISBN 0-582-06380-9

Set in 10/11 Linotron Bembo

Printed and bound in Great Britain
at the Bath Press, Avon

Betting, Backers and Bookmakers

'Never in the field of human endeavour
has so much been given
by so many
to so few'

CONTENTS

Foreword by Tony Stafford   xi

Acknowledgements   xiii

1   THE SELECTION PROCESS   1

   Form   2

   Fitness   2

   Class   2

   Conditions   3
      *Distance   Going   Weight   Courses   Draw   Jockeyship
      Sundry factors*

2   HORSE-RACING THROUGHOUT THE YEAR   5

   Flat racing – the season   5

   The Flat-race horse   6

   National Hunt racing – the season   7

   The National Hunt horse   8

3   TYPES OF RACE   11

   The types of 'level weight' race   11

   Flat races   12
      *Two-year-old level weight races   Three-year-old level weight races
      All-age (3 y.o. and upwards) condition races – over all
      distances*

   National Hunt Races   17
      *Novice hurdles   Condition hurdle races up to 2½m   Condition
      chases up to 3½m   Novice chases*

Handicaps   22
Types of handicap and principles   Nursery handicaps   Handicap chases   Handicap hurdles   Summary of handicaps

Comments on various types of race   28
The Classics   Early season Classic race trials   Selling races   Auction races Claiming races   Apprentice races/conditional jockeys races Amateur races   Hunter chases   National Hunt Flat races

4   TOOLS OF THE TRADE   36

Definitions   36
Workmanship   Materials   Tools

Details of the race   37
A daily newspaper   A daily racing newspaper

Details of form   45
The Form Book   Form sheets

A horse's biography   47

Tools for betting   49

5   BETTING   50

To win at betting   50
The modifying factors

Betting technique   51
The 'if'   The 'how' to bet   Single selection bet Staking systems

Odds   54
The three types of odds   Bookmaker's percentage   The right odds

Betting value hints   60
Tote odds   Staking   Accumulative staking

Summary of betting   63

Betting and bookmakers   64
Bookmaking   Bookmakers

6   THE SELECTION FORMULA ANALYSED: FORM   73

Grades of form   73

Proof of form   74

Date of form   75

Winning form   77

Changing form   78

Form commentaries   86

Form for age   90

National Hunt form   91

Handicap form   94

Collateral form   95

Time form   95
  Speed

Form ratings   98

Favourites' form   99

Summary of form   99

7   THE SELECTION FORMULA ANALYSED: FITNESS   101
Seven-day race fitness   104

'Fitness' by looks   108

8   THE SELECTION FORMULA ANALYSED: CLASS   114

9   THE SELECTION FORMULA ANALYSED: CONDITIONS   118
Distance   118

Going   120

Weight   122

Courses   129
  Flat racing   National Hunt

Types of obstacle   137

The draw   137

Jockeyship   139
  Apprentices and conditional jockeys
  Jockeys (Flat racing)   National Hunt jockeys

10   THE SELECTION FORMULA ANALYSED:
     SUNDRY POINTS   159
Blinkers and visors   159

Breeding   161

Trainers 165
Trainers' records

Owners 190

11 THE PRACTICAL APPROACH TO MAKING
A SELECTION 196

Selection of the race 196

Assessment of the race 196

Using the selection formula 197
Form – the keynote

The modalities: fitness, class, conditions 199
Fitness Class Conditions
Summary of star ratings

12 PRACTICAL EXAMPLES OF THE SELECTION
FORMULA AS APPLIED TO ACTUAL RACES 204

Flat race season 1989 205

National Hunt season 1988–89 228

13 CONCLUSION 250

SUMMARY 251

References 252

Further Reading 253

Index 254

FOREWORD

The millions of racing fans who either daily or weekly invest their pounds on the horses come in many shapes and sizes as do their bets. As someone who has lived with the betting ideal for two decades, it is easy to identify the born winners and born losers.

The race-track and the betting shop are a minefield through which the backer must move in order to survive. Either painful lessons are acted upon or the result is penury.

The borderline between the poorhouse and prosperity where gambling is concerned is a thin one. But the serious backer needs to discipline himself to avoid the obvious pitfalls.

I believe that over the years, as the wounds have healed, I have managed an *ad hoc* safety system. Peter Braddock, by contrast, in his *Guide to Horse-Race Selection and Betting*, has systematically laid down rules which he found helpful in his own considerable success as a selector of horses.

The size of the work should not scare the reader. Logic is the thread which runs through these pages; common sense and analytical care the criteria for employing his thoughts.

Only the serious person should apply. Racing success only comes to those willing to work at it. As Fred Hooper, breeder of the year for 1982 in the United States said at the Eclipse Awards in San Francisco in February 1983, 'People say I'm lucky, it's true, I'm very lucky. In fact, the harder I work, the luckier I get.'

I think that speech is the most appropriate sentence or two I could use to apply to Peter Braddock's *magnum opus*. Luck comes to those prepared to work for it. I can guarantee that from the minute I changed my own approach from that of the lazy guesser to the keen form student, the winners began to roll in.

While it might be inappropriate to add my own private coda to someone else's work, I feel I must.

Two rules I always follow. Never bet odds-on, though I realize that a 5–4 on chance with nothing to beat on the Braddock system could for others be a betting proposition *par excellence*.

Second, never be afraid to win too much. I have found that when a horse is a better price than your research tells you it should be, the appropriate action is to increase your bet. If much shorter than you think, either drastically reduce or even abandon it. You will find that even a winner below the expected odds causes little irritation to the disciplined backer.

But now I leave you in the capable hands of Peter Braddock, and his superb statistical tables. They will give you plenty of food for thought, and just the right mixture of awareness and dexterity to win the battle with the bookies.

Good luck, work hard and accept the rewards which will follow.

Tony Stafford
Racing Editor
Daily Telegraph

ACKNOWLEDGEMENTS

We are indebted to the following for permission to use copyright material:

The Jockey Club and Daily Mail for Figs 4.1, 4.2; The Jockey Club and Racing Post for Figs 4.5 and 4.6; The Jockey Club and The Sporting Life for Figs 4.3 and 4.4; Sporting Chronicle Publications Limited and Raceform Limited for Fig. 4.7; Timeform and Portway Press for Fig. 4.8, The Jockey Club and Racing Post and The Sporting Life for the racecards featured in Chapter 12, and Ed Byrne, George Selwyn, Alec Russell and Associated Sports Photographers, Leicester, for the photographs.

Cover photograph: by Associated Sports Photographers, Leicester.

1 THE SELECTION PROCESS

The aim of this book is simple – to promote the rational process of picking winners. It identifies the factors responsible for producing successful selection results encapsulating these elements in an easy-to-apply selection formula.

The principles of selection are simple, encompassing four basic issues: *Form, Fitness, Class, Conditions*, as a reliable framework to race assessment. The formula promotes the questioning of assumptions, the establishing of facts and encourages a development in the powers of logical reasoning. The book makes no claim to hold the key to an easy or instant fortune from betting. It does, however, provide a reliable framework for the thorough understanding of horse-racing. By this means and by the backer's own application to the task can the book-makers' advantage be nullified. Then, and only then, will a regular profit from horse-racing become a reality.

'To bet or not to bet', is the question facing every backer. Before every betting decision a vital factor – *choice* – distinguishes the attitude of the bettor from that of the punter. He alone decides whether or not to bet, and what, when and how to bet. The punter is oblivious of having a choice.

The bettor bets always with the sole purpose of winning money. It is an activity with a clearly defined and limited aim. Betting is a financial investment of the highest-risk money with the possibility of most lucrative returns. The bettor bets only when in his judgement the chances of winning are most favourable. It is always an act of free will in response to the merits of a situation.

The punter is a victim in the world of gambling. Allured by the prospect of winning money, but depressed, disheartened and disap-pointed at the actuality of losing, the punter gambles whenever he can no longer resist the temptation. It is never an impassive act, but always a response to retrieve past losses or fulfil a dream of having a big win.

In practice the backer is likely to fluctuate between the two approaches, more easily being drawn into the weak acts of the punter than the strong posture of the bettor.

1

Betting is a hard struggle in which only the most able survive. And so with this stern warning it must be left to the backer's own counsel to accept the challenge and decide whether 'To bet or not to bet'.

While there may be various methods of non-independently achieving successful selection results (ranging from 'informed tips' to a computerized evaluation of selection), it is intended here to provide the backer with an independent *selection method* that produces successful results. This selection method is encapsulated in a *selection formula*, which incorporates four cardinal principles – *Form, Fitness, Class* and *Conditions*.

FORM

Form is the major consideration in selection, with the other factors serving only as modifying agents. Form is the undisputable record of performance, a record of what a horse has or has not achieved, the sole means of reliably assessing and comparing *ability*. *Top-class form* is extremely reliable and evokes the statement: 'Form beats everything.' Form is the factor in selection which should never be underestimated.

FITNESS

This is the second element in the formula and is always likely to have a major influence on form. 'Peak race fitness' must never be assumed without some proof. The most reliable evidence that a horse is 'fit' will be indicated from a race performance within the previous 14 days. A horse should, however, not be automatically considered 'fit' because it has run within the previous 14 days if the quality of that performance is not up to a prescribed standard. Fitness is a balancing factor which can invalidate form.

CLASS

This is the third element of the formula, and can have a most powerful modifying influence on selection. In terms of horse-racing, class can be defined as the quality of competition a horse races against.

For selection purposes:

- A horse when raised in class has to improve upon its own ability and form.
- A horse in the same class has to reproduce form equivalent at least to what it has shown in that class.
- A horse lowered in class has merely to repeat its normal level of ability as shown in the higher class to have a winning chance.

Class, therefore, in selection assumes a negative, neutral or positive character.

CONDITIONS

This is the fourth and final element of the selection formula. Conditions will act as an important balancing mechanism in the selection decision when other factors appear equal. The conditions for consideration are: distance; going; weight; penalties; course; draw; jockeyship; sundry factors.

DISTANCE

A horse's ability to stay a distance cannot be accepted until proven by the test of a race. Most horses have only one distance at which they can produce their best form.

GOING

This is the term referring to ground conditions of the race-track. Most horses have a preference for a certain type of going and may be unable to produce their true form on other going.

WEIGHT

The more weight a horse carries the slower it will run – it is the leveller of ability. In handicaps the weight of horses is constantly being reassessed and changed to correspond to their performances.

Penalties of weight are given to horses after they have won a race. Weight conditions and penalties in a race must always be very seriously considered.

COURSES

Racecourses in the British Isles vary as much in size, shape, sharpness and stiffness in undulation as they do in location, and on National Hunt courses the fences that will be encountered also vary in size and stiffness. The peculiarity of courses produces course-specialists; whether a track suits a horse's style of racing and action may be an important consideration in certain instances.

DRAW – *(applies only to Flat Racing)*

The draw is the position across the racecourse where a horse is placed to start a race. The draw is mainly of significance in sprint races when there are large fields, and one side of the course gives a particular advantage to a horse. *The draw in these instances will be a distinct advantage* to a horse, often to the extent of completely nullifying the chances of a badly drawn horse.

JOCKEYSHIP

The performance of a quality jockey can be the difference between winning and losing a race. Jockeyship at all levels and types of racing is often the margin between victory and defeat.

SUNDRY FACTORS

These include the fitting of blinkers or a visor, which can have a devastating or detrimental effect on a horse's performance. A trainer's record and the stable's current form are also factors to be carefully noted; as are a horse's breeding and ownership.

This selection formula has been designed to make the process of selecting winners a more exact and less hazardous operation. It identifies the constantly important elements which affect the results of races. By careful formulation of the relevant factors and the orderly presentation of this vital information the selector can make logical selection decisions.

2 HORSE-RACING THROUGHOUT THE YEAR

Throughout the British Isles there are two major types of horse-racing: Flat racing and National Hunt racing. Flat racing principally concerns younger horses, and is ostensibly oriented to improve the speed qualities in the thoroughbred horse. National Hunt racing concerns older horses with an emphasis on qualities of strength and endurance as well as speed.

There are separate racing seasons for each type of racing. The Flat race season in the United Kingdom lasts approximately 8 months, beginning in late March and finishing in the early part of November, although the introduction of Flat racing on all-weather surfaces in autumn 1989 means a limited Flat race programme continues outside the recognized season. Meanwhile, the National Hunt season lasts approximately 10 months, starting in the first week in August and ending in the first week in June of the following year.

The Flat race season allows for the younger horses (colts and fillies still in a process of growth and development) and much affected by climatic conditions, to reach their natural physical peak during the more clement weather of late spring, summer and early autumn.

The National Hunt season in contrast, encounters the extremes of climatic conditions; meetings in midwinter may be cancelled due to the harshness of frost, snow or rain, while early in the National Hunt campaign, meetings may be cancelled due to the hard ground and equally dangerous conditions for racing.

FLAT RACING – THE SEASON

There are good-class (valuable) Flat races throughout the season, commencing with the competitive 1m Lincoln Handicap at Doncaster in March in the first week of the season and culminating with the equally competitive 1½m November Handicap in the last week. In between there is a carefully planned programme of racing, highlighted by the three Classic meetings of: the Guineas (at Newmarket in early May); the Derby (at Epsom in June); and the St Leger (at Doncaster in September). Similar competitive prestigious and valuable race meetings are held at: Ascot (in June) the Royal Meetings; at Goodwood (in July); and the York Festival in August. Many of the leading Flat-race stables focus their training schedule on these events, and are aided in a balanced programme of other races which serve as, and are often recognized as, trials for the major events. Throughout the Flat-race season, there will be opportunities for horses of all classes and preferences to find a race particular to their needs where they should be able to display their true ability.

THE FLAT-RACE HORSE

Flat racing and Flat-race horses are essentially concerned with *speed* – speed in races, and a demand for swift physical development, so a horse's abilities at racing may be quickly exploited resulting in many horses being quickly 'burnt out' after a few races and ensuring a short and sharp Flat-race career.

A Flat-race horse's racing life usually begins as a 2 y.o. All thoroughbred racehorses are given an official birthday of 1st January irrespective of what date in the year they are actually foaled – a horse foaled in February and a horse foaled in June will both be officially considered a year old on the 1st January of the following year when one is approximately 10 months old and the other 6 months old.

This can lead to considerable physical disparity in the horses in the early part of their lives, especially as 2-year-olds and this imbalance may not be properly resolved even later during their 3-year-old season at racing. A survey of the foaling dates for winning 2-year-olds during the 1988 season shows the advantage that relatively older horses have.

Month foaled	Wins	Runners	Percentage
January	40	390	10.3%
February	171	1,797	9.5%
March	281	2,782	10.1%
April	293	3,316	8.8%
May	110	1,695	6.5%
June	2	134	.7%
July	0	6	—

Most horses that begin racing as 2-year-olds end their Flat-racing lives by the time they are 5-year-olds. This is either due to injury, complete lack of ability, because they have been retired for breeding purposes (this happens to most fillies, and the best colts will stand as stallions), or more generally because their waning powers of speed means a generation of younger horses supersedes them.

- As a 2 y.o. a horse is physically immature (comparable to a child in human terms).
- As a 3 y.o. its maturity begins (ossification will begin to occur) and it is like a teenager becoming a young adult.
- At 4 years of age a horse is reaching its physical peak – and is usually considered to be at its prime for Flat racing.
- As a 5 y.o. a horse is fully mature – a colt is considered a horse and a filly is considered a mare – there will unlikely be further physical development which would aid a horse's Flat-race career.

Flat-racing has a rapidly and constantly changing population in horses as a new crop of 2-year-olds appear every season and replace other and older horses. The fortunes of most Flat-race stables revolve around their yearly intake of new fresh young horses from the sales and private studs. These horses arrive as unbroken yearlings, and each trainer has the often unenviable task of attempting to turn these raw recruits into efficient racing machines. The pressures on a trainer are likely to be high – many of these horses may represent a high financial investment by their owners who will get little or no return on their outlay unless these horses become winners. The risks, therefore, are great, but similarly the rewards to the successful will be enormous for top/good-class Flat-race horses have a considerable value at stud as potential brood mares and stallions.

It will be only the comparative few who are successful and whose future may seem pleasantly assured; the remainder are likely to encounter varying fates. Some will be sold to race abroad in racing of lower standard. Some will be sold out of racing altogether and some will enter a new career as novice National Hunt horses.

NATIONAL HUNT RACING – THE SEASON

The National Hunt season is long and protracted, lasting 10 months and encountering the best and worst extremes of weather conditions. Beginning at the height of summer in the first week of August, it slowly unfolds throughout the autumn, reaching a zenith of activity during the winter months of December, January and February (weather permitting).

The climax of the season comes in March with the 3-day Cheltenham

Festival meeting which serves as a championship decider for horses of all types (hurdlers/chasers, novices and experienced horses) over varying distances. Competition is extremely fierce, for not only are the best English horses contesting these most valuable and prestigious races but also the best of Irish horses as well. Irish-bred and trained National Hunt horses for many years have held sway over the British National Hunt scene, and each year they continue to display their influence by capturing a high proportion of races at the Festival meetings. The Aintree (Liverpool) meeting follows a few weeks later and includes the running of the Grand National. This meeting, held similarly over 3 days, signals the progressive slowing down of the National Hunt season during April and its culmination at the end of May.

Throughout the season there should have been opportunities and conditions to suit every type and class of horse, i.e. early and late season provides chances for the more moderate horses and those specializing on firm ground, while the bog-like conditions of winter should allow the heavy-going specialist chances to excel.

The better-class and champion horses will usually not be risked on anything but the best going, and this will certainly be found at some stage during the season. Good-class and valuable races are programmed throughout most of the season, but they tend not to commence until November, when public attention will be focused fully on National Hunt racing, as by this time the Flat season has ended. Many races will serve as trials in the build-up to the Cheltenham Festival, giving the public and trainers ample information upon which to assess ability.

THE NATIONAL HUNT HORSE

National Hunt racing is an extreme test of basic physical qualities in a horse – soundness, endurance and durability. Although speed and jumping ability are essential requirements of any winning performance, these talents will never be fully realized unless a horse is able to withstand the constant rigours inherent in this code of racing. The ever-present unpredictable element posed in a race by obstacles and injury conspires to make National Hunt racing a powerful leveller of horses and men. This ensures it retains its original sporting flavour, attracting its supporters (owners, etc.) from farming and hunting communities where there is an appreciation of the difficulties, uncertainties and patience required to bring a National Hunt horse to full racing maturity. Many successful National Hunt horses have been bred and reared by their owners whose sympathetic interest and involvement has made certain the horse be given unhurried consideration to establish a racing career. Success emanating from such an approach cannot be simply bought, and therefore this aspect of the National Hunt horse has no attraction for the business-orientated Flat-race entrepreneur of blood-stock who seeks a fast and assured return on investment.

While the racing life of a Flat-horse is likely to be short, by contrast the National Hunt horse avoiding serious injury may expect five or six seasons, involving a two-part career, first as a hurdler then as a chaser. The length of time a horse spends as a hurdler or chaser will be determined by the age at which it embarked on a National Hunt career and what was considered initially as its possible forte. A hurdler is considered to be at its peak at 6 or 7 years and a chaser is thought normally to be at the height of its powers at 9 or 10 years.

Horses taking part in National Hunt races have come into this type of racing from two different sources: ex-Flat-race horses and those horses bred primarily for National Hunt racing (often called 'store' horses). Ex-Flat horses with any ability at all are usually quickly able to learn the requirements of their new career and develop into efficient hurdlers. However, they tend to lack the physical scope and resilience that is necessary to become top-class chasers. The 'store-type horses' bred on more stoic lines whose long-term objective is to 'make up' into chasers develop more slowly, sometimes being unable to win a hurdle race before they achieve success as chasers. A horse's ability as a chaser may bear no resemblance to its ability as a hurdler (for better or worse) and it is therefore necessary to consider objectively the progress of a novice chaser.

All horses when first entering either mode of National Hunt racing are considered novices, novice hurdlers/novice chasers – and initially for their first season compete in novice events against similar horses. If a horse wins in its first season of National Hunt racing, it will no longer be considered a novice, and will graduate to handicap class in its second season. A horse that does not win can seasonally remain in the novice class until it achieves a success. Similarly, a horse – whether an unsuc-cessful novice hurdler or an experienced handicap hurdler or a pre-viously unraced National Hunt horse – when tried as a chaser will compete in the novice chase class.

A horse cannot compete in a National Hunt race until the August of its 3-year season, so officially it will be at least 3½ years old (and ossification will have taken place, or will be taking place in its development).

A 3 y.o. can usually only compete in juvenile hurdles against horses of the same age until it reaches its official fourth birthday at the turn of the year, midway through its first season. A horse may also not compete in chases until it is 4 years 8 months old (officially). This will occur in the August of its second season of racing.

Horses will vary in capacity and rate of development as National Hunt performers – learning how to jump quickly and accurately and gaining the physical strength necessary to endure the stress of National

Hunt racing will be factors comparable with speed in the make-up of a successful National Hunt horse. (This is why horses of moderate Flat-race ability can become stars at the winter race game for it requires different qualities.) National Hunt horses are generally geldings, because entire horses are usually less than inclined to maintain an interest in racing if certain sensitive parts of their anatomy are endangered – this means that a horse's future and value outside racing is limited. (Unsuccessful National Hunt horses will be sold out of racing altogether, as hunters or as potential point-to-point hunter-chasers.)

It is therefore necessary for a National Hunt horse to maintain and/or increase its value entirely from its participation in racing (this will be closely associated with its earning potential as a racehorse) and is best served by the consideration of its long-term rather than short-term future. National Hunt horses will normally be raced on this basis, and it is a factor that should always be carefully considered when making a selection.

3 TYPES OF RACE

The betting usually reflects the horses with the best form and the most probable chance of winning. Overall about a third of favourites are successful, so on a typical six-race card it can be expected that two will win. However, some types of race hold a better ratio than this and are likely to be more predictable.

This fundamental consideration places all races into two distinct categories:

1. *Level weight races.* Races where horses carry (basically) the *same* weights, irrespective of their ability.

   These are the more easily assessed as they entail only direct comparison of abilities. They are the most favourable type of race for selection.

2. *Handicaps.* Races where horses carry different weights according to their ability.

   These races are usually more difficult to assess as they involve more than mere comparison of ability. Therefore they should be contemplated only by the more experienced selector.

THE TYPES OF 'LEVEL WEIGHT' RACE

There are level weight races for horses of all ages, class and distance in both codes of racing (Flat/National Hunt).

There are acceptable variations in the literal interpretation of the term 'level weights'. These are:

1. *Sex allowance* (Flat racing). Colts, geldings and horses are expected to give fillies and mares a 5 lb* weight allowance to offset their expected physical superiority. (National Hunt racing.) Colts, horses and geldings give a weight concession of 5 lb to fillies and mares in all chases, hurdles and National Hunt Flat races.

   * *but* 3 lb for 3 y.o. + in Group races.

2. *Weight-for-age allowance* (applies to Flat and National Hunt). Horses of different ages racing against each other are set to carry different weights according to the time of year and distance of the race to take account of the maturity advantage. (See Tables 9.1 and 9.2.)

3. *Condition races* (Flat/National Hunt). Races where horses are set to carry weights solely in accord with the particular entry conditions of the race, and subject to sex and weight-for-age allowance should they apply.

The 'level weight' types of race most favoured for purposes of selection are, in order of preference and reliability:

Flat races
(i) 2 y.o. and 3 y.o. and condition races
(ii) 2 y.o. and 3 y.o. – maiden races

National Hunt
(i) Novice hurdles – condition hurdles
(ii) Condition chases
(iii) Novice chases

FLAT RACES

TWO-YEAR-OLD LEVEL WEIGHT RACES

There are two types of basically level weight race for 2-year-olds – condition races and maiden races.

Condition races are open to previous race winners with the allocation of weight set in the entry conditions and varying from the strict level weight principle. Maiden races, by contrast, are strictly level weight events except for sex allowance and limited to horses yet to win a race.

Two-year-old condition races which include all the major prizes for the juvenile generation are likely to be the more reliable selection medium with winning form holding a strong influence on the outcome. In the 1988 Flat season 46.1 per cent of 2 y.o. condition races were won by horses who won their previous race. Two-year-old maiden races, although less demanding to win, can be more problematic as many horses have no previous form. In the 1988 Flat season 37.4 per cent of 2 y.o. maiden races were won by horses making their racecourse début.

Two-year-old races are the most reliable type of races in which to make selections, for 2 y.o. horses usually run consistently, and there are fewer discrepancies in the evolution of form.

5f races – contested all season are races demanding pure speed.
6f races – are contested from mid–May onwards and are similarly focused towards the speed element.

TABLE 3.1   Winning favourites in races for 2 y.o. during 1988 Flat season

Distance	2 y.o. races Wins – runs	2 y.o. maidens Wins – runs	Total Wins – runs
5f	42 – 130 = 32.3%	56 – 157 = 35.7%	98 – 287 = 34.1%
6f	56 – 123 = 45.5%	55 – 135 = 40.7%	111 – 258 = 43.0%
7f	34 – 89 = 38.2%	32 – 85 = 37.6%	66 – 174 = 37.9%
8f	11 – 27 $\left.\right\}$ = 39.3%	13 – 35 $\left.\right\}$ = 35.1%	24 – 65 = 36.9%
9f	0 – 1	0 – 2	
Total	143 – 370 = 38.6%	156 – 414 = 37.7%	299 – 784 = 38.1%

7f races –   are contested from June onwards and while requiring a strong element of speed allow an opportunity for the horse bred to stay middle distances (1m 2f).

1m+ races –   are staged from August onwards. For a 2 y.o., even those bred to be stayers, 1m can be an extreme distance. Maiden races for 2 y.o. of 1m are not reliable mediums for making a selection. They are notoriously difficult races to assess as most horses competing have unproven form and are unproven over the distance, and many are horses which, having proved too slow over shorter distances, are being run in the final hope that their lack of speed was the strength of stamina in disguise.

THREE-YEAR-OLD LEVEL WEIGHT RACES

Three-year-old level weight races rival only 2 y.o. races in their reliability as good mediums for selection. Similar to the 2 y.o. level weight contests there are condition and maiden races. Of the two, 3 y.o. condition races are the better and will include some of the premier races in the calendar (e.g. the Classics, their trials, etc.) and range down in class to races formerly known as maidens at closing. Three-year-old condition races contested by good horses with proven and winning form are attractive vehicles for selection.

Maiden races attract horses of less ability. 'Maiden' is the term used to describe a horse that has not yet won a race. Yet 3 y.o. maiden races are a reliable type of race for selection. They are races designed for horses that did not win a race during their 2 y.o. season. The better-class 3 y.o. maiden races up until the end of July or August are good mediums for selection (a horse still a maiden after this time, except in special circumstances, is likely to be at best moderate).

These races can involve well-bred and potentially good horses that were backward as 2-year-olds and unable to be given serious race opportunities, but who are likely to develop and display their ability over longer distances as 3-year-olds.

There are three types of 3 y.o. level weight races:

(a) *Maiden races* – limited strictly to horses that have not won a race.

(b) *Graduation races* (formerly referred to as maidens at closing). These races are contested by both maidens and previous winners, allowing a winner of a race to continue in basically maiden company before graduating to more competitive races.

(c) *Condition races* – open to all horses allowed by the entry conditions which prescribe the weights. Will range from Pattern races to lower class races.

Overall, 3 y.o. level weight races are second only to 2 y.o. races as reliable mediums for selection. However, some races according to distance are better than others, and the selector is advised to become acquainted with and identify their characteristics (see Table 3.2).

5f, 6f (usually referred to as sprints)

The basic quality necessary to win races over these distances is speed and this is an attribute that is usually readily discernible, especially in condition races, where horses are likely to have prior winning form. It should be noted that the longer a 3 y.o. remains a maiden competing at sprint distances the more moderate it is likely to be. For most horses numerous opportunities occur to win as 2-year-olds over these distances.

7f

This is an in-between distance, neither a pure sprint nor a test of stamina. It is best regarded as a specialist distance and selection should be limited to proven performers in condition races rather than unproven maidens.

1m

The quality to win a 1m race will be one of some excellence, requiring a horse to have the speed to remain in contention throughout the race yet possess further acceleration within the final 2f to enable it to win. This calls for an almost perfect balance between speed and endurance exemplified in the demands of the first Classic races, the 1,000 and 2,000 Guineas. Mile condition races attracting good-class horses which have

TABLE 3.2 Winning favourites in races for 3 y.o. during 1988 Flat season

Distance	3 y.o. conditions races Winners – races	3 y.o. maidens Winners – races	Total Winners – races
5f 6f	3 – 10 12 – 41 } 15 – 51 = 29.4%	8 – 11 5 – 16 } 13 – 27 = 48.1%	28 – 78 = 35.9%
7f	10 – 34 = 29.4%	8 – 27 = 29.6%	18 – 61 = 29.5%
8f	23 – 72 = 31.9%	23 – 59 = 39.0%	46 – 131 = 35.1%
9f 10f 11f	7 – 14 19 – 70 0 – 5 } 26 – 89 = 29.2%	0 – 2 14 – 50 6 – 8 } 20 – 60 = 33.3%	46 – 149 = 30.9%
12f 13f 14f 15f 16f	31 – 49 — 0 – 6 1 – 3 2 – 2 } 34 – 60 = 56.7%	19 – 51 1 – 3 3 – 7 1 – 1 3 – 6 } 27 – 68 = 39.7%	61 – 128 = 47.6%
Total	108 – 306 = 35.3%	91 – 241 = 37.8%	199 – 547 = 36.4%

these desired qualities offer reliable selection opportunities, while 1m maiden races attracting unproven performers need to be approached more cautiously. The influence of American breeding on British racing during the 1980s with five winners of the 2,000 Guineas (1983–89) American bred has produced a general rise in standard of milers, and promises that these races should remain dependable se'ection mediums.

1m 1f–1m 3f

The attributes necessary to win races between 1m 1f and 1m 3f often referred to as middle distances) are not so readily definable for they are neither a test of pure speed nor a true test of stamina. Although some horses successful at these distances are specialist bred, many more are horses that have failed at other distances (i.e. horses bred for sprinting that have stayed longer distances and potential stayers that have won over shorter distances). As a result these events can prove less predictable and provide some unexpected outcomes.

1m 4f+

These are staying races and require that a horse has stamina to last out the longer distances. This is usually an easily discernible quality, making these reliable mediums for selection, especially in condition races. However, the extreme distances (1m 6f+) for maidens are likely to attract moderate horses who, it is hoped, will finally prove their forte in a test of stamina. These should be approached with caution.

Three-year-old races can therefore be approached on this broad basis of characteristic requirements according to distance.

Races for 3 y.o. maiden fillies are definitely to be approached with caution because fillies with promising 2 y.o. form often fail to 'train on'. Meanwhile many fillies train on at different speeds and consequently their form is not always consistent, resulting in unlikely and unexpected results.

ALL-AGE (3 Y.O. AND UPWARDS) CONDITION RACES – OVER ALL DISTANCES

These range in class from important Group races down to much less prestigious prizes which may give a horse badly treated in handicaps the chance to win a race against inferior horses at basically level weights. They are all suitable races for selection.

NATIONAL HUNT RACES

NOVICE HURDLES

Novice hurdles are always level weight races with concessions only for weight-for-age (when it applies), sex allowances and penalties for previous winners. Novice hurdles are the most reliable type of National Hunt races to consider for selection. They are usually contested by horses in their first season of National Hunt racing, but remain also open to any horse which had not in a previous season won a hurdle race (see Table 3.3). Although all National Hunt races (except National Hunt Flat races)★ require the jumping of obstacles – hurdles are smaller obstacles, the least encumbrant and therefore produce fewer fallers.

Novice hurdles are a reliable selection medium because horses of different and usually easily discernible abilities compete against each other at basically level weights.

All novice hurdles are run over a minimum distance of 2m and range in distance up to 3m approximately. The minimum age for any horse contesting a novice hurdle is as a 3 y.o. at the beginning of the National Hunt season in August, with these juveniles being considered 4-year-olds on their official birthday at the turn of the year midway through the season. There is no maximum age for horses competing in novice hurdles.

In consideration of age and distance for novice hurdles, 3 y.o./4 y.o. (juvenile novice hurdles) and 4 y.o. + (novice hurdles) stand almost on a par with each other in terms of reliability for selection.

Juvenile novice hurdles, broadly speaking, are contested by horses which have recently graduated to National Hunt racing from varyingly successful Flat race campaigns. Their National Hunt form will therefore be quite recent and demand no great scrutiny.

Novice hurdle races for older horses (4-year-olds+) tend to be contested by horses more specifically bred for the winter sport and whose ambitions as hurdlers are likely to be set within the long-term aims of their jumping career. Ex-Flat race horses do sometimes compete in these races after an unsuccessful first season as a juvenile hurdler or as an older ex-Flat-race recruit. The form of novice hurdlers for older horses sometimes appears more complex, as horses with considerable racing experience (albeit Flat race) may meet completely inexperienced newcomers to racing, while previous season novice hurdle form may have to be reconciled with the present season's performances.

Novice hurdle races over a distance of 2m are usually the most readily

---

★ Races run on National Hunt courses with the hurdles removed – limited to claiming jockeys and amateur riders and horses that have never competed in any flat races.

TABLE 3.3   (a) Novice hurdles during the 1988–89 National Hunt season, (b) Condition hurdles during the 1988–89 National Hunt season

(a) Novice hurdles

	2m–2m 2f	2m 3f–2m 5½f	2m 6f–3m	Total
Fav.	252 (42.1%)	44 (31.9%)	10 (19.2%)	306 = 38.8%
2nd fav.	123	32	15	170 = 21.5%
3rd fav.	73	21	9	103 = 13.1%
Non-fav.	151	41	18	210 = 26.6%
Total	599	138	52	789

(b) Condition hurdles

	2m–2m 2f	2m 3f–2m 5½f	2m 6f–3m+	Total
Fav.	48 (43.6%)	6 (26.1%)	1 (9.1%)	55 = 38.2%
2nd fav.	20	8	7	35 = 24.3%
3rd fav.	16	4	2	22 = 15.3%
Non-fav.	26	5	1	32 = 22.2%
Total	110	23	11	144

assessed as the speed element necessary to win them is fairly easy to recognize.

Novice hurdles in excess of 2m but only up to 2½m approximately are similarly reliable selection vehicles although often they take horses into unproven areas in regard to stamina, and thus need to be approached with caution.

NB Four-year-olds competing in 2½m novice hurdle races should be treated with *great caution* as this is an extreme distance for a young horse, who is likely to lack the strength and stamina to cope with twelve flights of hurdles over a distance of 20f, particularly should the ground be soft or heavy. Four-year-old novice hurdlers, however, do improve month by month with age when tackling 2½m hurdles and by the final month of the year and their official fifth birthday are likely to be on a par with older rivals.

2m 6f novice hurdles

This is a specialized distance for any class of horse and presents a number of selection problems. It is not a satisfactory distance for most horses but an intermediary stage for horses moving up from 2½ to 3 miles.

18

3m novice hurdles

These are likely to be difficult races for selection. There are not many such races in the calendar and the form in those that exist tends to be moderate or unreliable. These races are contested primarily by horses of slow maturing or decidedly moderate ability. It is hoped that the slow maturing types may 'make up' into chasers, but they often lack the technique or speed to be successful as hurdlers. Others, meanwhile, are entered in the vain hope they may have the strength of stamina to compensate for their proven non-ability over shorter distances. Results can therefore be unpredictable and this type of race *must not* be contemplated for the purpose of selection. (It should, however, be noted that horses with ability in these contests are likely to so easily overshadow their rivals that they may win a number or sequence of long-distance hurdles, but usually at increasingly unrewarding odds.)

CONDITION HURDLE RACES UP TO 2½m (4 Y.O. AND UPWARDS)

Basically level weight races with the only concessions being weight-for-age and sex allowance and any particular entry conditions, these types of races for selection are on a par of reliability with novice hurdles. They will include the Champion Hurdle and recognised trials.

Form is consistent, although top-class hurdle races may be competitive and provide a searching test for skilful selection.

CONDITION CHASES UP TO 3½m (5 Y.O. AND UPWARDS)

Basically level weight races with the only concessions being weight-for-age and sex allowance and any particular entry conditions. All chases require a horse to jump the larger obstacles provided in National Hunt racing. The size and concentration of fences can act as formidable hazards and may prevent horses who are jumping at racing speed from completing the course. This has therefore given rise to the assumption that all chases are hazardous ventures which should be avoided for selection purposes. However, this is *not* a fair assessment and experienced good-class horses are extremely reliable jumpers.

Thus condition chases may be considered a good medium for selection.

Horses of unequal ability will race against each other at basically level weights providing the test of selection to be a clear assessment of comparative ability.

The very top-class condition races will include the non-handicap races at the Cheltenham Festival and other races which will serve as trials for these. These races involve top-class experienced horses which are reliable and provide a fair test of the selector's skills (see Table 3.4).

TABLE 3.4   Condition chases during the 1988–89 National Hunt season

	2m–2m 2f	2m 3f–2m 5½f	2m 6f–3m+	Total
Fav.	5 (33.3%)	14 (40.0%)	12 (41.4%)	31 = 39.2%
2nd fav.	6	5	10	21 = 26.6%
3rd fav.	0	5	3	8 = 10.1%
Non-fav.	4	11	4	19 = 24.1%
Total	15	35	29	79

NOVICE CHASES

Novice chases are basically level weight races with the only concessions being weight-for-age and sex allowance and penalties for previous winners. They are restricted to horses which before the start of the National Hunt season had not won a steeplechase. Although contested by horses inexperienced over the more formidable obstacles, in certain instances these are acceptable races in which to make a selection.

Proficient jumping is the essential quality which wins novice chases – a horse that does not complete the course has no possibility of winning the race. The fear of horses falling (which has to be strongly considered) has dissuaded many astute judges from selection in novice chases. This view gains support from the fact that all novice chasers by their nature will be inexperienced jumpers of the larger obstacles and that some will have been put to chasing after their failure in other aspects of racing (Flat racing and hurdling). This type of horse can be clearly identified and *must be avoided*. However, accepting that novice chases are often principally contested by slow and indifferent jumpers, it then becomes obvious that these types of race often take very little ability to win. Therefore a horse of proven hurdling ability (i.e. a good–class handicap hurdler) if 'put to' chasing (providing it has been properly schooled and can adapt its jumping technique to fencing) will have too much speed and ability for the average slow-moving novice chasers.

Handicap hurdlers (of ability) set to chasing are horses that must always be strongly considered in selection of novice chasers.

2m–2¼m novice chases

These are usually the more attractive type of novice chase for the purpose of selection. They are contested frequently by horses with proven abilities in other spheres of racing (i.e. a previously successful hurdle or Flat race record) who from the speed aspect are therefore likely to outclass their rivals.

2m 3f–2m 5½f novice chases

Considered National Hunt's middle-distance races. This basically 2½m trip focuses on speed yet places a demand on stamina. Hence it is often a specialist or in-between distance that can be problematic.

2m 6f+ novice chases

Described as long-distance novice chases, these may be seen as less desirable mediums for selection because they are contested principally by horses of moderate or unproven ability who lack this aspect of speed. The accent in long-distance novice chases is that of stamina, strength and steady, proficient jumping, especially as there are many obstacles to negotiate. These races attract contestants either specifically bred for this task and whose career is focused on their development to become staying chasers, or else horses of mediocre ability whose lack of speed render longer-distance chases as their last hope for redemption. It can therefore often take little ability to win these races, being contested as they are usually by inexperienced or moderate horses. With recent results showing an above-average record for the most favoured horses in long-distance novice chases, this may suggest them to be attractive mediums. However, a closer examination and realization of the nature of these races (i.e. long-distance races, over many large obstacles, often contested in extremes of ground conditions by horses usually without sound credentials of form who are frequently offered at unattractive short odds) show these races in their truer perspective of holding many selection pitfalls and from a long-term betting viewpoint to be uneconomic (see Table 3.5).

TABLE 3.5　Novice chases during the 1988–89 National Hunt season

	2m–2m 2f	2m 3f–2m 5½f	2m 6f–3m+	Total
Fav.	85 (55.2%)	54 (39.4%)	74 (47.7%)	213 = 47.7%
2nd fav.	32	29	27	88 = 19.7%
3rd fav.	12	18	18	48 = 10.7%
Non-fav.	25	37	36	98 = 21.9%
Total	154	138	155	447

HANDICAPS

Handicap races can be full of enigmas and therefore it is usually difficult to predict their outcome. *They should be considered for serious purposes of selection only by the more experienced selector.*

It is, however, advisable to examine some of their aspects to gain a wider understanding and realize their context in racing. Handicaps are designed to give horses of different abilities an equal chance of winning the same race by carrying different amounts of weight. Weight is allotted to each horse in accordance with its abilities; the best horse(s) carrying most weight and the worst horse(s) least weight. Handicaps are compiled by an experienced handicapper appointed by the Jockey Club.

Handicap races exist for horses of all types, ages, classes and for all distances, for Flat races and for National Hunt. Official handicappers tend to specialize in either Flat races or National Hunt.

TYPES OF HANDICAP AND PRINCIPLES

Age

Handicap races restricted to 2-year-olds are called nursery handicaps and are staged from July onwards. Older horses compete throughout the whole season in either all-age handicaps or handicaps confined to horses of a certain age group (i.e. for 3-year-olds only; for 4-year-olds and upwards, etc.). In National Hunt races there are handicaps restricted to novices whilst others are unrestricted.

Class

From selling class to horses just below group class. In flat racing selling handicaps are restricted to horses rated 0–65 and the best class handicaps are for horses rated 0–115.

Distance

From a minimum 5f to the marathon 4m 865yd of the Grand National.

Horses become eligible for handicaps under the following conditions:
- Two-year-olds if they have been placed second, third or fourth in a race and run three times unless having won a race.
- Other horses – Flat and/or National Hunt – must have run in three races or have won one race. National Hunt horses wishing to run in handicaps, but who have not qualified, are given an automatic top weight.

Initially, a horse is handicapped on the best form which it has shown. To win from that allotted weight a horse must repeat and/or improve upon its best performance. A horse's form is constantly being reassessed by the handicapper, and where and when necessary the horse is rehandicapped, i.e. a horse that has improved on its best form and/or won a race since being originally handicapped is moved up the handicap and given increased weight.

Horses that no longer seem to be able to reproduce their best form from their current weight have their weight reduced and moved down the handicap.

If a horse wins a race and then runs again (in a race where it has been handicapped on its previous best form) it is usually required to carry a winner's weight penalty (appropriate to the value of the race won).

Weight is the great leveller of the abilities of horses, and this coupled with the change in abilities (improvement and deterioration) contrive to make handicap races the most difficult races to predict confidently. To be confident of winning a handicap requires that a horse is handicapped with a lower weight than is the true reflection of its ability. This situation occurs for a number of reasons:

1. A horse improving with and after every performance, yet can only be rehandicapped on what it has done; therefore it remains ahead of the handicapper.
2. A horse which has improved since its initial handicap assessment, and is better than its current handicap mark.
3. A horse that has been lowered in the handicap from its initial assessment, but has still retained the ability of its appropriate original handicap weight.

These occurrences, especially when a horse is considered remarkably leniently handicapped, are known as a 'blot in the handicap' – they occur very rarely as seldom does the handicapper make serious errors in judgement.

Deliberately losing a horse's form has long been a device used to gain a handicapped horse's winning opportunity. Before the horse is considered 'a good thing' it must be considered that similar conditions of legitimate improvement or malpractice apply equally to other horses in the race.

The consideration of these issues further complicates the difficulties and contrary elements which are present in handicaps.

Horses handicapped for Flat racing are rated by the official Jockey Club handicappers on a scale from 0 (the lowest) to 140 in steps of 1 lb, and in National Hunt from 0 to 175. Thus, a horse rated 70 is thought to be 2 st better than a horse rated 42. Because the normal weight range in Flat handicaps is from 7 st 7 lb to 10 st, handicap races are graded to confine them to horses of broadly similar ability. A handicap of grade 0 to 90 (0.90) would therefore not be open to horses rated above 90.

The scale of grades for Flat racing handicaps covering all distances are: 0.65, 0.70, 0.75, 0.90, 0.100, 0.110, 0.115. A horse rated above 115 is ineligible to run in a handicap. As horses improve they may be raised in class in accordance with their rating, and if they deteriorate are then lowered. The range of handicaps allows for a horse rated at 65 to be given top weight in a 0.65 handicap yet a low weight in a top-class (0.100) handicap. A guiding rule to handicaps is – *The best horse on proven form is the top weight.* (If in doubt select the top weight.) Although a horse will not be top weighted without having shown some performances of merit, it is rather too sweeping a statement without consideration of other factors. These include:

1. Is the top weight clearly top weighted, i.e. having to give 7 lb, 14 lb, 21 lb to the second and third weight horses, or is the difference merely 1 lb, 2 lb or 3 lb in which case the difference of ability is likely to be negligible? If the horse is clearly top weighted, are the conditions favourable to concede the weight (its current form, fitness, going, distance and jockey)? It must then be considered how the horse has achieved top weight in the particular handicap.
2. Has the horse been promoted to top weight on the evidence of its most recent performances (i.e. an automatic weight penalty for winning or recent regrading as top weight as the resulting assessment of recent performances)? To defy this newly incurred top weight a horse must be capable of further improvement – only the horse that is constantly improving and thereby keeping just ahead of the handicapper's rating can overcome the weight burden.
3. Has the horse top weight because it has been lowered in grade (i.e. a horse rated 75 – previously carrying low weights in 0.100 handicaps, dropped in grade 0.75 and required to carry top weight)?
4. The size and conformation of the horse will be a factor, some horses running better with lighter burdens against good-class opponents while others perform better carrying heavy weights against inferior opponents.
5. Ground conditions will similarly have great influence. It is more difficult for horses to carry big weights on soft or heavy ground because the weight has a more telling effect when conditions are testing. Conversely, when the ground is firm weight matters less and top weights are more likely to prevail.
6. If a horse remains top weight (without being downgraded) yet has no recent winning form, the handicapper in this instance still considers there is not enough evidence to constitute a lower rehandicapping of the horse. This may be because the horse has had an absence from racing, but is handicapped on its very best old form and therefore has had no recent opportunity to show whether its current ability still warrants its previously assessed handicap weight. Alternatively the horse may be readily holding its form but not

making the necessary improvement to better it. In these circumstances, to gain a winning opportunity, the top weight must have the horses below handicapped to the limit of their ability and capable of no further improvement.

7. To win a handicap a horse must be on a weight level that is most favourable to its current fitness, form and ability.

It may be necessary because of the intricacy of handicap form to specialize in particular handicaps, in respect of their distances:

5f/6f – 3 y.o. – all age
7f/1m 1f – 3 y.o. – all age
1m 2f/1m 5f – 3 y.o. – all age
1m 6f+ 3 y.o. – all age

Similarly, National Hunt racing:

2m hurdle – ¾ y.o. – all age
2½m hurdle – 2m 7f – 4 y.o. – all age
3m+ hurdle – all age
2m chase
2½m chase
3m+ chase

The selector will then become familiar with the particular value of form, a task almost impossible to someone trying to understand every type of race. Even the Jockey Club's official handicappers specialize according to age and distance.

NURSERY HANDICAPS

Nursery handicaps are handicaps exclusively for the 2 y.o. and are not staged until the middle of July. Form is always recent, the oldest form even by October will not be more than 6 months old. Form of the top-weighted horses tends to work out consistently, although late-season (late October and November) horses that have had a hard season and reached the top of the handicap can become jaded. Opportunities then arise for lighter-weight opponents who appreciate the softer ground conditions.

The success of top-weighted 2-year-olds in nursery and penalized 2-year-olds generally, has given credence to the assumption that all 2-year-olds must be good weight carriers. This has no particular truth, although 2-year-olds (in company with other horses) that win races and gain top weight in handicaps or penalties in stakes races are invariably the fastest, strongest and healthiest. They tend to have the best conformation, and are thus able to withstand the rigours of racing better than their peers and produce good consistent form.

The 5f–6f nurseries normally see a good display from the top-weighted horses. Races over these distances have been available for contention from the beginning or early season, giving an opportunity to most horses if good enough. The variances occur in races over 7f–1m, these races being staged for the first time later in the season.

Often, horses handicapped on their form over shorter distances are unable to reproduce it over longer distances while other horses improve considerably over longer distances.

HANDICAP CHASES

Like all chases, handicaps are won primarily due to jumping ability. They are seldom run at full racing pace from start to finish yet place a prerequisite on fast, accurate jumping especially as the pace quickens in the later stages; consequently weight is of less account.

The horses who have reached the top of the handicap possess this ability, while the horses lower down the handicap tend to be poor, slow and/or erratic jumpers. Dependable jumping ability always gives a horse a possibility of winning, because if a horse does not complete the course it has no possibility of winning (see page 84).

The best horses are those at the top of the handicap, and in many instances they can be clearly seen to have a winning chance, the modifying factors being:

Current form (does it merit handicap weight?)

Fitness (is there proof of current fitness?)

Going (are conditions favourable? – weight is a greater burden to concede on heavy or soft going)

TABLE 3.6   Handicap chases during the 1988–89 National Hunt season

	2m–2m 2f	2m 3f–2m 5½f	2m 6f–3m+	Total
Fav.	82 (33.7%)	54 (27.0%)	113 (34.3%)	249 = 32.3%
2nd fav.	57	58	70	185 = 24.0%
3rd fav.	46	33	58	137 = 17.7%
Non-fav.	58	55	88	201 = 26.0%
Total	243	200	329	772

HANDICAP HURDLES

Handicap hurdles are usually run at a good racing pace throughout, demanding quick accurate jumping plus a fair degree of acceleration in the closing stages. The fastest and best horses obviously get promoted to the upper part of the handicap. In the shorter-distance races carrying higher weights holds no particular disadvantage but in the longer-distance races, also run at a fast pace, extra weight becomes a more gruelling test. A general below-average record of favourites and high success rate of outsiders, shows handicap hurdle results to be difficult to predict.

TABLE 3.7   Handicap hurdles during the 1988–89 National Hunt season

	2m–2m 2f	2m 3f–2m 5½f	2m 6f–3m+	Total
Fav.	109 (28.3%)	49 (26.3%)	40 (27.7%)	198 = 27.7%
2nd fav.	82	36	19	137 = 19.2%
3rd fav.	47	22	24	93 = 13.0%
Non-fav.	147	79	61	287 = 40.1%
Total	385	186	144	715

SUMMARY OF HANDICAPS

Handicaps are designed to be competitive. The handicapper has sought to nullify the different abilities of horses by allowing each a weight in accordance with its abilities. Horses are then considered to have an equal chance of winning, weight being the great leveller of ability. Sufficient weight will defeat any horse and this constant consideration places a fine balance of judgement in selection and assessment of any handicap.

Handicaps on the Flat and National Hunt racing are popular spectacles, usually providing nail-biting finishes for excited punters, as frantic whip-waving jockeys are seen to drive their horses towards the winning post in a frenzy of action and colour.

Bookmakers often sponsor the more competitive types of handicap quite substantially, gaining business prestige and publicity in the process. Races of such a competitive nature enable the bookmakers to make a 'nice round book' (this means they show a very good profit whoever wins) beguiling the naive punter with generous odds.

The willingness of bookmakers to involve themselves in the sponsorship of handicaps must confirm to the selector that 'Handicaps can't be all good'.

COMMENTS ON VARIOUS TYPES OF RACE

THE CLASSICS (FLAT–LEVEL WEIGHTS + SEX ALLOWANCE)

The Classics are the top races for 3 y.o. colts and fillies. There are five Classic races programmed to take place throughout the season:

2,000* and 1,000 Guineas, for colts and fillies respectively, run at Newmarket over a distance of 1m in the spring.

Derby* and Oaks, for colts and fillies respectively, run at Epsom over a distance of 1½m in June.

St Leger, a race open to and regularly contested by both colts and fillies run over a distance of 1¾m at Doncaster in September.

The five Classic races are the Blue Riband events of the Flat race season; they are a stern and true test of ability, the most prestigious and among the most valuable in prize money of any events in the racing calendar. Only the best horses compete in the Classics, they are usually trained by the best trainers and ridden by the best jockeys and are therefore always fiercely competitive races. The challenge to selection in these events is to select the very best from the best – a daunting task – when

- the size of the field may be large;
- most of the runners will have at least a semblance of a chance of winning;
- each horse will be at peak fitness (time in preparation will not be spared).

The main point in favour of selection in such circumstances is that it will be made of top-class horses who reliably hold their form and can consistently reproduce their best performances. A note of caution, however, must be exercised in the consideration of form especially for the first two Classics (1,000 and 2,000 Guineas).

Form for the two early Classics will be based on two sources, the previous seasons 2 y.o. form (which will normally be over distances short of a mile) and the early season Classic trials; both require careful examination because their face value often proves deceptive and unreliable.

2 y.o. form in the consideration of 3 y.o. Classic contenders

Some horses vastly improve from their 2 y.o. days as they gain strength and maturity, while other more precocious individuals fail to develop further. This seems particularly to apply to fillies who were 'flying

* It is worth noting that although fillies are eligible they rarely take part.

machines' as 2-year-olds over distances of 5f, 6f or 7f but fail to 'train on' as 3-year-olds and truly stay the distance of 1m.

EARLY SEASON CLASSIC RACE TRIALS

The early season trials in April often involve only partially fit horses on soft going and this form may be reversed as other horses obtain peak fitness and race on the normally fast dry ground of Newmarket Heath on Guineas days. Unless an unchallenged contender emerges with outstanding proven form – the first two Classics are likely to produce results which are difficult to forecast.

The Derby and Oaks pose other problems in selection. In June, Flat race form will have begun to be settled and the Classic trials will have produced a number of contenders for the premier Flat race crowns. The two major factors which consistently emerge as being responsible for a horse's failure at Epsom are: (i) its inability to stay the distance; (ii) the inability to act on the gradients and undulations of the course. Horses with the latter characteristic completely fail to negotiate the steep climbs, uphill and downhill gradients and the bends, while horses of speed with unproven stamina tire quickly in the last 2½–3f of the race. Another factor which only to a slightly lesser extent spoils a horse's chances is temperament – a horse becoming upset and overwrought before the race in the preliminaries in response to the noise and size of the crowd (100,000 people) thronging the course and downs.

The Derby and Oaks normally produce winners from among those horses which are considered the leading challengers of form and rarely provide shock outsiders. The English Derby 1975–89 has been won by first or second favourite thirteen times. The English Oaks nine times. The winner of these premier Classics will normally be bred in the purple (by a British Classic winner or foreign equivalent) and will need the priceless ability to be able to accelerate almost instantly when asked in the last 2f of the race.

The St Leger can be considered the Classic race which is the most discernible for selection. It is staged in September, and by this time Flat race form at Classic level is well exposed and the abilities, stamina, limitations and requirements of the leading candidate is almost fully exposed. The only shadow to be cast on the consideration of a selection is that some horses who throughout the season may have proven their abilities in hard-fought races over shorter distances may have reached their peak and be unable to withstand the gruelling challenge over this extended distance. This is a factor that should be particularly noted, especially with the failure in recent St Legers of DIMINUENDO (1988), SHERGAR (1981), ILE DE BOURBON (1978), ALLEGED (1977).

SELLING RACES (FLAT AND NATIONAL HUNT-LEVEL WEIGHTS AND HANDICAPS – FOR 2-YEAR-OLDS AND UPWARDS)

Selling races are contested by horses with the poorest racing ability. *They cannot be recommended* as satisfactory mediums for the purposes of selection. They were designed to give opportunities to horses of the most moderate ability, the winner being offered for sale at public auction after the race (hence 'selling' races) and so providing an owner with the chance to sell slow and unwanted horses for a reasonable price. The conditions of many selling races allows for any horse competing in the race to be claimed afterwards (sold to anyone) for a sum of fixed value in accord with the conditions of entry. These type of races therefore attract the worst type of horses who either have:

1. Little or no racing ability;
2. Are physically and/or temperamentally unsound and who cannot be depended upon to reproduce consistent performances.

In these circumstances there can never be any basis for confident selection and they are races that should normally be avoided.

The only positive factor in favour of selling races, for selection or any other purpose, is that they are races which require very little ability to win. This has led over the years for them to become a popular medium (especially by trainers and connections) for tilts at the betting ring and led to the adage 'follow the money in selling races'. Some of the less fashionable trainers who struggle to make a living from training alone subsidize their income with carefully planned and concealed coups in selling races. They retain in their stable a horse or two imperceptibly better than selling class who, when skilfully prepared and entered, can be guaranteed to collect the spoils. Such attitudes and approaches further undermine confidence in making selection in selling races, as sudden turnabouts in form can be incomprehensible. While stating that nefarious practices can occur in selling races, most often expectations fail to materialize because of the unreliability of bad horses. Although usually not a suggested medium for selection, the selector occasionally, in very rare instances, finds a horse of proven ability somehow inexplicably dropped into selling class and is presented with a golden opportunity to take advantage of such fortune.

AUCTION RACES (FLAT-LEVEL WEIGHT SEX ALLOWANCE FOR 2-YEAR-OLDS AND UPWARDS)

Auction races are maiden and condition races principally for 2-year-olds, and limited to those that were bought at public auction as yearlings for below a prescribed maximum price (usually 10,000 guineas, with the first sale to govern should the horse have been subsequently reauctioned). Auction races for 2-year-olds are run over all distances from 5f up to 1m and staged throughout the season. They are designed to allow the inexpensively purchased yearling, as a 2 y.o., to race against similar rivals rather than being forced to contest races against very expensively purchased yearlings who would be expected to outclass their humbler opponents. The weight allotted to each horse will vary according to the entry conditions of the race with the provision of each horse receiving a weight in accord with the purchase price – the lower the purchase price the greater the allowance. This gives a good opportunity for unfashionably bred and consequently usually cheaper purchased horses to display their abilities on the race-track by receiving a weight allowance which may not reflect their form (for better or worse). Occasionally maiden auction races can provide a golden opportunity for a bargain-basement horse which has racing ability far in excess of anything expected or reflected by its original purchase price. Auction races can be seen as an interesting and sometimes profitable selection medium.

TABLE 3.8   Record of Favourites in Auction races during the 1988 Flat season

Distance	Wins – Runs	
5f	12 – 33	36.4%
6f	4 – 18	22.2%
7f	2 – 13	15.4%
8f	1 – 4	25.0%
9f	1 – 1	100.0%
12f	2 – 5	40.0%
13f	1 – 1	100.0%
Total	23 – 75	30.7%

CLAIMING RACES (FLAT-LEVEL WEIGHTS, SEX ALLOWANCE WITH PENALTIES FOR WINNERS FOR 2-YEAR-OLDS AND UPWARDS)

Claiming races are basically level weight contests where any horse entered may be claimed (or bought) after the race for the claiming price set in the entry conditions of the race. Claiming races, in class, are a grade or two (depending on the maximum claiming value) above selling races where all winners are offered for sale by auction and other horses may be claimed for a fixed sum. Whereas in selling races horses receive weight strictly according to the handicap, or on a level weights basis in stakes races, in claiming races horses deviate from the level weight principle directly in response to the claiming value placed upon them by their connections. Therefore, from the maximum claiming price, horses receive corresponding weight allowance as their claiming value is lowered – the higher-valued horses carrying most weight, the lesser valued ones least. Claiming races can be seen to provide an opportunity for a good horse (perhaps otherwise difficult to place due to its high position in the handicap) to win a less than fiercely competitive race against inferior rivals without fear of the horse being lost at auction for a 'silly' price; or having to be bought back in for a very high price should the stable want to retain it, as is the case when a good horse wins a seller. However, if some buyer should emerge to claim the horse after the race this can only be for the agreed realistic sum set as the claiming price.

Claiming races open to both maidens and previous winners (which are penalized) allow horses often with quite a considerable disparity in their abilities to meet each other at basically level weights with concessions only in regard to their claiming price. In this respect claiming events are often quite easy to assess for selection, holding the possibility of a reasonable profit for the astute backer.

Claiming races have for many years had a high profile on the American horse-racing scene, and now with their popularity growing on this side of the Atlantic promise to assume a greater role here.

APPRENTICE RACES (FLAT-LEVEL WEIGHTS AND HANDICAPS)/CONDITIONAL JOCKEYS RACES (NATIONAL HUNT – LEVEL WEIGHTS AND HANDICAPS)

These races are staged to give young riders experience competing against their peers rather than against the senior and more experienced jockeys. They can be divided into different types:

1. Races limited to apprentices riding only for the stable they are apprenticed to. (This applies only to Flat racing and is designed to give the newest and youngest apprentices an early racecourse riding experience – many apprentices make their début in such races.)
2. *Races limited to apprentices/conditional jockeys* who have not ridden more than a prescribed number of winners.
3. *Non-conditional apprentice/conditional jockeys* – open to all claiming jockeys. These races whatever type, class or distance tend to be won by the most experienced rider competing (especially when there are considerable differences in experience), who is likely to be offered the mount on the horse with the best winning chance.

All these races must be judged on their merits for selection purposes, but conforming strictly to the criteria suggested for race selection – level weights receiving first consideration.

NB. Do not engage in selection in races where inexperienced horses (who may require strong and skilful handling) are ridden by young, equally inexperienced riders.

AMATEUR RACES (FLAT AND NATIONAL HUNT – LEVEL WEIGHTS AND HANDICAPS)

Amateur races, once the almost exclusive preserve of National Hunt racing, have with the introduction of lady riders into the sport become increasingly popular and grown in number in the Flat race calendar.

Amateur races initiating from the hunter chases in the National Hunt programme have spread to include handicap chases, hurdles and novice events, as well as now running the full gamut of distances and types of races in the Flat programme. Amateur races are largely supported by, and provided for, owners who wish to ride their horse(s) in public and by other dedicated and often more proficient enthusiasts who cannot or have no wish to enter the professional riding ranks in racing. Similarly to apprentice races, the most proficient and experienced riders gain the mounts on the best horses, and carefully noting the jockeys in these races often holds the key to selection. The top leading amateur riders (National Hunt) rank with many of their professional counterparts, and many leading professional riders have graduated from the amateur ranks.

Leading amateur riders during recent National Hunt seasons are:
Mr M. Armytage (10 st 0 lb)
Mr P. Fenton
Leading lady amateur riders during recent Flat race seasons are:
Elaine Bronson
Carolyn Eddery
Amanda Harwood (9 st 0 lb)
Maxine Juster (8 st 7 lb)
Franca Vittadini (8 st 3 lb)

Amateur races play a useful role and provide variety in racing – amateur races of level weights (Flat and National Hunt) can be an extremely reliable medium for selection.

HUNTER CHASES (NATIONAL HUNT – LEVEL WEIGHTS; DISTANCE 2½m +)

Hunter chases begin in the National Hunt programme on 1 February, continuing for the remainder of the season. They are limited to horses that have been certified as hunters during the hunting season and have not taken part in any National Hunt or Flat races after 1 November. These races are supported by the farming/hunting community who provide the backbone to National Hunt racing and are contested by point-to-point horses and ex-racehorses who have been sold out of racing.

(*NB.* Some professional stables retain horses that have been hunted by their owners during the winter to compete in hunter chases.)

The form of hunter chases normally works out extremely well and they can be recommended as a reliable medium for selection (see Table 3.9).

TABLE 3.9   Hunter chases during the 1988–89 National Hunt season

	2m 4f+	%
Fav.	42	32.8
2nd fav.	30	23.4
3rd fav.	21	16.4
Non-fav.	35	27.3
Total	128	

NATIONAL HUNT FLAT RACES

These are limited to horses that have never competed in Flat racing, and are ridden by claiming jockeys and amateur riders only. They are level weight races, with weight-for-age allowances and penalties for previous winners. Distance usually 2m (see Table 3.10), although during the 1988–89 National Hunt season 1½m races were introduced.

TABLE 3.10   National Hunt Flat races during the 1988–89 season

	2m+	%
Fav.	31	46.9
2nd fav.	7	10.6
3rd fav.	8	12.1
Non-fav.	20	30.3
Total	66	

National Hunt Flat races or 'bumper' races as they are sometimes known have been established to allow purpose-bred National Hunt horses without previous racing experience to gain their first taste of competition against similar opponents. Usually they are programmed as the final event at a National Hunt meeting, being run over the hurdle course with the obstacles removed from the track. The popularity of these races with their growth in entries has meant that a horse is not allowed to compete in more than three such races. Any horse competing in these 'bumper' races will therefore be very inexperienced and usually offer the strict form student little upon which to base a selection. In 1988–89 52 per cent of the winners of National Hunt Flat races won on their racecourse debut. However, the form of National Hunt Flat races tends to be sound, as 42 per cent of winners who contested a subsequent 'bumper' race won again.

4 TOOLS OF THE TRADE

The successful execution of any trade is subject to three factors – the workmanship, the materials and the use of the best and most appropriate tools.
'The trades of selection and betting are no exception to the rule.

DEFINITIONS

WORKMANSHIP

This will be the reflection of the abilities of each selector in such skills as: (i) assessing information; (ii) formulating judgements; (iii) taking calculated action in response to these judgements. Good workmanship demands consistently practising the trade to the highest standard of personal ability and this is particularly aided if enthusiasm can be maintained in the approach to performing the selection/betting skills.

MATERIALS

These are the basic information requirements which make a well-considered selection possible; these will include:

1. Details of race – time, venue, value, distance and going. A list of the declared runners, riders, trainers, owners and weights.
2. Details of the form of each declared runner.
3. Details in a concise biographical account of each runner with particular reference to breeding and conformation.

TOOLS

The *tools of the trade* are the sources from where the essential information is obtained.

1. *Details of race*. Most national daily newspapers or a national daily racing newspaper.
2. *Details of form*. The official Jockey Club form books (supplied in weekly parts), and daily racing newspapers.
3. *Horses' biographies*. Weekly or annual specialized horse racing publications (e.g. Timeform books).

With selection firmly dependent for success upon the quality of the information received it is essential that this information be derived from only the most dependable of sources – these sources, if of quality, may be considered as being the best tools of the trade.

DETAILS OF THE RACE

A DAILY NEWSPAPER

Although a list of the declared runners, riders, etc. can be found in most of the national daily newspapers, it is a matter of personal choice as to which newspaper is preferred; the factors which have to be considered and offer considerable assistance in selection are: (i) the clarity of the print of the newspaper; (ii) the general layout and presentation of facts; (iii) any unique of features of the newspaper which provides vital information that is not otherwise readily obtainable without more involved investigation. The daily newspaper which is found consistently to fulfil the above requirements in respect of its horse-race coverage is the *Daily Mail*. This is a newspaper of tabloid size, excellently printed with clean, clear lettering thereby giving the reader immediate visual access to information (see Fig. 4.1). Its layout and presentation enable the selector to receive a direct yet comprehensive impression of the race-card at a glance; different race meetings are neatly separated, with races arranged in time order and sequence descending down the length of the page. This allows for relevant information (e.g. trainers' arrangements and jockey engagements) to be quickly recognized. Prestige races are usually given more detailed coverage. A typical example is given in Fig. 4.1. A special and originally unique feature of the *Racing Mail* has been its daytime information (the number of days since a horse last ran) which is represented by a figure after the horse's name. *This is vital information* (a recent race performance is the most positive indication of a horse's present fitness

Epsom card

ROBIN GOODFELLOW	GIMCRACK
2.15 Dancing Music	2.15 Naval Party (nb)
2.45 Greensmith	2.45 Magical Strike
3.45 Prince of Dance	3.45 NASHWAN (nap)
4.40 PERION (nap)	4.40 Restless Don
5.10 Inaad	5.10 Main Objective
5.45 Compleat	5.45 Young Inca

JIMMY LINDLEY'S TV TIPS: 2.15: Naval Party; 2.45: Greensmith; 3.45: Cacoethes; 4.40: Perion.

FIVE-YEAR RECORD

Jockeys: S Cauthen 26, Pat Eddery 25, W Carson 16, B Rouse 11. **Trainers:** G Lewis 21, R Hannon 13, M Stoute 11, H Cecil 11.

PRINCIPAL MEETING. DRAW ADVANTAGE: High numbers are favoured on the 5f course. STALLS: 5f: stands side; 6f & 7f: outside; remainder: inside. TOTE JACKPOT: All six races. 5.10 & 5.45 races on SIS. GOING: Good.

RADIO 2: 2.15, 2.45 & 3.45.

---

8 (21) 612610 **RACEMAIL (B)** 18 (C&D BF) A Tryin 5-9-7 .....S Cauthen ●78

KEY to all-in-a-line card: Racecard number; draw; six-figure form to sixth place, plus S – slipped up, R – refused, F – fell, P – pulled up, C – carried out; horse's name, B – blinkers, H – hood, V – visor; Daytimer – the number of days since horse last ran; C – course winner (different distance), D – distance winner, C&D – course and distance winner, BF – beaten favourite; trainer, age and weight; jockey; and Formcast rating.

2.15 — 183rd WOODCOTE STAKES (2-Y-O) £15,000 added (£10,796.25)6f (12)

101	(5)	2412	ACROSS THE BAY 13	S Dow 9-2	S Cauthen	76
102	(7)	1	BOLD RUSSIAN 11	B Hills 9-2	M Hills	74
103	(11)	211	CHAMPAGNE GOLD 12	Denys Smith 9-2	W Carson	●78
104	(8)	12	DANCING MUSIC 46	J Berry 9-2	G Duffield	76
105	(6)	1343	LORD GLEN 16	R Boss 9-2	Pat Eddery	77
106	(1)	1	NAVAL PARTY 19 (D)	M Stoute 9-2	W R Swinburn	75
107	(12)	014	PALABORA 16 (D)	P Arthur 9-2	R Cochrane	73
108	(9)	5	INDIAN CHIEF 46	R Hannon 8-11	B Rouse	—
109	(4)		PETMER	N Mitchell 8-8	W Shoemaker	—
110	(3)		STATE OF AFFAIRS	R Hollinshead 8-8	K Darley	—
111	(2)	234	SUPER VIRTUOSA 23	M Haynes 8-6	R Fox	66
112	(10)		ZIZANIA	C Brittain 8-3	M Roberts	—

Probable SP: 9-4 Bold Russian, 5-2 Naval Party, 4 Dancing Music, 6 Champagne Gold, 8 Lord Glen.   **FAVOURITES:** — — — — — 0.
1988: Sno Serenade 2-9-2 (M Roberts) 25-1 R Boss 8 ran.

GOODFELLOW'S GUIDE

Bold Russian's Haydock win over the minimum and **Naval Party's** over this distance at Newmarket were scored with something to spare from other youngsters appearing for the first time. In the meantime, the opponent who finished last, 11 lengths down, in Naval Party's race has got his head in front in a modest event at Brighton. **Champagne Gold,** clearly too good for two previous winners at Pontefract, finished full of running and will not be troubled by the extra furlong. The runner up in that race, and the third to Bold Russian at Haydock, were saddled by Jack Berry, who now starts **DANCING MUSIC** in a bid to bring to 30 his tally in two year olds' contests this season. The eased ground will suit this one, who, after overcoming inexperience to run away with his first race, stayed on to be clearly best of still unbeaten Princess Taufan's pursuers on a yielding surface at Ascot.

EPSOM TRACK FACTS — Left-hand U-shape of 1m 4f, rising 150ft over the first 4f going downhill to Tattenham Corner, with a final sharp rise. An extension provides the 5f course, mainly downhill, and the fastest in the world.

FIG. 4.1   Extract from a typical racecard as displayed in the *Daily Mail.*

• THE EVER READY DERBY •

3.45 — (Group 1) £500,000 **C4** **Formcast**
(£296,000) 1m 4f
(12)

301 (5) 3-11 **CACOETHES**25 (D) G Harwood 9-0 .... **G Starkey** 77
b c Alydar-Careless Nation. Light Green,Dark Blue and Light Green hooped sleeves,striped cap.

302 (3) 111-5 **CLASSIC FAME**18 M O'Brien 9-0 ....**J Reid** 66
b c Nijinsky-Family Fame. Emerald Green,Orange sash,White cap.

304 (6) 2-26 **FLOCKTON'S OWN**21 (V) J Shaw 9-0 .... **R Hills** 57
b c Electric-Tree Mallow. Light Blue,Red star,Red and White quartered cap.

305 (1) 353-14 **GRAN ALBA**14 R Hannon 9-0............................**B Rouse** 56
gr c El Gran Senor-Morning Games. Black and Yellow diamonds,striped sleeves,Yellow cap,Black spots.

306 (12) 1-1 **ILE DE NISKY**11 G Huffer 9-0 ....**G Duffield** 55
b c Ile de Bourbon-Good Lass. Yellow and Blue diamonds,Yellow sleeves and cap,Blue diamond.

308 (11) 21 **MILL POND** 15 (D) P Biancone 9-0.............. **Pat Eddery** 50
ro c Mill Reef-Royal Way. Red,Light Green cap.

309 (10) 11-1 **NASHWAN**32 Major W Hern 9-0.....................**W Carson**●78
ch c Blushing Groom-Height of Fashion. Royal Blue,White epaulets,striped cap.

312 (7) 124-22 **POLAR RUN**26 G Harwood 9-0............................**A Clark** 53
b c Arctic Tern-Melodina. Light Green,Dark Blue and Light Green hooped sleeves,striped cap.

313 (9) 1D11-1 **PRINCE OF DANCE**33 Major W Hern 9-0.. **S Cauthen** 73
b c Sadler's Wells-Sun Princess. Pale Blue,Yellow and White check cap.

314 (8) 46-2231 **TERIMON**9 C Brittain 9-0 .... **M Roberts** 44
gr c Bustino-Nicholas Grey. Beaver Brown,Maple Leaf Green cross-belts and cap.

315 (4) 2-11 **TORJOUN**21 L Cumani 9-0 ....**R Cochrane** 72
ch c Green Dancer-Tarsila. Green,Red epaulets.

316 (2) 11-31 **WARRSHAN**14 M Stoute 9-0................. **W R Swinburn** 63
b c Northern Dancer-Secret Asset. Maroon,White sleeves,Maroon cap,White star.

Probable SP: 5-4 Nashwan, 13-8 Cacoethes, 6 Warrshan, 7 Prince Of Dance, 10 Torjoun, 25 Ile de Nisky, 33 Mill Pond, 40 Classic Fame, 50 Gran Alba, 200 Polar Run, 500 Flockton's Own. **FAVOURITES: 1 1 0 1 2 1 0.**
1988: Kahyasi 3-9-0 (R Cochrane) 11-1 L M Cumani 14 ran.

FIG. 4.2 Typical presentation of a more prestigious race as displayed in the *Daily Mail*.

and well-being). Another positive feature of the *Racing Mail* is in its form figures preceding a horse's name, where up to the first six placings are recorded. Included at the foot of each race is the record of market leaders over the past seven seasons (i.e. whether the race was won by 1st, 2nd or 3rd favourite or by a non-favourite). This is a most important feature, alerting the selector to the likely predictability of the race. These features mean the *Daily Mail* can be highly recommended.

A DAILY RACING NEWSPAPER

While the basic needs for making a selection (i.e. the declared runners and riders) will be accommodated in the daily national newspaper of preference, the selector desiring a wider acquaintance with horse-racing is also recommended to obtain a national daily racing newspaper. There are two, the historic *Sporting Life*, established in 1859, and the recently founded *Racing Post*.

The *Sporting Life* retains its traditional large broad-sheet size while the *Racing Post* is a tabloid. The design and layout of the two papers are therefore somewhat different and the reader who has come to favour one will be unfamiliar and perhaps even disorientated when referring to the other. Both, however, give a comprehensive coverage of horse-racing and are packed with information essential for making a considered selection. This includes full description of entry conditions for each race, the prize-money awarded to the first three or four finishers, weight-for-age scale (when appropriate), complete long handicap and raising of weights (when it applies), the draw and its effect, and stalls location, plus of course the form of each runner in their last three races and numerous statistical tables. Extracts from the *Sporting Life* and *Racing Post* (Figs 4.3 to 4.6) show their typical layouts for a race.

Both newspapers in their contrasting styles have layouts that are clear and concise and present all the relevant information. This includes information on ownership, which is not found in most national daily papers and can be quite an important consideration for the experienced selector conversant with the influential connections and training methods of some trainers. Both papers also identify the racing colours of each owner and this is a most useful aid for the racing fan visiting the racecourse or for those watching on colour television.

The *Sporting Life*, which for so long had stood as the major or sole presenter of British racing, responded quickly to meet the challenge of its new rival by sharpening its presentation and generally shaking itself from the lethargy and predictability in which its tradition and monopoly had threatened to engulf it.

The *Racing Post*, as the young upstart, has brought a fresh and

3.45 Ever Ready Derby (Group 1) CH 4 1½m

guaranteed minimum value £500000 Distributed in accordance with Rule 194
(ii)(a) (Includes a fourth prize) **for three yrs old only, entire colts and fillies**
£1320 to enter, £1750 ex unless forfeit dec by MAY 23 £930 ex if entry confirmed;
Weights: Colts 9st; fillies 8st 9lb EVER READY LIMITED have generously
sponsored this race, the prize money for which includes a golden trophy value
£6500 for the winning owner (£200000 minimum added to stakes) The Stewards of
the Jockey Club have modified Rule 121 (ii)(a) for the purposes of this race THERE
WILL BE A PARADE FOR THIS RACE, ff dec for 16.

Penalty value £,296,000; 2nd £,111,000, 3rd £53,500, 4th £23,500

1 3-11 **CACOETHES (USA)**(25) (D)
(Lady Harrison) .... G Harwood   9 0 .... G Starkey 5
Light green, dark blue and light green hooped sleeves, striped cap.

2 111-5 **CLASSIC FAME (USA)**(18)
(Classic Thoroughbred Plc) M V O'Brien
in Ireland   9 0 .... J Reid 3
Emerald green, orange sash, white cap.

4 2-26 **FLOCKTON'S OWN**(21) (Ian
Flockton Developments Limited)
J R Shaw   9 0 ......R Hills (VV) 6
Light blue, red star, red and white quartered cap.

5 353-14 **GRAN ALBA (USA)**(14) (C R
Kilroy) .... R Hannon   9 0 .... B Rouse 1
Black and yellow diamonds, striped sleeves, yellow cap, black spots.

6 1-1 **ILE DE NISKY**(11) (H H Prince
Yazid Saud) .... G A Huffer   9 0 ......G Duffield 12
Yellow and blue diamonds, yellow sleeves and cap, blue diamond.

8 -21 **MILL POND (FR)**(15) (D) (Marquise
de Moratalla) ..... P L Biancone in France   9 0 .....Pat Eddery 11
Red, light green cap.

9 11-1 **NASHWAN (USA)**(32) (Hamdan
Al-Maktoum) .... Major W R Hern   9 0 ...... W Carson 10
Royal blue, white epaulets, striped cap.

12 124-22 **POLAR RUN (USA)**(26) (Lady
Harrison) .... G Harwood   9 0 .... A Clark 7
Light green, dark blue and light green hooped sleeves, red cap.

13 11D11-1 **PRINCE OF DANCE**(33) (Sir
Michael Sobell) .... Major W R Hern   9 0 ......S Cauthen 9
Pale blue, yellow and white check cap.

14 46-2231 **TERIMON**(9) (The Dowager Lady
Beaverbrook) .... C E Brittain   9 0 ....M Roberts 8
Beaver brown, maple leaf green cross-belts and cap.

15 2-11 **TORJOUN (USA)**(21) (H H Aga
Khan) .... L M Cumani   9 0 ..... R Cochrane 4
Green, red epaulets.

16 11-31 **WARRSHAN (USA)**(14) (Sheikh
Mohammed) .... M R Stoute   9 0 ...W R Swinburn 2
Maroon, white sleeves, maroon cap, white star.

Twelve runners

FORECAST: 6-4 Nashwan, 2 Cacoethes, 7 Prince Of Dance, 8 Warrshan, 12
Torjoun, 25 Mill Pond, 28 Ile De Nisky, 40 Classic Fame, 50 Gran Alba, 250 Polar
Run, 500 Terimon, Flockton's Own.

Last Year: KAHYASI, 9-0, R Cochrane, 11/1 (L Cumani). Drawn 13 of 14.

FIG. 4.3   Extract from a racecard as displayed in *Sporting Life.*

3.45 🏇🏇🏇 Ever Ready Derby (G.1) (3-y-o) 1½m (£296,000) 12 runners

3-11 CACOETHES (USA) (9-0) (G Harwood) b c Alydar (USA) [9.3f] - Careless Notion (USA) by Jester [6.0f] 1989, 1¼m firm (Brighton), 1½m firm (Lingfield). £38,460.00 (£38,460.00).

DW: 5

May 13, Lingfield, 1½m (3-y-o) (Listed Race), firm, £35,380.00: 1 CACOETHES (USA) (9-0, G Starkey,2), made all, shaken up to quicken clear two furlongs out, stayed on strongly. (5 to 2 op 3 to 1) 2 Pirate Army (USA) (9-0,1), 3 Spitfire (9-0,3),; 7 Ran. 4l, 8l, nk, 3l, 6l, 2l. 2m 30.89s (b 2.11s). SR: 79/71/55/54/48/36.

April 24, Brighton, 1¼m (3-y-o) , firm, £3,080.00: 1 CACOETHES (USA) (8-11, G Starkey,4), led over five furlongs out, ridden and quickened clear two furlongs out, easily. (6 to 5 on op Evens tchd 5 to 4) 2 Dolpour (8-11,2), 3 Child Of The Mist (8-11,3),: 10 Ran. 7l, 4l, 4l, 1½l, 4l, 7l, 6l, 4l, nk. 2m 2.70s (a 3.30s). SR: 29/15/7/-/-/-.

Oct 8 1988, Ascot. See NASHWAN (USA)

1-1 ILE DE NISKY (9-0) (G A Huffer) b c Ile de Bourbon (USA) [12.0f] - Good Lass (FR) by Reform [9.9f] 1988, 1m good (Newmarket) 1989, 1¼m 50yds good to firm (Doncaster). £6,405.00 (£1,710.00).

DW: 12

May 27, Doncaster, 1¼m 50yds (3-y-o), good to firm, £1,710.00: 1 ILE DE NISKY (9-4, G Duffield,1), tracked leaders, shaken up to lead over two out, soon clear. (9 to 4 tchd 5 to 2 and 2 to 1) 2 Sharardoun (9-4,7), 3 Vinstan (8-4,7*,6),: 8 Ran. 6l, 1½l, 12l, 1½l, 1½l, 3l. 2m 8.26s (a 0.76s). SR: 56/44/34/10/7/1.

Oct 13 1988, Newmarket, 1m (2-y-o), good, £4,695.00: 1 ILE DE NISKY (8-7, B Lane,7*,15), with leaders, led one and a half out, edged left inside final furlong, ran on. (16 to 1 op 12 to 1 tchd 20 to 1) 2 Peace King (9-0,10), 3 Bitone (9-0,8),: 17 Ran. 1½l, 2l, hd, 2l, ½l, 1½l, sht-hd, 2l, ½l, ¾l. 1m 42.77s (a 4.17s).(After a stewards' inquiry and an objection by the rider of the second, the objection was overruled and Val Recit was demoted to fourth place.) SR: 49/44/38/37/31/29.

-21 MILL POND (FR) (9-0) (P L Biancone) ro c Mill Reef (USA) [11.0f] - Royal Way (FR) by Sicambre 1989, 1½m good to firm (St-Cloud (Fr). £7,117.00 (£7,117.00).

DW: 11

May 23, St-Cloud (Fr), 1½m (3-y-o) mdn, good to firm, £7,117.00: 1 MILL POND (FR) (8-11, G W Moore), 2 Model Man (8-11), 3 Marzano (7-11,7*),: 3 Ran. 3l, ¾l, 5l, 1½l. 2m 38.00s.

May 14, Longchamp (Fr), 1m 3f (3-y-o), good, £8,703.00: 1 Guillaume de Tyr (9-2), 2 MILL POND (FR) (8-11, G W Moore), 3 Karawaan (9-2),: 3 Ran. ½l, 1½l, 1½l, sht-hd. 1m 19.90s.

11-1 NASHWAN (USA) (9-0) (Major W R Hern) ch c Blushing Groom (FR) [10.0f] - Height Of Fashion (FR) by Bustino [11.3f] 1988, 7f good to firm (Newbury), 1m good to soft (Ascot) 1989, 1m good to firm (Newmarket). £117,572.80 (£103,262.50).

DW: 10

May 6, Newmarket, 1m (3-y-o) (Group 1), good to firm, £103,262.50: 1 NASHWAN (USA) (9-0, W Carson,12), pressed leaders, led over two furlongs out, stayed on well. (3 to 1 fav op 3 to 1 tchd 11 to 4 and 100 to 30) 2 Exbourne (USA) (9-0,10), 3 Danehill (USA) (9-0,13),: 14 Ran. 1l, 1½l, nk, 3l, 1l, sht-hd, nk, 3l, 1½l, 10l. 1m 36.44s (b 1.56s). SR: 82/79/77/76/67/64.

Oct 8 1988, Ascot, 1m (2-y-o) (Listed Race), good to soft, £8,984.80: 1 NASHWAN (USA) (8-11, W Carson,1), tracked leader, smooth headway to lead over two out, strode clear, comfortably. (6 to 4 on op Evens) 2 Optimist (8-11,3), 3 CACOETHES (USA) (8-11, G Starkey,2), headway well over two furlongs out, fourth straight, stayed on, never nearer. (11 to 1 op 8 to 1 tchd 12 to 1); 6 Ran. 4l, 1½l, 5l, ¾l, 1l. 1m 47.29s (a 7.19s). SR: 55/43/38/18/21/18.

Aug 13 1988, Newbury, 7f (2-y-o) mdn, good to firm, £5,325.50: 1 NASHWAN (USA) (9-0, W Carson,21), chased leaders stands side, sustained headway to lead inside final furlong, ran on well. (6 to 4 fav op 2 to 1) 2 Young Turpin (9-0,4), 3 Child Of The Mist (9-0,10),: 27 Ran. ¾l, nk, 4l, 2½l, nk, 2l, sht-hd, ½l, ½l, nk. 1m 28.28s (a 2.68s). SR: 60/58/57/45/37/36.

0246-2231 TERIMON (9-0) (C E Brittain) gr c Bustino [11.3f] - Nicholas Grey by Track Spare [8.6f] 1989, 1¼m good to firm (Leicester). £1,884.00 (£1,884.00).

DW: 8

May 29, Leicester, 1¼m (3-y-o) mdn, good to firm, £1,884.00: 1 TERIMON (9-0, B Procter,9), held up, improved halfway, strong run to lead near line. (9 to 2 op 4 to 1 tchd 11 to 2) 2 Marcinkus (9-0,12), 3 Carnival Spirit (8-11,11),; 12 Ran. Nk, sht-hd, 6l, 2½l, 3l, 2l, 2l. 2m 6.80s (a 3.30s). SR: 52/51/47/38/33/27.

May 9, Chester, 1¼m 85yds (3-y-o) mdn, good to firm, £3,915.00: 1 Sharardoun (9-0,4), 2 Rudjig (USA) (9-0,5), 3 TERIMON (9-0, S Cauthen,10), close up, kept on well final three furlongs. (9 to 2 op 3 to 1 tchd 5 to 1); 9 Ran. 2l, 2l, 2l, 7l, 1½l. 2m 10.16s (a 0.16s). SR: 52/48/44/40/26/25.

April 15, Thirsk, 1m (3-y-o) , good to soft, £5,299.00: 1 Braiswick (8-4,5), 2 TERIMON (8-7, M Birch,3), tracked leader, led well over one furlong out, hard driven and just caught. (10 to 1 tchd 12 to 1) 3 Travelling Tryst (USA) (8-7,1),: 6 Ran. Sht-hd, 3l, 2l, 4l, 4l. 1m 44.20s (a 6.20s). SR: 45/47/38/40/20/8.

April 1, Doncaster, 7f (3-y-o) h'cap (0-100), good, £3,850.00: 1 Tymippy (8-10,7), 2 TERIMON (9-0, S Cauthen,12), always leading group, every chance over one out, not quicken close home. (15 to 2 op 6 to 1 tchd 8 to 1) 3 Admiralty Way (8-6, inc 6lb extra,8),: 13 Ran. Sht-hd, ¾l, 1½l, 4l, nk, 1l, 1½l, hd, nk, ¾l. 1m 27.19s (a 2.69s). SR: 24/27/17/24/-/-.

Sept 28 1988, Newmarket, 6f (2-y-o) (Group 1), good to soft, £56,592.00: 1 Mon Tresor (9-0,1), 2 Pure Genius (USA) (9-0,7), 3 Northern Tryst (USA) (9-0,4), 6 TERIMON (9-0, Pat Eddery,5), flat away, speed for over two furlongs, soon lost touch. (33 to 1 op 25 to 1); 6 Ran. ¾l, ¾l, 7l, 7l, 6l. 1m 12.27s (b 0.43s). SR: 66/63/60/32/4/-.

Aug 12 1988, Newbury. See PRINCE OF DANCE

July 15 1988, Newbury, 6f (2-y-o) mdn, good, £4,935.50: 1 Tatsfield (9-0,9), 2 TERIMON (9-0, S Cauthen,13), always in touch, switched left approaching final furlong, ran on well. (12 to 1 op 8 to 1) 3 Pivot (9-0,11),: 19 Ran. Hd, nk, ¾l, sht-hd, ¾l, ¾l, 1½l, ½l, ½l, 1½l. 1m 18.11s (a 5.11s). SR: 22/21/20/17/16/13.

FIG. 4.4 Extract of horses' previous form as displayed in *Sporting Life*.

Going: GOOD   **Live on Ch4 & Radio 2**

3.45	**Ever Ready Derby (Group 1)**			**1m4f**	**TV**
12 DECLARED					**CH4**

£500,000 guaranteed **For** three yrs old only, entire colts and fillies **Weights Colts.**9st; fillies 8st 9lb **Entries** 169 pay £1,320 **Forfeit** 32 pay £1,750 **Confirmed** 16 pay £930
Penalty Value 1st £296,000 **2nd** £111,000 **3rd** £53,500 **4th** £23,500

1	3-11	**CACOETHES (USA)**25 D		G.Harwood	3 9-00		G Starkey 5
		LadyHarrison –*light green, dark blue and light green hooped sleeves, striped cap.*					
2	111-5	**CLASSIC FAME (USA)**18		M.V.O'Brien (IRE)	3 9-00		J Reid 3
		ClassicThoroughbredPlc –*emerald green, orange sash, white cap*					
4	2-26	**FLOCKTON'S OWN**21		J.R.Shaw	3 9-00 v1		R Hills 6
		IanFlocktonDevelopmentsLimited –*light blue, red star, red and white quartered cap.*					
5	353-14	**GRAN ALBA (USA)**14		R.Hannon	3 9-00		B Rouse 1
		MrC.R.Kilroy –*black and yellow diamonds, striped sleeves, yellow cap, black spots.*					
6	1-1	**ILE DE NISKY**11		G.A.Huffer	3 9-00		G Duffield 12
		H.H.PrinceYazidSaud –*yellow and blue diamonds, yellow sleeves and cap, blue diamond.*					
8	-21	**MILL POND (FR)**15 D		P.L.Biancone (FR)	3 9-00		Pat Eddery 11
		MarquisedeMoratalla –*red, red and green hooped cap.*					
9	11-1	**NASHWAN (USA)**32		MajorW.R.Hern	3 9-00		W Carson 10
		MrHamdanAl-Maktoum –*royal blue, white epaulets, striped cap.*					
12	124-22	**POLAR RUN (USA)**26		G.Harwood	3 9-00		A Clark 7
		LadyHarrison –*light green, dark blue and light green hooped sleeves, red cap.*					
13	11d11-1	**PRINCE OF DANCE**33		MajorW.R.Hern	3 9-00		S Cauthen 9
		SirMichaelSobell –*pale blue, yellow and white check cap.*					
14	46-2231	**TERIMON**9		C.E.Brittain	3 9-00		M Roberts 8
		TheDowagerLadyBeaverbrook –*beaver brown, maple leaf green cross-belts and cap.*					
15	2-11	**TORJOUN (USA)**21		L.M.Cumani	3 9-00		R Cochrane 4
		H.H.AgaKhan –*green, red epaulets.*					
16	11-31	**WARRSHAN (USA)**14		M.R.Stoute	3 9-00		W R Swinburn 2
		SheikhMohammed –*maroon, white sleeves, maroon cap, white star.*					
LAST YEAR:	**KAHYASI**			L M Cumani	3 09 00		R Cochrane

BETTING FORECAST: 11-8 Nashwan, 13-8 Cacoethes, 7 Warrshan, 8 Prince of Dance, 12 Torjoun, 25 Ile de Nisky, 33 Classic Fame, Mill Pond, 50 Gran Alba, 200 Polar Run, 500 Flockton's Own, Terimon.

TOPSPEED	**Prince Of Dance 127**	**Nashwan 125**	**Torjoun 125**

FIG. 4.5   Extract from a racecard displayed in *Racing Post.*

EPSOM FORM

3.45

£296,000

Gp13yo   **1m4f**

Cacoethes (USA)

3-11   **3-9-00**
G.HARWOOD   b c Alydar (USA)

Starts 1st 2nd 3rd	Win & Pl	Careless Notion (USA)
3	2 — 1	£39,749	(Jester)

89 Lingf 1m4f 3yoGp3 FIRM	.... £35,380
89 Bghtn 1m2f 3yoGrad FIRM	.... £3,080
	TOTAL: £38,460

13 May Lingfield Park 1m4f	3yoGp3 £35,380
7 ran	FIRM	TIME 2m30.89s (fst3.7s)

1 CACOETHES (USA) 3 9-00 .... G.Starkey[2] 5/2
made all, quickened over 1f out, easily [op 3/1]
2 Pirate Army (USA) 3 9-00 .. R.Cochrane[1] 4/7F
3 Spitfire 3 9-00 .... T.Ives[3] 14/1
DISTANCES 4-8-nk-3-6-2

24 Apr Brighton 1m2f	3yoGrad £3,080
10 ran	FIRM	TIME 2m02.70s (slw3.0s)

1 CACOETHES (USA) 3 8-11 .. G.Starkey[4] 5/6F
led 6f out, quickened over 2f out, very easily [op
Evens tchd 5/4 and 4/5]
2 Dolpour 3 8-11 ...... W.R.Swinburn[2] 9/4
3 Child of The Mist 3 8-11 .... M.Hills[3] 11/2
DISTANCES 7-4-4-1½-4-7-6-4-nk

8 Oct[88] Ascot 1m	2yoList £8,985
	third, see NASHWAN (USA)

Ile de Nisky

1-1   **3-9-00**
G.A.HUFFER   b c Ile de Bourbon (USA)
                 — Good Lass (FR)

Starts 1st 2nd 3rd	Win & Pl	(Reform)
2	2 — —	£6,405	

89 Donc 1m2f50y 3yoGrad GD-FM	...... £1,710
88 Nmkt 1m Mdn2yo GOOD	.... £4,695
	TOTAL: £6,405

27 May Doncaster 1m2f50y	3yoGrad £1,710
8 ran	GD-FM	TIME 2m08.26s (slw0.4s)

1 ILE DE NISKY 3 9-04 .... G.Duffield[1] 9/4
*tracked leaders, 2nd straight, led 3f out, ran on
easily* [tchd 5/2 and 2/1]
2 Sharardoun 3 9-04 ...... G.Carter[7] 8/15F
3 Vinstan 3 8-04 .... P.Dalton [7]6 33/1
DISTANCES 6-1½-12-1½-1½-3

13 Oct[88] Nmkt 1m	Mdn2yo £4,695
17 ran	GOOD	TIME 1m42.77s (slw4.4s)

1 ILE DE NISKY 2 8-07 .... B.Lane [7]15 16/1
*led well over 1f out, edged left inside final fur-
long, pushed out* [op 8/1 tchd 20/1]
2 Peace King 2 9-00 .... G.Starkey[10] 8/1
3 Bitone 2 9-00 .... R.Cochrane[6] 4/1
DISTANCES 1½-2-hd-2-½-½-½-2-shd-½-¾-¾
*Following a stewards' inquiry, the objection by
Roberts to the winner was overruled and Val Recit,
who finished second, disqualified and placed
fourth. Roberts was suspended for four days for
careless riding. Peace King and Bitone wre promoted to second and third respectively.*

Nashwan (USA)

11-1   **3-9-00**
MAJORW.R.HERN   ch c Blushing Groom
                 (FR) — Height of

Starts 1st 2nd 3rd	Win & Pl	Fashion (FR) (Bustino)
3	3 — —	£117,574	

89 Nmkt 1m 3yoGp1 GD-FM	.... £103,263
88 Ascot 1m 2yoList GD-SFT	.... £8,985
88 Nbury 7f Mdn2yo GOOD	.... £5,326
	TOTAL: £117,574

6 May Nmkt 1m	3yoGp1 £103,263
14 ran	GD-FM	TIME 1m36.44s (fst2.0s)

1 NASHWAN (USA) 3 9-00 .. W.Carson[12] 3/1F
always prominent, led over 2f out, ridden out [op
3/1 tchd 11/4 and 10/3]
2 Exbourne (USA) 3 9-00 .. C.Asmussen[10] 10/1
3 Danehill (USA) 3 9-00 .....PatEddery[13] 9/1
DISTANCES 1-½-nk-3-1-shd-nk-3-½-10-2½-8-
dist

8 Oct[88] Ascot 1m	2yoList £8,985
6 ran	GD-SFT	TIME 1m47.29s (slw6.4s)

1 NASHWAN (USA) 2 8-11 .. W.Carson[1] 4/6F
2nd straight, led well over 1f out, ran on well [op
evens]
2 Optimist 2 8-11 ...... W.R.Swinburn[3] 11/1
3 CACOETHES (USA) 2 8-11 .. G.Starkey[2] 11/1
4th straight, shaken up 2f out, one pace [op 8/1
tchd 12/1]
DISTANCES 4-1½-5-¾-1

13 Aug[88] Newbury 7f	Mdn2yo £5,326
27 ran	GOOD	TIME 1m28.28s (slw3.5s)

1 NASHWAN (USA) 2 9-00 .. W.Carson[21] 6/4F
*ridden over 1f out, led well inside final furlong,
driven out* [op 9/4 in odd place, then 2/1]
2 Young Turpin 2 9-00 ......S.Cauthen[4] 14/1
3 Child of The Mist 2 9-00 ....M.Hills[10] 10/1
DISTANCES ¾-nk-4-2½-nk-2-shd-½-½-nk-nk-
nk-2½-shd-½

Terimon

8246-2231   **3-9-00**
C.E.BRITTAIN   gr c Bustino — Nicholas
               Grey (Track Spare)

Starts 1st 2nd 3rd	Win & Pl	
8	1 3 1	£7,216	

| 89 Lestr 1m2f Mdn3yo GD-FM | .... £1,884 |

29 May Leicester 1m2f	Mdn3yo £1,884
12 ran	GD-FM	TIME 2m06.90s (slw2.8s)

1 TERIMON 3 9-00 .... B.Procter[9] 9/2
*headway halfway, 5th straight, ran on to lead
near finish*
2 Marcinkus 3 9-00 ......R.McGhin[12] 14/1
3 Carnival Spirit 3 8-11 ...C.Asmussen[11] 6/4F
DISTANCES nk-shd-6-2½-3-2-2

9 May Chester 1m2f85y	Mdn3yo £3,915
9 ran	GD-FM	TIME 2m10.16s (slw0.1s)

1 Sharardoun 3 9-00 .. W.R.Swinburn[4] 11/10F
2 Rudjig (USA) 3 9-00 ..... G.Starkey[5] 5/1
3 TERIMON 3 9-00 ......S.Cauthen[10] 9/2
*pulled hard, prominent, 3rd straight, one pace
from below distance* [op 3/1 tchd 5/1]
DISTANCES 2-2-2-7-1½

15 Apr Thirsk 1m	3yo £5,299
6 ran	GD-SFT	TIME 1m44.1s (slw6.4s)

1 Braiswick 3 8-04 .... G.Carter[5] 13/2
2 TERIMON 3 8-07 .... M.Birch[3] 10/1
*chased leaders 2nd straight, ridden to lead 2f
out, ran on, just caught* [op 10/1 tchd 12/1 in places]
3 Travelling Tryst (USA) 3 8-07 ...T.Ives[1] 8/1
DISTANCES shd-3-2-4-4

FIG. 4.6   Extract of horses' previous form as displayed in *Racing Post*.

alternative view of racing to the average fan, providing easy access to the most relevant information. The competition engendered by having more than one daily national racing newspaper can only be good for the sport, enlivening the scene, and reminding the racing establishment that in changing times no one can rest on the laurels of past glories for ever.

A national racing newspaper is an important accessory to the basic needs of selection, providing the general news of racing plus articles and opinions which enable the selector to remain constantly abreast of events in the racing world.

DETAILS OF FORM

In the assessment of form, the serious selector requires the fullest information of form and for this there can be no substitute for the Form Book.

THE FORM BOOK

This is the officially accepted Form Book printed annually in a bound volume, but received by subscribers throughout the season in weekly up-to-date editions. It is called *Raceform Up-to-Date* – there are separate volumes for Flat and National Hunt racing – one referred to as *Flat Racing Season 19*– and the other called *Chaseform*.

The Form Book is the selector's most important and indispensable tool; it is a publication which has a record of every British racehorse's race performance(s) and is indexed and presented as a book. The Form Book contains the result of every race run and/or that was programmed in the British racing calendar. The results recorded always show the first four placed horses in each race and usually the first nine horses (the size of the field permitting, of course). The official distances between the first six finishers is also normally recorded, together with a commentary on their running and any other horse(s) who figured prominently during the race. A page from the Form Book is illustrated in Fig. 4.7. Altogether the Form Book records:

The meeting – the going, the time of the race (and time of the 'off').
The value of the race, and its distance.
The horses competing, in finishing order, with respective trainer and jockey.
The weights carried, including overweight and allowances.
The draw (where applicable – Flat), blinkers and hoods.
The winning owner, trainer and breeder.

365—**EPSOM (L-H)**
Wednesday, June 7th [Good]
Going Allowance: minus 0.15 sec per fur (F)   Wind: nil
Stalls: high 4th, remainder low

1060   EVER READY DERBY STKS (Gp 1) (3-Y.O.C & F) £296000.00 (£111000.00: £53500.00:
            £23500.00) **1½m**
                                                                                                 3-45 (3-50)

510* **Nashwan (USA)** (Fav) *(MajorWRHern)* 9-0 WCarson (10) (lw: 4th st: led over 2f
        out: drvn out: r.o wl) .... —1
895* Terimon *(CEBrittain)* 9-0 MRoberts (8) (lw: gd hdwy fnl 2f: fin wl) 5.2
643* Cacoethes (USA) *(GHarwood)* 9-0 GStarkey (5) (lw: 2nd st: led over 3f out to
        over 2f out: r.o) 2.3
873* Ile de Nisky *(GAHuffer)* 9-0 GDuffield (12) (lw: 3rd st: r.o one pce fnl 2f) ½.4
    Mill Pond (FR) *(PLBiancone,France)* 9-0 PatEddery (11) (str: gd hdwy 3f out:
        one pce fnl 2f) 2.5
797⁴ Gran Alba (USA) *(RHannon)* 9-0 BRouse (1) (hdwy 3f out: one pce fnl 2f) 2.6
822a⁵ Classic Fame (USA) *(MVO'Brien,Ireland)* 9-0 JReid (3) (w'like: str: no hdwy fnl
        3f) 6.7
697* Torjoun (USA) *(LMCumani)* 9-0 RCochrane (4) (swtg: led 6f out to over 3f out: sn
        wknd) ¾.8
697⁶ Flockton's Own (v) *(JRShaw)* 9-0 RHills (6) (5th st: wknd 3f out) 3.9
502* Prince of Dance *(MajorWRHern)* 9-0 SCauthen (9) (lw: hdwy 5f out: sn rdn: wknd
        3f out) hd.10
797* Warrshan (USA) *(MRStoute)* 9-0 WRSwinburn (2) (6th st: wknd over 3f out: t.o) ... 15.11
635² Polar Run (USA) *(GHarwood)* 9-0 AClark (7) (lw: led 6f: sn wknd: t.o) 25.12

5/4 NASHWAN (USA), **3/1** Cacoethes (USA), **11/2** Prince of Dance, **11/1** Warrshan
(USA), **16/1** Mill Pond (FR), **20/1** Ile de Nisky, **33/1** Classic Fame (USA), **80/1** Gran Alba (USA), **250/1** Polar
Run (USA), **500/1** Ors. CSF £153.32, Tote £2.60: £1.40 £20.20 £1.80 (£298.20). Mr Hamdan Al-Maktoum
(WEST ILSLEY) bred by Hamdan Al Maktoum in USA. 12 Rn   2m 34.90 (U1.1)
                                                                      SF—93/83/79/78/74/70/58

1061   NIGHT RIDER H'CAP (0-115)   £13810.00 (£4180.00: £2040.00: £970.00)
            5f
                                                                                                 4-40 (4-41)

805⁴ **Gallant Hope** (bl) *(LGCottrell)* 7-7-10 WShoemaker (9) (lw: mde all: r.o wl) .... —1
805⁵ Ski Captain *(PHowling)* 5-7-9 TyroneWilliams (10) (a.p: ev ch over 1f out: nt
        qckn) 3.2
848* Restless Don *(DWChapman)* 4-7-11⁽²⁾ WCarson (8) (hdwy & hrd rdn over 1f
        out: r.o ins fnl f) nk.3
805² Absolution *(DWChapman)* 5-8-7 MHills (5) (a.p: nt qckn fnl f) ½.4
761 Grand Prix *(RAkehurst)* 4-7-8⁽¹⁾ RFox (7) (nvr nr to chal) 1½.5
805⁶ Micro Love *(HO'Neill)* 5-7-7 JLowe (4) (no hdwy fnl 2f) 1½.6
511⁵ Perion (Fav) *(GLewis)* 7-10-0 PatEddery (6) (hld up: rdn 2f out: wknd fnl f) 7
910² Tachyon Park (bl) *(PJArthur)* 7-7-11 CRutter (3) (lw: prom 3f) 8
373 Clarentia *(MDIUsher)* 5-8-2 AMcGlone (1) (b.nr hind: spd 3f) 9
805 Ashtina (bl) *(APIngham)* 4-8-10 SCauthen (2) (lw: spd over 2f: t.o) 10
    LONG HANDICAP: Grand Prix 6-13, Micro Love 7-3.

7/2 Perion(5/1—3/1), **5/1** Absolution, **11/2** Restless Don, **6/1** GALLANT HOPE, Ski Captain, **9/1** Ashtina,
10/1 Tachyon Park, **16/1** Micro Love, **25/1** Grand Prix, **50/1** Clarentia. CSF £37.32, CT £187.46. Tote £10.70:
£2.80 £1.90 £1.50 (£29.60). Mrs Nerys Dutfield (CULLOMPTON) bred by Mrs A. W. F. Whitehead. 10Rn
A.O.R.—78   54.89 sec (U.11)
                                                                      SF—69/56/57/65/46/39

FIG. 4.7   Extract from the Form Book.

The race time is also recorded with comparison to standard time and
    speed figures calculated on these times.

The betting market and starting prices are recorded plus the equivalent
    Tote prices including the daily double, treble and placepot, etc.

Such detailed coverage of races, which are so clearly marked, make the
Form Book a trusted asset in the sometimes involved process of form
selection.

    The *Sporting Life* also produces a form book which serves as a rival to
the well-established and officially accepted *Raceform* publication. It
appears in two separate annuals covering each code of racing: *Flat
Results 19–* and *National Hunt Results 19–*. They are produced in glossy

paper-bound covers and contain each season's racing results originating from those printed daily in the newspaper.

These annual form books also contain a full list of jockeys' weights, and average times for each course, providing further information for the racing fan.

The results of the races themselves are set out in two columns down the page, in date and time sequence, with the title, type of race, prize-money and distance at the top of each race, and beneath, the first nine horses (size of the field permitting) identified in finishing order. By the side of each horse is the weight it carried, its jockey, a close-up commentary of its race performance, plus its starting price and any betting fluctuations. At the foot of each race the margins between the first six finishers are recorded with their corresponding speed rating, and the trainer of the winner. All the English and Irish fixtures in the racing calendar are included plus some of the leading European races. The index at the back of the book contains every horse which raced during the season, its age, pedigree, a full record of the races it contested and who trained it, thus setting off this publication as a useful addition to the armoury of racing information.

FORM SHEETS (from daily racing newspapers)

These are the abbreviated version of the Form Book provided in the national daily racing newspapers (see Figs. 4.4 and 4.6). They can be used as a substitute for the more complete information contained within the Form Book, or may serve in the role of an eliminating agent in the initial review of form. In this respect form sheets act as reference points, requiring that the selector undertake a more searching investigation with the aid of the Form Book.

Form sheets present the selector with a useful outline of form, but cannot be confidently accepted as providing the complete picture as they may withhold almost as much information as they reveal.

A HORSE'S BIOGRAPHY

This is the in-depth information which may finally confirm or deny the impression of a horse's ability that has been developing in the form evaluation process. It will be found most easily and reliably in the specialist racing publications of Timeform – namely the weekly *Black books* and the more detailed *Annuals* (Flat and National Hunt).

The Timeform book contains a brief or detailed account of every horse that has raced, plus some as yet untraced (see Fig. 4.8). There is a

December: 20/1, last of 8 finishers in novice hurdle won by Texan Cowboy at Plumpton 6 weeks later. *J. A. B. Old.*

BARGE POLE 8 b.g. Pollerton–Bargy Music (Tudor Music) [1988/9 c20sᴘᵁ] good-bodied, useful-looking gelding: lightly-raced winning hurdler/chaser: stayed 2¹/₂m: acted on heavy going: was a dependable jumper: dead. *Capt. T. A. Forster.*   c—
—

BARKIN 6 b.g. Crash Course–Annie Augusta (Master Owen) [1988/9 16m 16s⁴ 16g 20d 20fᴘᵁ] lengthy gelding: second foal: dam unraced half-sister to several winning jumpers: best effort in novice hurdles when around 9¹/₂ lengths fourth behind Another Coral at Bangor in December: trained until after third start by J. Edwards. *T. H. Caldwell.*   86

BARKMILLS 6 b.g. Maculata–Fairy Show (Prefairy) [1988/9 F17d⁴ 16s⁴ F17d 16d² F17d 16v* 20v² 16v³ 19s⁴ 19s 22v* 19v⁶ 20d⁴ 24v⁵ 20d²] Irish gelding: first foal: dam lightly-raced maiden: won maiden hurdle at Gowran Park in October and minor event at Thurles in February, showing much improved form when beating Shannon Spray a neck in latter: neck second to Sutica in 25-runner handicap at Punchestown in April, best subsequent effort: suited by 2¹/₂m or more: acts on heavy going. *Patrick Mullins, Ireland.*   132

BARNABY BENZ 5 b.g. Lochnager–Miss Barnaby (Sun Prince) [1988/9 16sᶠ 16g 16d] dipped-backed, good-quartered gelding: modest middle-distance handicapper on Flat, winner twice in 1988: never placed to challenge when in mid-division in novice hurdles at Catterick in December and Southwell in January: not knocked about either time and gives impression capable of better. *M. H. Easterby.*   — p

BARNACLE BILL 6 ch.g. Nicholas Bill–Matsui (Falcon) [1988/9 16f 16gᴘᵁ] leggy gelding: races much too freely to stay 2m over hurdles: has twice sweated up badly. *I. Campbell.*

BARN BRAE 7 b.g. Derek H–La Raine (Majority Blue) [1988/9 c16d c16s² c20v⁵ c20dᴘᵁ c21v⁶ c17m³ c16s* c16sᶠ c16s² c21f³] angular, workmanlike gelding: clear most of way when winning amateur riders novice chase at Market Rasen in March: stays 21f at least when conditions aren't testing: below form on heavy going, acts on any other: usually amateur ridden. *J. P. Leigh.*   c95

BARNBROOK AGAIN 8 b.g. Nebbiolo–Single Line (USA) (Rash Prince) [1988/9 c17s* c20m* c20g* c16d*]   c168
—

A new name went on the trophy for the Queen Mother Champion Chase in 1989, Barnbrook Again. Offered a golden opportunity by the injury to the past two years' winner Pearlyman and the switching of Pearlyman's old rival Desert Orchid to the Gold Cup, he seized it by four lengths and the same from Royal Stag and Beau Ranger. In so doing Barnbrook Again ended his season, his second over fences, unbeaten in four starts. He has developed into a top-class chaser and though not yet so good as Pearlyman or some of the other dual winners the race has become noted for, he is young enough and may well be good enough to emulate them.

Barnbrook Again started 7/4 favourite at Cheltenham ahead of Beau Ranger, whose effectiveness over the distance was questionable, and the previous year's fourth Midnight Count, apart from Panto Prince the only horse in the line-up to have contested the Champion Chase before. Vodkatini, like Royal Stag much improved, Wolf of Badenoch and Prideaux Boy completed the field. Barnbrook Again and the Irish-trained Wolf of Badenoch had each shown themselves leading novices in 1987/8 despite injury set-backs, Barnbrook Again having the better form which included a superb twenty-length win from Prideaux Boy in the Hurst Park Novices' Chase at Ascot. On his final outing as a novice Barnbrook Again was beaten ten lengths into third behind Danish Flight in the Arkle Challenge Trophy. He didn't look himself that day, jumping out to the right and making mistakes. Those inclined to discount his rather disappointing performance, among them ourselves and his trainer, would have taken great encouragement from Barnbrook Again's first run in 1988/9, against Panto Prince, Long Engagement and Western Sunset in the Plymouth Gin Haldon Gold Challenge Cup, a well-conceived start-of-campaign race for above-average chasers at Devon & Exeter in October. He was a very convincing winner by four lengths from Panto Prince. After this, all sorts of targets were announced for Barnbrook Again, among them the Mackeson, the H & T Walker Gold Cup

71

FIG. 4.8   Extract of a typical page from *Timeform Annual, Chasers & Hurdlers 1988–89.*

brief biography of a horse's breeding, its foaling date and cost if bought at public auction (in the case of 2-year-olds), a description of its conformation – plus an analysis and rating of performance(s) by their experts. The Timeform publications have rightly gained a high reputation for their consistently sound analysis and judgement and will prove extremely useful in providing important background detail for the selector who has little or no visual contact with horse-racing.

TOOLS FOR BETTING

The backer, having made a confident well-chosen selection, seeks access to the best facilities to make betting an easy and profitable practice. These are described in Chapter 5.

5 BETTING

The purpose of betting is to win money!

Betting is defined: 'To risk money on the result of an event – to back an opinion with money.'

Betting can be described as the practical act which confirms commitment to a decision.

Betting seeks to exploit for profit a correct opinion. Successful betting is therefore subject to correct selections.

Horse-race selection is subject only to its own process and can exist without betting.

Selection must remain separate from and dictate to, betting. An intrusion of betting considerations in the selection process undermines the selection decision and thereby defeats its purpose.

Betting will only be financially viable if practised as part of a calculated, reasoned act.

TO WIN AT BETTING

The obvious and fundamental necessity is betting on winners. If selections recorded are 100 per cent correct there are no modifying factors that can prevent winning at betting. This is an ideal to be aimed for with selections but is an unlikely practical reality.

THE MODIFYING FACTORS

The factors which prevent winning at betting are as follows:

1. The percentage of winners to losers;
2. The *odds* of winners backed;
3. The staking method used.

BETTING TECHNIQUE – 'If' and 'How' to bet

Betting technique is basically simple; it revolves around one question that must always be asked: 'To bet or not to bet.' Even with a confident reasoned selection decision this question is evoked, because the factor still to be considered that will limit successful betting is 'the odds'.

In the assessment of odds the following should be considered:

- The purpose of betting is to win and the odds place a limit on what can be won.
- The backer has no control in the formation of odds – odds are controlled by the layers (layers of odds bookmakers) who manipulate the odds for the distinct purpose of restricting winnings and limiting their own financial liabilities.
- The backer has only one action to combat this power of fixing the odds that is held by the bookmaker – he has the power of veto.

THE 'IF'

'Not to bet until the odds be considered fair, reasonable or completely in the favour of the backer is an advantage which must never be surrendered. The bookmaker has to lay odds all the time for each and every race – but the backer can choose if and when to bet.

In assessing the odds the backer, supported by a confident reasoned selection, needs to pose the monetary question: 'What can I win?' Specifically, 'How will the money returned be comparable to the money risked?' Money used for betting is very high risk capital and it is suggested that the minimum acceptable return be at least equal to outlay – 'even money'. *The backer must consider odds of less than evens unacceptable in all circumstances.*

Successful betting is dependent upon the following:

1. *Selecting winners.* Selections formulated without prejudice or enticement to bet, based upon factors of reasoned probability, are selections that hold the most likelihood of winning.
2. *Betting at fair and reasonable odds.* Only betting at odds where gain is appropriate or favourable to the amount of money risked.
3. *Staking system.* One which places no undue emphasis on one particular bet to the detriment or enhancement of the previous betting record.

A successful outcome to betting requires that betting be conducted as a calm reasoned act, paying due regard to these modifying factors. This will mean applying discipline to refrain from betting in unfavourable circumstances and practising only good betting habits.

Selection, odds and staking are theoretically the only factors in the betting process, but in practice there is another all-pervading aspect which can conspire to play a dominant role. This is the *financial consideration*. Although the purpose of betting is to win money, betting entails the risk of losing money. Lucid betting requires the removal of that fear of losing, whether in the form of hard cash, markers, credit or encapsulated ego and pride. The financial involvement, therefore, must be considered, realized and placed in its true perspective.

Money used for betting is high-risk money

It is therefore essential that a bank or pool of money be set aside to be used solely for the purposes of betting. The size of the bank may be large or small, but with the prerequisite that losing the whole or part of the bank places no financial burden on the backer.
- It must be money that the backer can afford to lose.
- It must be money that the backer is not attached to.
- It must be money the backer considers already lost.

A weakening from this rigid viewpoint will serve only to promote the unwelcome influence of the financial consideration. Unchecked, this influence will grow to affect the selection process adversely and thereby undermine the basis upon which successful betting is founded.

THE 'HOW' TO BET

The way

Betting is the simple act of supporting an opinion/selection with money. Placing a bet is an uncomplicated operation – writing instructions on a slip/voucher or verbally giving instructions by telephone.

There are three ways to bet on a single selection: (1) to win; (2) place (only); (3) each way (win and place combine). Single selections may be joined together to form doubles, trebles and accumulators in myriad combinations.

Besides single selection bets there are forecast bets:
- Straight forecast – predicting the first two finishers in correct order.
- Dual forecast – predicting the first two finishers in either order.
- Forecasts can be similarly joined together to form doubles, trebles, etc.
- Tricasts – selecting the first three finishers in correct order in handicap races of 8 or more runners.

SINGLE SELECTION BET

To win   is the simplest and most economic bet. It demands decisive selection.

Place only   is an uneconomic bet; SP and Tote place bets of selections with positive chances of being placed are normally odds-on. It encourages timid and indecisive selection.

Each way   the place part of the bet is uneconomic at one-fifth of the odds. If the selection wins, half the stake has been wasted in an endeavour to protect whole or part of the stake.

Tote odds are not guaranteed for any type of bet.

The single win bet is the best possible way to bet. It is uncomplicated, economically sound and no part of the stake is wasted if the selection is successful. Selection is focused on predicting decisive positive results; its aim is unmistakably understood from the outset.

There are other methods besides single selection bets which include the following. Combined selection bets (doubles, trebles, etc.) designed to give a large return on a small outlay by multiplying the odds together. The increase of odds signifies a decrease in the chances of winning and should be considered an over-ambitious, uneconomic way of betting. Forecasts similarly have the attraction of multiple odds and large possible gain for small outlay, but the inherent weakness of numerous combinations of possible results. Forecasts can only be economically viable when the possibilities of the result are numerically small and the multiplication of odds large (i.e. in small fields of five or less – a combination forecast made of the highest-priced runners. This is a proposition based on mathematical speculation and without any regard necessarily to selection based on reasoned probability).

Single selection bets contain enough unpredictable factors without the further uncertainties introduced when combining selections. It is said that doubles were invented for anyone not satisfied with one loser but preferring two.

STAKING SYSTEMS

The obvious and most simple to operate 'level stakes' is the best method. In level stakes every bet is of the same value, every bet is of equal importance and no particular relevance is attached to any single bet. Therefore, no single selection decision is less or more important than the previous, and one loser places no financial loss out of proportion to other losers.

ODDS (PRICES)

Odds are the degree of probability of winning. Prices are shown as odds *against* the chance of winning. For example with odds of 2–1, one is risked to gain two. Odds are also the means by which the layers of odds make a profit whatever the result. Bookmakers make a book of prices/ odds on an event, giving each competitor or runner price or odds against its chances of winning. These prices are carefully mathematically balanced against the money betted, so after settling payment of all winning bets the bookmaker takes a percentage profit on the overall money that has been taken.

The odds are formulated and controlled by the major bookmakers at a race meeting. After an initial write-up or opening 'show' of prices, market forces operate, with prices adjusted to accommodate varying amounts of money wagered. This betting market continues until the start of the race. The starting price odds are the mean average price for each horse calculated by independent assessors, from the lists of the leading bookmakers at the end of trading. They are a fair representation of the amount of money wagered on each horse. In the market exchanges before the start of the race, prices continually fluctuate according to supply and demand and a bet struck during these exchanges will be at a 'board price' which may be more or less than the final or starting price.

THE THREE TYPES OF ODDS

Starting price (SP) odds

The official, independently calculated average odds, that were offered by Course bookmakers at the close of trading at the start of the race.

Board price odds

The odds laid and taken in the market exchanges before a race. These odds are fixed, guaranteed and not subject to any later market fluctuations.

Tote odds

The odds calculated after the division of the pool of money wagered on a race with the Totalisator Board. These odds are not fixed or guaranteed. They are sometimes unpredictable, depending on the size of the pool and how this relates to the number of winning ticket holders (i.e. a large pool with few winning ticket holders pays high odds, a small pool with many winning ticket holders pays low odds).

Tote odds are presented in the form of dividend to a £1 unit staked. For example, £3.50 returned wins £2.50, or odds of 5–2. Tote dividends are the actual amount paid to the backer and are not subject to any further reductions (such as betting tax, rule 4 on withdrawals, etc.) that occur in SP betting.

NB. Some bookmakers do not accept bets at Tote odds, so the backer can bet with the Tote only when visiting a racecourse, or a Tote-owned betting shop, or as a Tote account customer.

BOOKMAKER'S PERCENTAGE

Bookmakers win in the long run and most backers lose in the long run because the odds available are balanced in favour of the bookmaker. Take the most simple case of all, the two-horse race where both animals are believed to have equal chances of winning. The situation is exactly the same as spinning a coin, heads and tails are both even-money chances. That gives the bookmaker no profit margin, so in a two-horse race if one horse, A, is evens the other, B, will be odds-on say 4–5, to give the bookies their percentage. If the odds-makers have got things exactly right their book on the race may look like this:

£55.55 to win on B at 4–5 – liability £99.99
£50 to win on A at Evens – liability £100.00
Total £105.55

Whichever horse wins, the bookie wins £5.55.

The more runners there are in the race the bigger the bookmaker's percentage can be without it appearing bad value to the backer. On average the bookmakers will have around 30 per cent built into the odds in their favour, but in a two-horse race that would mean odds of approximately 8–15 on both horses which would be completely unacceptable. So they are prepared to accept around 5 per cent on two horse races but ask for, and get, more than 50 per cent in big fields.

The discerning backer must be able to calculate when the bookmakers' margins are unacceptable and be able to work out the odds. To do this requires a little skill in arithmetic, but it is well worth while practising on a few races.

The odds of each horse must first be worked out in terms of a percentage that it represents towards the bookies' profit. To do this write down the odds of a horse as a fraction, putting the left-hand part of the odds on the bottom and the right-hand part on top. Then add the top part of the fraction into the bottom part, divide it out and show the answer as a percentage. A few examples are shown overleaf:

2–1 is $\frac{1}{2}$ becomes $\frac{1}{1+2} = \frac{1}{3} = 33.3\%$
3–1 is $\frac{1}{3}$ becomes $\frac{1}{1+3} = \frac{1}{4} = 25.0\%$
4–6 is $\frac{6}{4}$ becomes $\frac{6}{4+6} = \frac{6}{10} = 60.0\%$
13–8 is $\frac{8}{13}$ becomes $\frac{8}{8+13} = \frac{8}{21} = 38.1\%$

The most commonly used prices (up to 10–1) in terms of odds percentages are given in Table 5.1.

TABLE 5.1   Odds expressed as percentages

Odds-on	Price	Odds-against
50.00%	Evens	50.00%
52.38	11–10	47.62
54.55	6–5	45.45
55.56	5–4	44.44
57.89	11–8	42.11
60.00	6–4	40.00
61.90	13–8	38.10
63.64	7–4	36.36
65.22	15–8	34.78
66.67	2–1	33.33
68.00	85–40	32.00
69.23	9–4	30.77
71.43	5–2	28.57
73.33	11–4	26.67
75.06	3–1	25.00
76.92	10–3	23.08
77.78	7–2	22.22
80.00	4–1	20.00
81.82	9–2	18.18
83.33	5–1	16.67
84.62	11–2	15.38
85.71	6–1	14.29
88.67	13–2	13.33
87.50	7–1	12.50
88.24	15–2	11.76
88.89	8–1	11.11
89.47	17–2	10.53
90.00	9–1	10.00
90.91	10–1	9.09

To calculate the theoretical percentage profit for the bookies in a given race, calculate the percentages for every runner and add them up. The resulting figure is the so-called *overround* figure or the percentage in favour of the bookies. An example taken from the 1989 St Leger is given in Table 5.2.

In broad terms the bookmakers are prepared to work on smaller margins in small fields, at big meetings and on the first race at a

TABLE 5.2   Bookmakers' percentage on the 1989 St Leger

Horse	Starting price	Percentage towards profit
MICHELOZZO	6–4	4/10 = 40.0
ROSEATE TERN	5–2	2/7 = 28.6
TERIMON	7–2	2/9 = 22.2
N.C. OWEN	12–1	1/13 = 7.7
ALPHABEL	14–1	1/15 = 6.7
SAPIENCE	15–1	1/16 = 6.3
BLAZING TOUCH	100–1	1/101 = 1.0
SKISURF	250–1	1/251 = 0.4
Total		112.9
Percentage in bookmakers' favour		= 12.9

meeting. They work on big margins in large fields, on bank holidays and in sellers.

It is also important to note that the bookmakers make least out of bets on favourites and short-odds horses and most on long-odds chances. An analysis of the prices of all the horses that ran on the Flat in 1988 and National Hunt 1988–89 is given in Table 5.3.

TABLE 5.3   Analysis of prices of horses that ran on (a) the Flat in 1988, (b) the National Hunt in 1988–89

(a)

Prices	Wins	Runs	Profit or loss
Odds-on	275	442	+£2.18
Evens – 2–1	1,047	14,862	−£5,945.34
9–4 – 5–1	525	7,927	−£3,035.45
11–2 – 9–1	370	7,088	−£2,940.50
10–1 +	95	1,953	−£445

(b)

Prices	Wins	Runs	Profit or loss
Odds-on	432	726	−£32.86
Evens – 2–1	1,211	16,625	−£6,965.38
9–4 – 5–1	282	4,112	−£1,559.91
11–2 – 9–1	232	4,701	−£1,735
10–1 +	73	2,096	−£721

Odds are the factor which decides how little or how much is returned on the money staked. Winning money demands betting successfully at the right odds.

THE RIGHT ODDS

This can be termed as getting 'value for money', when it is clearly understood to mean obtaining fair and reasonable odds on a well-formulated selection which has a positive reasoned chance of winning. However, value for money often tends to be a term totally misunderstood. Attractive sounding odds are worthless if a horse has no chance of winning.

It is impossible to state categorically what are the right odds without examining the factors particular to any given situation. It can only be left to the personal judgement of the backer to decide what odds in the circumstances are appropriate, always placing supreme importance on two questions: What can I win? and What do I stand to lose? And how these two factors relate to the practical chances of the selection winning.

Before suggesting what may be considered the right odds it can be emphatically stated what can be considered 'bad odds'. 'Odds-on' are bad odds as they are unfair and unreasonable.

They can never favour the backer, who stands to lose more than can be gained.

They always favour the bookmaker, whose risk is less than his possible gain.

At odds-on the onus is firmly placed on the backer being correct in selection. At 'evens' less than a 50 per cent winning ratio produces financial loss. In such circumstances the only viable response to bad, unfair, restrictive odds is not to bet.

A guide to the 'right odds'

Getting the 'right odds' can be termed as the fine balance of the odds that can be fairly and reasonably demanded by the circumstances and the odds realistically likely to be offered by the bookmakers.

The circumstances reveal and are subject to the following factors:

1. The proven quality of the form of the selection.
2. The number of runners, particularly the number with probable chances of winning (i.e. the more competitive the race, the more open should be the betting odds).
3. The type of race (e.g. condition races basically have a reliable predictability value. All types of handicaps are by their nature

unpredictable. Chases are similarly laced with drama and surprises that can thwart even the most reasoned of selections).

These prominent factors have to be carefully considered when making a calculated assessment of true, fair, appropriate odds – which may not bear close relationship to the odds offered and calculated solely to favour the layers!

The realistic view of the odds actually offered by the bookmakers is subject to the following:

1. The popular predictability of the selectors (i.e. how strongly have the racing press tipped or ignored the selections).
2. Information/rumour private to bookmakers, of a horse's chances which causes them cautiously to shorten or speculatively lengthen prices.
3. Weight of money wagered before the opening show of prices, which restricts the possibility of a fair price being offered.

After giving due regard to the odds which may be realistically offered, a guide can be suggested upon which to base the 'fair' right odds. This should be constructed on the understanding that 'evens' are the lowest acceptable odds, and that upward price adjustments be made to accommodate competition and conditions.

A 'fair price' for a horse in a race in which there is no foreseeable competition is evens. When betting tax and unforeseen circumstances are taken into consideration there will still remain a good profit for the backer in this situation. Odds-on is not acceptable because the profit for the backer is reduced to unacceptable or non-existent levels.

If there is a serious danger to a selection the backer must look for longer odds to compensate for the additional risk; 2–1 is the least acceptable odds.

Two serious rivals, the backer must look for 3–1 or more; three serious rivals warrants 4–1 or more and so on.

NB. It is considered that a race comprising three or more serious rivals is too competitive to contemplate a selection, and any betting in these circumstances is likely to be most injudicious.

Favourable conditions such as weight, distance and/or going require the reduction of odds by a fraction of a point. Similarly, if these and/or other elements are to the disadvantage of a selection, then fractions of a point should be added.

By this method the backer can calculate odds that are fair and equivalent to the practical elements influencing the winning chances of a selection. The backer with this formed and detached assessment of the odds can readily make a reasoned comparison with the actual odds offered by the bookmaker, and not be unknowingly beguiled to accepting less than a fair value. The value offered to backers does vary considerably from course to course according to the strength of the market.

BETTING VALUE HINTS

Every backer knows how difficult it is to beat the bookie, because the satchel man fixes the odds. Ask a bookmaker if you can have a bet on the toss of a coin and he will offer you 4–5 for each of the two so he can make his profit.

What few backers realize is that the bookie's profit margin varies from race to race and that the off-course bookmaker and backer are in the hands of the on-course bookmaker who fixes the prices.

Backers can obtain a vital edge by knowing when the odds are in their favour and avoiding betting on races when the bookies' take is high.

A survey was made of flat races run in 1988 and National Hunt races of 1988–89 and, using a computer to make the many thousands of calculations involved, produced the following results. The average mark-up was just over 34 per cent, which gives the odds fixers a reasonable profit. However, in some races the mark-up went to over 60 per cent, yet in others was less than 10 per cent.

By and large, the more runners there are in a race the bigger the bookies' margin becomes. In our coin-tossing example, the layers would have to go to 4–6 heads and tails to get their average 20 per cent margin, and who would bet at those odds? It can be seen from Table 5.4 that betting in fields of 5 runners or less is a much better proposition than betting in fields of 16 or more runners.

TABLE 5.4

Size of field	% Mark-up	
	Flat 1988	National Hunt 1988–89
5 and under	8.4	9.0
6–15	21.8	21.4
16 and over	49.1	48.1
All races	35.0	33.9

A useful rule-of-thumb guide to gauge the bookmakers' likely margin is to add 2 per cent for each runner. Hence in a five-horse race expect a 10 per cent mark-up while in a ten-runner field the profit margin will be about 20 per cent.

TOTE ODDS

These are not guaranteed. They are declared after the race when the number of winning tickets is measured against the size of the Tote pool. A dividend for win, place and dual forecast is then announced. Few winning tickets in a large pool will produce long odds whilst many winning in a small pool will produce short odds. This uncertainty persuades some backers to seek the guaranteed return of a 'board price' offered by bookmakers.

However, the Tote, using the latest technology in its racecourse operations, now informs backers of its on-going betting odds. This has done much to dispel the unpredictability. Current Tote odds are clearly displayed on screens above the betting windows, with changes flashed every few moments to show any fluctuations. The actual 'pay out' dividend is usually approximate to that shown just before betting stops at the 'off'.

Sizeable bets on any runner (representing 10% or more of the Tote Pool) can depress the eventual dividend unless counterbalanced by a proportionate amount for other runners. Unlike bookmakers, who respond swiftly to rumour and money from inspired sources to reduce the odds, the Tote reacts only to weight of money. Therefore nominal bets (of 2% or less of the Tote pool) have little impact on their odds.

Advice to backers at the racetrack must be to compare the odds of the Tote with those in the ring and bet with whoever offers the better value.

As a general rule the Tote will be likely to offer the better value on:

(i)   larger fields – (here the bookmakers' margin is known to be highest);
(ii) horses not tipped in the press or published form guides;
(iii) unfancied horses from unfashionable stables;
(iv) mounts of lesser known jockeys.

STAKING

Stakes

The amount of money bet is of equal importance and fully complementary to odds. Winning money is the outcome of developing a successful betting technique, and this will only be established by maintaining a disciplined staking method. Although many staking plans abound, the best, most efficient, obvious and simplest to practice is *level stakes betting*. Level stakes ensures every bet is treated with equal importance.

The size of the stake

This essentially must be left to the personal consideration of each backer. For practical guidance it is recommended that a bank of money (set aside for betting purposes) be divided into 20 equal parts to represent 20 bets at level stakes. Such an approach enables the betting to commence without any financial pressure or looming insolvency.

Level stakes may appear a cautious, mundane method of betting – but results testify to its effectiveness and sound economic basis.

Favourable odds

When odds are offered that are well above their real value (e.g. 5–1 is offered for a selection whose realistic odds should be 2–1) such favourable odds demand an increase of the stake. The amount of increase can only be left to the personal judgement of the backer; the guiding factor being: 'the greater the value the greater the increase in the stake'.

The occasions when bookmakers generously err in the odds offered is extremely rare – they do exist – but only enforce the wisdom of maintaining level stakes at most times. Real over the odds value from bookmakers is comparable to 'solid gold' watches being sold cheaply – it is a situation to be viewed with great scepticism.

In the fluctuations of the betting market, drifting odds can become favourable odds if they reach well above a level thought to represent fair value. This situation justifies making another bet, if one had already been struck at lower odds, or increasing the stake if a bet has yet to be made.

In the charged atmosphere of the betting ring the drifting or lengthening of odds are the bookmakers' only method of attracting money to balance their 'book'. The drifting of the odds of any carefully formulated selection should not cause the backer to lose nerve but rather to take full advantage of the opportunity to obtain extra value by increasing the stake.

Shortening odds are unfavourable odds

If odds shorten no attempt must be made to increase stake to compensate for loss of the price value. If a bet was not made at the fair 'right odds' a bet must not be made later at shorter odds (especially when there is a temptation to increase stakes).

An increase of stakes to offset shortening of odds is at best an extreme method of buying money, which if habitually practised will quickly lead to betting bankruptcy.

ACCUMULATIVE STAKING (BASED ON THE LEVEL STAKES PRINCIPLE)

Level staking makes no immediate use of winnings.

Accumulative staking seeks to make full use of winnings by immediate reinvestment to produce further profit.

The bank – divided into 20 equal units representing 20 equal bets – allows for 20 consecutive losers before the bank is lost completely. The profit from winnings is added to the bank, which is divided immediately to raise the level of stakes of the remaining bets.

If the first bet is a 2–1 winner, e.g. 2 pts profit:

    2 pts + bank 20 pts = 22 pts

    22 pts ÷ 20 (bets) = 1.1 pts (20 remaining bets)

If the first bet was a loser and the second bet a 2–1 winner, e.g. 2 pts profit:

    2 pts + (remaining bank) 19 pts = 21 pts

    21 pts ÷ 19 (remaining bets) = 1.105 pts (19 remaining bets)

If it were desired to keep the bank intact in the second instance, then:

    21 pts ÷ 20 (original no. of bets) = 1.05 pts (20 bets)

NB. The rate of increase in stakes is subject to the odds and consistency of winning selections.

SUMMARY OF BETTING

A guide to successful betting may be summarized in the following formula:

    S   O   S

  Selection   Odds   Stakes

These alone are the three factors which govern betting.

Selection

This is the first and fundamental element. Selection is the *means* – without winning selections there is no possibility of achieving successful betting results.

Odds

These are a modifying element, secondary to selection. Odds are the modality which impose a limit on how much can be won. Objectively they must evoke the question: 'Is the reward worth the risk?'

Stakes

These are the other modifying element – complementary to both odds and selection. Stakes are the method which serves to apply the means. Stakes raise the question: 'How much should be risked?' Stakes are the vital monetary aspect whose inconsistent or ordered application will frustrate or promote the successful outcome of betting.

The outcome of successful betting is to win money. This objective can only be consistently achieved by supporting successful selections at the 'right odds' with a rational system of stakes.

BETTING AND BOOKMAKERS

BOOKMAKING

This is the making of a book (set) of odds on the outcome of an event. The odds are mathematically calculated to provide the maker of the book with a percentage profit on turnover irrespective of the outcome of the event.

BOOKMAKERS

These are the layers of odds – they form the betting market, which they endeavour to control and manipulate to maintain an advantage over the betting public. The layer of odds seeks to obtain the minimum of liability (pay-out) coupled with the maximum of income from betting stakes. This therefore makes odds-on the most attractive and favourable bet to the bookmaker and the most unfavourable bet to anyone taking those odds.

Bookmakers operate through the British Isles 'on' and 'off' the course, some are strictly on-course or off-course boomakers, while others combine and are both kinds. The betting market, however, is formed and controlled solely at the racecourse (except for ante-post betting) by the on-course bookmakers.

Types of on-course bookmakers

There are three separate groups of on-course bookmakers who can be immediately recognized from the position where they trade on the racecourse: (i) the 'rails' bookmakers; (ii) the 'Tatts' bookmakers; (iii) the Silver Ring (or public enclosure) bookmakers.

The 'rails' bookmakers

These are the foremost and, at most race meetings, the group of bookmakers which holds a commanding influence in the betting market. They take their position on the racecourse lining the railings which divide the members' enclosure from the Tattersalls enclosure. They are the senior, longest established and largest firms of book-

The 'rails' bookmakers – stand on the railings dividing the members' enclosure from the Tattersalls Ring. In the foreground a principal of one firm is receiving instructions via cellular telephone while his clerk looks down their ledger of bets taken on the race. Meanwhile to their right a principal of another firm answers an enquiry of a client from the members' enclosure, as in the background tic-tac men frantically relay market moves to other bookmakers.

The 'Tatts' bookmakers display on blackboards the price on offer for each horse, which can vary between bookmakers.

Bookmakers
Opposite is a scene overlooking the action of the betting rings. On the left, the 'Tatts' bookmakers conduct business, their prices for each horse marked up in chalk on boards. To the right, the credit-oriented 'Rails' bookmakers line the members enclosure, taking bets from clients in both rings. Between the two lies the area known as 'no man's land' where 'tic-tac' men stand on wooden crates relaying the latest market moves, and men called 'bookies runners' await to rush and 'lay-off' bets taken by the 'rail bookmakers' with other bookmakers in the 'Tatts' ring, who may be showing that horse at a higher price.

makers, wielding considerable power in the trading activities of the betting market. Betting transactions are made verbally with them and recorded on large boarded sheets of paper which give them an immediate visual indication of their commitments. Business is conducted almost entirely on credit, and therefore only with clients that have been vetted and are of a reliable standing; these include other bookmakers, professional racing people who often bet in larger sums than the average 'Tatts' bookmaker can or wishes to lay, and racing stables who, when they place their commissions on course, prefer the credit facilities offered by the 'rails' bookmakers.

The 'rails' bookmakers do not visually display the odds they have on offer and it is necessary to ask or listen to their exalted barker-like calls to discover what odds they are prepared to lay. These odds will be subject to market fluctuations and therefore change in response to the on-course betting activities conveyed to the 'rails' bookmakers by strategically placed and frantically signalling 'tic-tac' men. Off-course betting developments are conveyed to the 'rails' bookmakers with equal swiftness and efficiency via the 'blower' (the racecourse–off-course direct telephone link) and will produce an appropriate response in odds.

The 'rails' bookmakers, with their off-course betting links and their facility to lay the larger on-course bets, command the most powerful and dominating influence in the betting market. Significant market activity which permeates through to affect prices in the other betting rings is sure to have emanated from trading moves of the 'rails' book-makers (i.e. 'laying off' money – the bookmaker's method of limiting liability by placing whole or part of an accepted commission with other bookmakers). Such moves, which bring a volume of money suddenly into trading activities, cause an immediate depression of prices as money chases odds and the market forces of supply and demand are intensified.

As the betting market closes at the 'off', it is from the 'mean' or average prices laid by the 'rails' and leading 'Tatts' bookmakers that independent assessors, who have observed and recorded the foregoing market trading, compile the SP odds.

The 'Tatts' bookmakers

The 'Tatts' bookmakers usually form the majority of bookmakers to be found on the racecourse; they are located in the Tattersalls Ring, which is the focal point of betting at a racecourse. The Tattersalls area represents the medium-priced entrance fee for racecourse enclosures, attracting the racing enthusiast who is non-professional and whose principal interest is likely to be a moderate flutter (i.e. betting in sums from £5 to £10 up to perhaps a maximum of £100). The Tattersalls bookmakers exist principally to accommodate these punters, offering 'cash-only' betting and visually displaying the prices they have on offer on boards.

'Tatts' bookmakers form the cornerstone of bookmakers in the betting market, they offer odds which are competitive among themselves and often with those on offer by the 'rails' bookmakers. It is necessary for them to be (as their well-earned reputation confirms), sharp in their dealings and forever vigilant of the constant change of currents in market trends which unheeded would quickly swamp them. 'Tatts' bookmakers have for long provided colour to the racecourse betting scene epitomized in the caricature of 'Honest Joe' standing beside a board of prices, with a satchel heavily laden with the money of losing punters.

The Silver Ring bookmakers

The Silver Ring bookmakers are the least influential of bookmakers found at a racecourse; they are located and operate in the Silver Ring or public enclosures (the cheapest entry admissions on a racecourse). They provide a betting service for the amateur racegoer more likely interested in a day's outing in the open air than any hearty ventures into betting. Silver Ring bookmakers, like their 'Tatts' counterparts, insist on cash-only bets and, being at the lower end of the market, take only the smaller bets. They compensate for this lower turnover by usually offering undervalue odds (prices that are lower than what is on offer in the other betting ring).

Silver Ring bookmakers play no influential role in the betting market, and will be given a wide berth by the more experienced racegoers and backers. Their role is to serve the needs of the amateur, inexperienced and indiscriminate backers; the prices offered by the Silver Ring bookmakers have no influence of the eventual SP odds.

The on-course betting market

The on-course betting market, except for the larger prestigious races and meetings (Flat and National Hunt), tends to be extremely sensitive and quite unable to withstand any sizeable bets without a violent depression of odds. This is because without strong market activity (a considerable flow of money), the aim of bookmaking (making a rounded book of prices, with money proportionally evenly spread to show a percentage profit whatever the result) is challenged and threatened.

In such circumstances any large influx of money in an active market will be met with the counterbalancing response of an immediate reduction in the odds. If the influx of money is too great for even this guarded response, the bookmakers will enforce their strongest weapon: 'We maintain the right to refuse a part or whole of any commission.' In other words they will choose what bets, and what size of bets they are prepared to lay – usually refusing whole or part of sizeable bets at odds which are attractive to the backer.

The bookmaking fraternity are extremely nervous when faced with the possibility of accepting – or even worse of having already accepted – sizeable bets at long odds on a horse with a real winning chance. Such fears by bookmakers have forced any determined backers who want sizeable bets at less than derisory odds to find undetectable methods of 'getting on'.

On-course or off-course, large single bets at long odds will just not be taken by bookmakers, except in the most competitive of races and where there is an extremely large and strong market (i.e. Derby, Grand National, or popular handicaps where there is ante-post betting). Large bets for other races at best will only be accepted in part and then only at reduced odds; occasionally bookmakers will accept them whole or in part at SP (if they have sufficient time to 'lay off' the bet). This will result in a sweeping depression of the SP as the bookmaker quickly lays off the bet and in the process gains free trading points profit.

Laying the bet off will immediately reduce the SP to lowly odds as money floods in one direction in a weak market. The SP returning perhaps at evens when, as the money was laid off (spread with a number of other bookmakers), the odds may have varied in this process from 5–1 to 2–1, giving the original bookmaker who laid the bet off 2, 3 or 4 points profit on a winning bet.

The only hope any intrepid backer has to defeat such ploys is to get the bet laid without the bookmakers being aware of its real size. It will mean 'spreading the money'. This can be achieved on-course or off-course, but will require careful planning and skilful execution. On-course it will require a team of people simultaneously to place small bets (in total equivalent to the large bet) and having them accepted at prices before the significance of such prices on the market is realized. Off-course money may be spread over a wide area in small amounts and with the hope of a reasonable SP, as the market activity on-course will be uneventful.

The off-course bookmakers

There are two types of off-course bookmakers representing cash or credit business, although some do combine both.

Cash bookmaking

This is the dominant feature of off-course bookmaking and is represented by betting shops/offices which cater for the needs of the majority of the betting population. Business which is strictly 'cash only', is conducted in a casino-like atmosphere where some events for betting (i.e. horse-racing or greyhound-racing) are normally occurring every 10 to 15 minutes throughout the late morning and afternoon. Commentaries of races may be interspersed with, and are supplemented by, betting shows conspiring to engulf the betting-shop customer in constant action and excitement. In 1986 liberalization of the law allowed bookmakers who so desired to turn their erstwhile Spartan premises into more comfortable surroundings, with live television coverage of racing and other events and the serving of non-alcoholic drinks, etc. The backer, however, should be under no illusion as to the purpose of this new public image – to extract the punter's money!

Bets of almost any size from a nominal minimum to a fairly high maximum will be accepted in betting offices, and there is no discrimination between the large or the small backer. The smaller backers are in fact encouraged to bet small stakes in myriad combinations which if successful at good/long odds would produce a considerable return on a small investment (a possibility which, to the dismay of the punter and the expectation of the bookmaker, seldom happens).

The cash bookmakers involved with betting offices play no significant role in the on-course betting market, although themselves always subject to the results of its trading in the SP. Occasional large bets taken in the offices may be phoned through to be 'laid off' on-course to depress the SP; or similarly threatening commitments from the final leg of a successful but incomplete accumulative bet may warrant the same response and have an influence in the on-course market. Normally, betting offices passively lay the Board prices shown which represent the 'on-course' market trading and rely completely on the SP to settle all other bets.

Off-course bookmakers are therefore very vulnerable to any coup in on-course trading which could inflate starting prices, and have to remain extremely alert in preventing such situations from arising.

Betting offices, the only legal places for off-course cash betting, have become social institutions providing warmth and a meeting-place for those of like mind and disposition among the betting classes.

Credit bookmaking

Although smaller in volume this is normally of greater significance than off-course cash betting and bookmaking. Credit bookmaking is usually conducted by telephone, with backers conveying their instructions verbally and betting in larger amounts than the normal cash customer. The larger credit bookmaker is likely to have as clients professional racing interests (trainers, owners, etc.) whose betting habits are likely to be a specific indication of a horse's real chances of winning. The value of such information to a bookmaker amply compensates the retaining of these possibly regular winning accounts which would otherwise not be tolerated because of their unsound economic basis. Precise reliable information from these sources will prompt bookmakers to anticipate market trends and act accordingly, being ready to hold or lay off bets as the situation demands. All the larger credit bookmakers have, or have access to, course representatives with whom they will be in constant contact, entrusting them to initiate or regulate market activity with the aim always of limiting the bookmaker's liability.

Credit clients are only accepted by bookmakers from reliable personal references or after scrutiny of financial references as to their credit-worthiness. Transactions of often such a delicate financial nature require goodwill and trust by both parties, of which bookmakers with their years of experience have designed safeguard systems which seldom give rise to any disputes over bets. Credit accounts work well and provide excellent service to the backer; accounts are rendered for settlement weekly or fortnightly and they can be recommended as the easy comfortable way of betting for all except the impulsive, and uncontrollable gambler.

Ante-post betting

Ante-post betting is the betting that takes place on an event some time before it actually occurs – any time from 24 hours up to a year or more before the event. All the big races (i.e. Derby, Guineas, and other Classics, Grand National, etc.) have an ante-post betting market and they are constantly engendered by bookmakers to create betting activity at all times. The rule of ante-post betting is that all bets stand whether a horse runs in the event or not. Horses entered a long time in advance for a race may become injured, ill or prove inadequate and be withdrawn from the race.

All bets on these horses are lost, and herein lies the weakness and uncertainty of ante-post betting. The only attraction to ante-post betting is the chance of obtaining good odds and the possibility of holding a winning voucher on a 20–1 chance whose starting price is returned at possibly 4–1 or 5–1. The advantage of a cleverly struck ante-post bet is that it offers the backer the opportunity to hedge (i.e. lay it off to someone else) at an assured profit should the odds tumble. If a bet is struck at 20–1 and the odds shorten to 10–1, it could be generously laid off at 12–1 to the original stake. This gives the first backer an 8 pt bet down to nothing, and the new backer a 2 pt advantage over the price now on offer. If the bet loses the first backer comes out unscathed, and should it win there is a win costing nothing at the horse's probable SP price. Ante-post betting, to be successful, usually requires professional racing knowledge as to a horse's aims and more than a fair share of luck. It cannot be recommended to the amateur, who will lose out more often than not, with the horse failing to run.

There are some concessionary ante-post bets on the morning of a race which offer possible longer than SP odds without risk of losing the stake if the horse be withdrawn. However, ante-post cannot normally be recommended as a good betting medium. Ante-post betting can fairly be said to be designed by bookmakers solely for their self-development and publicity.

Cash ante-post bets where bookmakers have the backer's money a considerable time before settling day must appear an extremely attractive proposition to bookmakers and be a conclusive argument against this form of betting.

6 THE SELECTION FORMULA ANALYSED: FORM

Form is the first and foremost constituent in the selection formula.

Form is the record of a horse's race performances and the factual evidence of racing ability.

Form is therefore the primary consideration in the analysis of a race and the fundamental element upon which to base selection.

In the evaluation of form it is necessary to ask: 'What horses has the horse beaten?' or, 'What horses have finished behind it?' The most satisfactory answer is previous and/or subsequent winners. Such confirmation establishes the form as of value. It means a horse has finished in front of horses which have previously or subsequently beaten many other horses. This is the best and most reliable criterion of form, the soundest foundation upon which to base selection and is applicable to races of all types and class.

GRADES OF FORM

In regard to the selection formula any horse considered a probable will have its form assessed in one of three grades: **proven**; **promising**; **improving**.

Proven is the first and most desirable grade. It applies only when a horse has form clearly better than its rivals. That is when:

(a) it has already beaten today's rivals by a very wide margin;
(b) a form line through another horse shows it to have the beating of today's rivals;
(c) it has form obviously superior to its present rivals even though it has never raced against them before (for example, it may hold an official handicap rating of 100 yet be meeting inferior rivals rated no higher than 80 at basically level weights);
(d) assessment in a handicap leaves it as the top-rated horse.

It should be said that the clear-cut proof demanded by the grade *proven form* occurs only rarely.

Promising is the second grade in the assessment of form. It occurs frequently, and wherever a horse has good or closely matched form yet which cannot be *proven* as the best. It happens when:

(a) a horse has never met its present rivals;
(b) there is no form link to make direct comparison;
(c) a previous meeting or form line shows the horses to be of similar ability, and the margin between them close enough to make a form reversal quite possible;
(d) official handicap ratings show them to be of similar merit.

A horse's form in this grade therefore *promises* to be the best but the evidence is not conclusive.

Improving is the third and lowest grade of form. It occurs sometimes when a horse suddenly shows form after previously having none. Although this may apply to a winner who has been unplaced in previous races it is perhaps more appropriate to a horse achieving a place for the first time, especially if this is a reversal of form with previous conquerors. Such a performance shows the horse to be *improving* yet the suspicion exists that it may have to improve still further to win this race.

Therefore improving form is a cautious appraisal of a horse's ability.

PROOF OF FORM

Assessment relying on factors of proven ability is the most reasoned approach to form analysis and the surest foundation upon which to base selection. Proven ability can only be assessed from past performances.

Proven positive ability

This is ability proven by race performances. It is where a horse produces a race performance of definable positive value (i.e. winning or being placed, etc.).

The more race experience a horse has, the more information there is upon which to judge ability; patterns in performance become established from which a horse will make only discernible and probable deviations (i.e. its racing style will be determined).

Proven positive ability is only what a horse has achieved in race performance, it is exposed ability, and it can be identified in horses of all types, ages and class.

Unproven ability

This is ability that is unexposed and can be said to exist where the evidence from race performance is insufficient. It applies to inexperienced horses, some of which display potential ability, and to horses that have not previously raced. The less experienced a horse, the less opportunity it has had, and the less information there is upon which to assess ability. In these circumstances it is judicial to consider a horse's ability as unproven.

Potential ability and supposed abilities emanating from off-course reputation all remain unproven until confirmed in race performance; this applies to horses of all types, ages and class.

Proven non-ability

This is where a horse of experience has shown no ability in its race performances, or at best moderate ability which shows no sign of improvement. In such instances the horse can be considered to have proven non-ability, this also applies to horses of all types, ages and class.

DATE OF FORM

Form is a record of past performances, and by its very nature it is always past form. This can be considered as: (i) current form; (ii) less recent form; (iii) older form. As can be seen from Table 6.1 the value of form decays progressively as it grows older.

TABLE 6.1   Grades of form

Days since last ran	Flat 1988			National Hunt 1988–89		
	Wins – Runners		%	Wins – Runners		%
1–28	2,567	– 26,787	9.6	2,594	– 23,211	11.2
29–42	380	– 4,278	8.9	322	– 3,432	9.4
43–70	183	– 2,506	7.3	203	– 2,233	9.1
71–99	54	– 804	6.7	55	– 820	6.7
100+	27	– 597	4.5	67	– 1,024	6.5

Current form (1–28 days)

Current form is one of the highest value: it is the most reliable indication of whether or not a horse is likely to reproduce its proven abilities, and undeniably reflects a horse's present form, fitness and general well-being. Ideally it should be as recent as possible but can go up to 28 days. In the 1988 Flat race season and the 1988–89 National Hunt season 80 per cent of winners had run within the previous 28 days.

Less recent form (29–42 days)

Form becomes less recent after 29–42 days. On average both Flat and National Hunt horses run every 23 days. Newer current form therefore is constantly emerging to challenge the assumptions of less recent form, which generally has to be regarded as less reliable.

TABLE 6.2   Date of last run comparisons

Days elapsed since the horse last ran	1988 Flat				
	2 y.o.			3 y.o.	
	Winners – Runners	%		Winners – Runners	%
1– 7	91 – 976	= 9.3		378 – 3,720	= 10.2
8–14	237 – 2,407	= 9.9		671 – 7,370	= 9.1
15–21	202 – 1,838	= 11.0		509 – 5,659	= 9.0
22–28	143 – 1,194	= 12.0		336 – 3,623	= 9.3
29+	180 – 2,360	= 7.6		464 – 5,825	= 8.0

Days elapsed since the horse last ran	1988–89 National Hunt				
	Hurdles			Chases	
	Winners – Runners	%		Winners – Runners	%
1– 7	284 – 2,382	= 11.9		210 – 1,458	= 14.4
8–14	518 – 5,427	= 9.5		475 – 3,597	= 13.2
15–21	383 – 4,094	= 9.4		328 – 2,527	= 13.0
22–28	222 – 2,365	= 9.4		174 – 1,360	= 12.8
29+	363 – 4,922	= 7.4		284 – 2,587	= 11.0

Older form (43–70 days)

Form should be treated as older form after 43–70 days. Most horses will have run two or three times during this period, seriously questioning its value in the light of less recent and current form which have emerged since.

Form after 71 days has to be considered as past form. While proof of what a horse may be capable statistically, it has been shown to hold a scant significance for the present. Any horse running again after this length of absence will usually have met with a training setback.

WINNING FORM

Simply said: the **best form** is **winning form** and **losing form** the **worst form**.

Such a statement may appear obvious, but in analysing form and making a selection this most basic approach is frequently overlooked. Unless the entry conditions of race preclude previous winners, previous winning form always demands the closest attention and is the area where the selector should immediately focus interest. In the 1988 Flat and 1988–89 National Season 22% of winners won their next race.

Winning form means that a horse has previously shown it has the ability to win a race and beat other horses in the competitive atmosphere of a racetrack. Horses often grow in confidence from the experience of a victory, which can lead to future triumphs if other factors such as class, going, course, etc. are similar.

Winners in horse-racing, as in other walks of life, are likely to win again.

In practical terms a winning racehorse is likely to receive that extra attention and encouragement when it returns home to its yard that a loser will not. Everybody in the stable will be affected as morale is lifted and hopes for the future raised. A horse, if only a winner of a minor prize, will for a short time get star treatment and be the focus of attention, and an interest in its future has been created. The stable lad who looks after the horse, having constant close contact with the animal (feeding it, riding it, grooming it and being aware of its health and moods) will be instrumental in lavishing renewed praise and care. This lad will be able to stand tall with peers who may not have had such recent success, bathing in the kudos and freshened by the optimism to carry out the routine tasks of stable duties, which are often arduous, with renewed vigour. The spice of victory will also be felt from the financial angle if the lad had backed this winner or received a present from a grateful owner. In contrast the frequent losers will get none of these benefits.

CHANGING FORM

Also involved in the assessment of merit are previously unmentioned elements of: **consistency**; **inconsistency**; **deterioration**; **improvement**. These have to be carefully considered when interpreting form. Their existence can be established by examination and comparison of recent with past form.

Consistency is shown by form which contains performances of constant equal merit.

Inconsistency is displayed in form where performances are unpredictable and of varying merit.

Horses of top-class ability are usually consistent in performance. Horses of moderate ability tend to be unreliable and inconsistent in performance.

Deterioration is form that is worsening and displays present performances which are inferior to past performances. It can be apparent in horses of all types, ages and class (but it is especially found in National Hunt horses who fail to recapture their previous form after injury, in younger horses (Flat and National Hunt) who suffered from physical ailments, and in horses whose enthusiasm for racing has been soured).

Improvement is form which shows that a horse's performance has become better. It applies to horses of all types and class, and is a particular prominent feature in the assessment and interpretation of the form of younger inexperienced horses. Improvement can be positively established and calculated in respect of past performances, but its existence in the present and future is purely speculation. It is this assessment of its future development which pose the imponderable issues. The issues to be considered are as follows:

1. Is further improvement necessary?
2. Is further improvement likely to continue or has a peak been reached?
3. If further improvement is likely or possible then by what degree?

1. Is further improvement necessary? Improvement is essential for horses that carry a weight penalty, and for horses raised in class. In both instances they must better their previous performance to have a winning chance.

Constant improvement is essential for all inexperienced horses if they are to maintain their status with their peers. This applies to 2-year-olds – many show early season promise but as the season progresses they fail to maintain it. Consistency alone in these events is likely to be inadequate (e.g. the form figures 33232 may reveal admirable consistency but insufficient improvement to win without a lowering in class).

The criterion for improvement being a necessity, applies to all horses (3–4 y.o. maidens, novice hurdlers, novice chasers – and even handicappers) if they are to maintain their status. It is, however, more particularly apparent when applied to 2-year-olds where rapid growth and improvement exist as very dynamic factors. The only time improvement is not a required necessity is when it is applied to a current proven champion (i.e. Classic champions, sprinters, milers, middle-distance horses, stayers and their National Hunt equivalents) where if challenged at equal conditions (weight – distance – going) it is the challenger who must improve – and the consistent reproducing of proven ability will be enough for the champion to win.

2. Is further improvement likely? The likelihood of improvement will be indicated in the previous performance and will depend on three factors:

(a) *Manner of performance.* A horse that has not won may be judged as having to improve to win. A horse that has won displays proven ability which can be assessed for further development.

The guiding principle in a horse improving upon its performance is the ease with which it wins. A horse that wins 'easily', 'unchallenged', can do no more – if an inexperienced horse (e.g. 2 y.o.) running for the first time this is a highly commendable performance which suggests in all probability it will improve. Although particular to 2-year-olds first time out, any horse winning easily suggests further improvement. The more hard fought the victory, the less obvious scope in ability a horse has for improvement.

(b) *Physical fitness* at the time of performance.

A horse that wins easily when not at peak race fitness can be almost guaranteed to improve.

A horse that wins in a hard-fought race when unfit is also very likely to improve as it obtains peak fitness.

A horse that wins easily when fit can still improve, especially if inexperienced.

A horse that wins in a hard-fought race when at peak fitness is less likely to improve.

The modifying factor here will be the scope for further physical development in the horse. This is not a factor that can be satisfactorily judged from form; it can only be assessed by seeing the horse and observing its physical condition.

(c) *The methods and ability of the trainer.* Improvement is always subject to training methods. It is noticeable that some trainers in their racing preparation of inexperienced and experienced horses allow themselves an area in which to improve a horse, i.e. racing it initially short of peak race fitness, allowing weaker horses (2-year-olds that are growing) time to recover from races and gain strength, and generally allowing a horse to fulfil its physical potentiality.

Form is the undisputed record of a horse's race performance. The smaller the margin of victory or defeat the more possible a reversal of form. The greater the margin of victory or defeat the less likely a reversal of form.

An example of a close margin finish. The official margin between first, second and third was a short-head and a neck.

An example of a wide margin finish. The official winning distance was 6 lengths, with a short-head dividing the second and third.

Close-up showing the proximity of horses – typical of a close margin finish.

Close-up showing distance between horses – typical of a wide margin finish.

Horses can gain a vital advantage by jumping fences and hurdles accurately and quickly.

While horses may brush through hurdles and only lose impetus . . .

. . . horses that hit the much sturdier fences in chases are likely to pay the higher price of falling.

Other trainers run their horses 'fully wound-up' (peak race fit), have less scope to improve them, and in fact will in some instances 'burn out' a horse (especially 2-year-olds).

Improvement is dependent upon the skill, method and, in some instances, patience of the trainer.

3. Degree or rate of improvement   If a horse is likely to improve, what degree of improvement could be expected? This is an almost unanswerable question. Improvement will be strongly influenced by:

(a) The horse's physical scope (allowing for the possibility of any rapid or slow development).

(b) The trainer's method, which may be to allow the horse to mature slowly and not be rushed (i.e. in the case of 2 y.o. who is bred to stay as a 3 y.o., or a backward National Hunt horse which is considered primarily as a staying chaser and is allowed as much as two seasons to develop).

Improvement can be compared to growth or learning; it is a gradual process that occurs in stages. There will be phases of progress and of consolidation.

The degree of improvement is not one of improbable and incomprehensible leaps.

● The improvement to winning form is normally from progressively better performances (this is not always apparent from mere abbreviated form figures – closer analysis may be required to establish this fact).

● The improvement on winning form often originates from the impetus of winning. (The experience of winning gives added confidence.)

The rate of improvement will be closely linked with the type of horse (i.e. Flat or National Hunt, sprinter, stayer, 2m hurdler, 3m chaser) and whether the horse is precocious or slow maturing.

As a rule, the shorter the distance the faster maturing the horse is likely to be, and the longer the distance the slower maturing the horse will be. Sprinters 'come to hand' quicker than potential stayers, and are likely to be trained with a short-term viewpoint. Stayers (especially National Hunt 3m chasers) are trained with a long-term viewpoint. Between the extremes there are numerous rates of progress.

Once a horse (of whatever type) begins improving, its rate and range should not be underestimated. For example, early season 2 y.o. 'sharp types', often run up a sequence of wins over the minimum 5f distance in the first month of the Flat season. Similarly, 2-year-olds without previous experience, or with moderate form over shorter distances suddenly improve extensively and rapidly when running over a distance 7f–1m (late season). Three-year-old maidens can, during their second season, improve quickly and considerably when racing at longer distances, although sometimes not developing until late in their

3 y.o. season. Novice hurdlers usually learn quickly after a few races, but some may take a whole season. Whatever its type, once a horse shows improvement, its *rate* of improvement will be closely attached to its *degree* of improvement and its abilities must then be considered carefully.

The misuse and misunderstanding of the term 'improvement'. Improvement is always a speculative judgement, and only exists as a proven fact when it is a comparison of past and recent form. The misuse and misunderstanding of the term 'improvement' often emanates from journalistic copy which has presented opinion as fact.

'Has improved' is a statement of fact that can be disputed or verified by examination of form. Correctly understood, this statement provides concisely defined information upon which to make a judgement.

'Has improved', however, can have the unfortunate connotation of implying more than it can represent, arousing speculation and exceeding the limit of accurate definition.

'Will improve' – 'sure to improve' – 'can only improve' have become commonly used and accepted terms in horse-racing parlance, but from the objective viewpoint are meaningless. They insinuate proven fact, but are and can only ever be subjective opinion.

'Is improving' is another misleading term from any objective viewpoint of form. It has been confused with and often mistakenly used instead of the term 'has improved' which is an observed comparison of past and recent form. 'Is improving' is an unproven assertion of no value to objective form selection, and can only be assumed as meaningful when it can be attributed to a trainer who has witnessed improvement in its ability since the horse last raced.

FORM COMMENTARIES

The form of a horse is the record of its race performances.

To assess form correctly the selector will need to read the records and fully understand how the real live flesh-and-blood issues of horse-racing relate to the abstract figures and words in the Form Book. Unfortunately, most racing fans fail to achieve even a basic skill in this. Video-recorders have given the racing fan an opportunity to recall live action at the flick of a switch, but this still demands reference to the Form Book for factual details.

To obtain the required skill it is necessary to interpret the language of the commentaries found in the Form Book. As abbreviated terms they are explained at the beginning of the form, and are largely self-explana-tory. The facts such as weight, age, jockey, trainer, going, prize-money, etc. are relatively uncomplicated, but sometimes with a deep significance that will only be understood with experience.

The commentaries of a horse's running in a race can be divided into two parts. The first part gives an indication of how active a role a horse took throughout the race, or its position at different stages (e.g. 3rd st: led wl over 1f out). The second part states how the horse finished the race (e.g. r.o.wl.).

The Form Book may also have opening comment describing a horse's pre-race physical condition (e.g. l.w. – looked well – meaning looking very fit; or adversely BKWD – backward – meaning the horse looked decidedly lacking in peak fitness). These observations may therefore explain how a horse subsequently ran in the race, thus modi-fying conclusions about its earlier form.

Although it is necessary to understand the whole of the form commentary, it is particularly important to focus attention on how a horse finished. In broad terms the better a horse's performance in the closing stages of a race the greater the value its form is likely to be.

The positive comments which denote a good performance at the finish of a race are:

r.o. = ran on – means the horse was running on or finishing in the closing stages;

r.o.wl. = ran on well – means running on well in the closing stages;

comf. = comfortably;

drew clr. = drew clear;

easily = easily;

qckned clr. = quickened clear;

unchal. qcknd. = unchallenged quickened.

The negative comments (especially if they are a consistent feature in a horse's form commentaries) which denote unsatisfactory performances at the end of a race are:

one pce = one pace: means a horse being unable to find extra accele-ration from the one speed;

a.bhd. = always behind: means always behind – a most unfavourable comment;

sn.btn. = soon beaten: means a horse's challenge was soon beaten off;

sn.wknd. = soon weakened: means a horse's challenge soon petered out.

Numerous other comments from the form commentary are much less concrete and open to varying interpretations. These comments, while not necessarily negative, would need to be interpreted in an extremely imaginative way to be considered very positive. Referring to winners they include:

all out – meaning the horse was all out to win;

driven out – meaning the horse had to be driven out to win;

pushed out – meaning the horse had to be pushed out to win;

rdn. out – meaning the horse had to be ridden out to win.

The latter two observations suggest the horse may have had more to give if asked – while the former suggest the horse was at full stretch and this may bode less favourably for the future.

Two other comments that fit in this neutral category seldom apply to winners:

kpt on = kept on: meaning the horse kept on with its challenge;

styd on = stayed on: meaning the horse stayed on ('saw out') the distance of the race.

Both these commentaries can be interpreted in a positive or negative light:

kept on – can mean that the horse kept on with its challenge and although not showing any marked acceleration produced a good performance; alternatively it may be viewed that by keeping on without showing any acceleration the horse displayed its deficiencies and demonstrated it was not good enough;

stayed on – means a horse lasted out the distance of the race well. This bodes well for the future if the horse faces a similar or greater test of stamina. However, a horse that merely stayed on may have shown that it lacks the vital quality of acceleration, and again may not be good enough.

Other comments from the form commentary can be placed in this neutral category because although they have a negative prefix they can also be understood to have a more favourable interpretation:

no ex. = no extra – meaning a horse had no extra (effort, acceleration) to give;

nt. qkn. = not quicken – meaning a horse could not quicken or accelerate;

no imp. = no impression – meaning a horse made no impression on winning rivals or was not close enough to challenge the winner or leading horses;

nvr. nrr. = never nearer – meaning a horse was never nearer winning than its finishing position;

wknd. = weakened – meaning a horse weakened at a particular distance during the race:

no extra: means a horse on the day was not good enough and had no extra to meet the challenge of the winner. More favourably viewed it could be because the horse was short of race fitness (i.e. making seasonal début or a reappearance after recovering from illness, injury, etc.) or due to the distance of the race, stiffness of track or testing going;

not quicken: this may be an observation that identifies a horse as one-paced. In its most negative aspect this is a damning accusation of a horse's lack of ability. More favourably, however, it may be explained as due to a horse being unfit and/or inexperienced (especially in the case of 2 y.o., 3 y.o. maidens, etc.) and therefore without the fitness or experience to respond at the crucial time in a race when the pace suddenly quickens.

no impression: means a horse made no impression in challenging the winner and on the day was certainly not good enough. However, there may be extenuating circumstances explained in the other part of the commentary (National Hunt: mistakes, blundered. Flat: started slowly) which give reasons for this and allows the performance to be seen more favourably. Sometimes it is also due to horses not quite staying the distance of the race;

never nearer – means a horse never being in a closer position than its finishing position which is some margin from the winner and leading horses. On that performance the horse is certainly not good enough. However, the extenuating circumstances here may imply a 'non-trier'. Horses are sometimes schooled in public (which is against the rules of racing and could result in a trainer losing his licence), but blatant disregard of the rule has to be tempered with the fact that backward and inexperienced horses may need an educational race or two to learn the business of racing, after which they often improve. The unacceptable side of this is where a horse's true ability is deliberately being concealed to provide connections of that horse with the ammunition for a future betting coup;

weakened – means the horse weakened at a certain stage in the race and obviously was not good enough. However, there may be other reasonable excuses for this performance that demand the form be given some consideration. A horse may 'weaken' due to lack of fitness, the burden of weight, 'greenness' – in the case of inexperienced horses, being raised in class and tackling a better-class opponent, or the most frequent case, racing over the wrong distance (usually one that is too far).

hld. up Held up – means a horse was held up at the rear of the field throughout a good part of the race. From a selection viewpoint this is not an encouraging sign, especially should this be a regular feature of a horse's running. A race will have to unfold quite favourably to give a horse ridden this way a winning chance. Occasionally a horse will be ridden this way because of the jockey's style but usually it is in response to the demands of the horse. It may be a problem of temperament but more commonly it indicates that the horse has just one short burst of acceleration which if used too early just peters out. Although such racing characteristics may apply to good horses, from the selection viewpoint this type of horse is best avoided especially if the horse is also conceding weight to its opponents. An old race saying is 'You can concede weight and you can concede ground but you can't concede both'.

These later form commentaries demonstrate a variety of interpretation and sometimes explain why the unexpected does occur.

FORM FOR AGE (FLAT RACING)

Some basic observations can be made about the form of Flat race horses of different age groups.

Two-year-old form is in essence about speed. The race distances are short. The longer distance races do not take place until late in the season (1m races commence in August and those of 7f not before late June). Therefore, early season races will be essentially contests of pure speed. Even later in the season racing experience and a horse's ability to learn quickly are of advantage. For example, TIME TO GO HOME (1988) won its first race on 22 April yet by 1 June had won five times.

Three-year-old form is in essence about improvement. The longer distances which horses may now be tackling give opportunities for the slower-maturing type of animal to show its worth. In handicaps especially early in the season when the going rides soft, over distances in excess of 1¼m, some lower-weighted horses often show a considerable improvement upon their 2 y.o. form, where in races over shorter distances they were not able to show their true ability. In contrast, previous winners as 2-year-olds are unlikely to be viewed lightly by the official handicapper, so in the early part of the season, until rehandicapped, they can be at a disadvantage with lighter-weighted rivals, who may have been underestimated.

Horses previously maidens as 2-year-olds usually compete in suitable maiden races as 3-year-olds with winners often graduating to stakes races before tackling handicap company. Three-year-olds often continue to improve and are the most difficult type of horse to assess accurately. As more and more handicaps from June onwards become open to horses of all ages the more difficult it can be to assess a 3 y.o. against older rivals. Three-year-olds on the upgrade who are skilfully placed by their trainers can often run up a sequence of victories before the handicapper catches up with them. KNELLER (1988), although a winner of its only race as a 2 y.o., won on its seasonal reappearance as a 3 y.o. in April. In its next race with a low weight it won the Ebor Handicap at York in August, before rounding off the season winning two group races, the Doncaster and Jockey Club cups.

Four-year-old form is in essence about horses confirming what they are known to be capable of. Horses at this stage of their lives are subject to less sudden, or rapid rates of improvement. Occasionally older horses chalk up an unexpected sequence of wins when a trainer first discovers how best to exploit their abilities. For example, in 1988 GLENCROFT as a 4 y.o. won nine races – and in 1989 KABCAST as a 4 y.o. won five consecutive races in 13 days. However, these are the exceptions. Both were sprinters, 5/6f specialists, are the type of horse that sometimes only really get their act together with age, learning by experience to explode from the starting stalls and how to time their final finishing spurt to a nicety. Older horses in general tend only to confirm rather than improve upon the abilities they have previously shown, and sometimes even these strengths will be swept aside by the talent of the rising stars of the younger generation.

NATIONAL HUNT FORM

The longer distances and the obstacles to be jumped in National Hunt racing means that the finishing margins between horses will be wider than in Flat racing. In a 3m chase the margin between the winner and the last horse to finish is commonly 30–40 lengths, while a competitive 5f sprint handicap on a fast down course like Epsom may see only 10–15 lengths between the first and last horse.

National Hunt form cannot be observed in terms of age-groups. Horses are intended to have a longer career than their Flat-race counterparts. A National Hunt horse usually has a dual career beginning first as a hurdler at the age of 4 or 5 years, and then progressing from the age of 6/7 years to become a chaser.

Hurdle form

This is principally about speed; similar in some ways to longer distance Flat races, the technique for jumping hurdles is different from that of fences. Horses need to be faster and hurdlers usually jump flatter than chasers, often brushing through the top of the hurdle without necessarily finding great hindrance to their progress (see p. 83).

Chase form

This is principally about safely negotiating the fences. Unless a horse is able to jump fences efficiently and therefore complete the course it will have no chance of winning. Horses have to jump higher in chases than in hurdles and horses which do not jump cleanly will pay the price either of falling (see p. 84) or at least of having their progress impeded.

Novice hurdles

These are basically level weight races open to horses which before the beginning of the season had not won a hurdle run. They can be contested by horses of all ages (4 y.o. and upwards) although some have conditions of entry limiting them to horses of a prescribed age – and in the autumn as the season commences there are juvenile hurdles – races confined to 3-year-olds. Therefore, novice hurdlers tend to be younger horses. This is the beginning stage in a horse's National Hunt career. Theoretically, older horses can compete in novice hurdles provided they have not won a hurdle race in previous seasons. Occasionally the strange occurrence is witnessed when an older experienced handicap chaser who had never won a hurdle race is sometimes put back to hurdling in a novice event to regain lost confidence after a series of falls or injury. However, such horses usually will not have the necessary speed to succeed over hurdles.

Speed and quickly gaining a technique to jump hurdles will be an essential requirement to win a novice hurdle. Ex-Flat-race horses with racing experience often adapt more quickly to these requirements, but usually have less scope for development for a further National Hunt career as chasers. Novice hurdlers, therefore, improve at varying rates. Some need a whole season of experience in novice contests and only show their ability in their second season as a novice hurdler. Others show good form quickly and win in their first season before graduating into handicap hurdle company in their second season. After a season's experience in novice hurdles gaining in strength and maturity, horses can sometimes become transformed performers in their second season. For example, TEN PLUS (1985/86), the devastating winner of the Sun Alliance 2½m Novice Hurdle at the Cheltenham Festival and unbeaten in its three prior races – failed to win and was placed only once in three races as a novice in the previous 1984/85 season. PERTEMPS NETWORK (1988/89), winner of eight hurdle races, including Saddle of Gold Novices Final 3m Hurdle at Newbury, was unable to win in five attempts the previous season.

Handicap hurdle races

These are the contests novice hurdlers graduate to – usually in the second season of their National Hunt career after winning a novice event in their first season. While novice hurdlers can and sometimes do compete in handicap hurdles, these races are principally contested by more experienced hurdlers. Handicap hurdlers are performers who have usually developed a most effective hurdle technique, such races usually being determined by a horse's ability to accelerate in the final stages and on the run-in to the winning post. Handicap hurdles are often competitive and sometimes not easy to predict, but broadly speaking in races of approximately 2m the best horses, with the speed to win, will be those at the top of the handicap. Their ability will not be easily negated by the burden of weight.

Longer-distance handicaps (2m 6f+ and 3m+ handicap hurdles) can be much more gruelling contests of stamina where even the fastest horses at the top of the handicap may be worn down by weight, especially on heavy or soft going. Handicap hurdles are essentially won by experienced horses, and therefore horses with winning form can never be discounted from selection calculations.

Novice chases

These are races where horses are required to carry basically level weights and are confined to horses which, at the beginning of the current season, have not won a chase. They constitute the second stage of a horse's National Hunt career and are contested by: (i) horses whose racing ambitions have always been to 'make up' into being chasers; (ii) horses whose powers as hurdlers are flagging; (iii) horses who failed completely as hurdlers and are being put to chasing as a last hope.

Horses contesting novice chases will obviously be inexperienced at jumping the larger obstacles, and the essential requirement to win a novice chase will be to negotiate the fences and complete the course. A ride on a novice chaser who is an erratic jumper is a most hair-raising and unwelcome engagement for any National Hunt jockey.

Jumping ability is the foremost quality necessary to win any novice chase.

Horses who successfully 'take' to novice chasing can sometimes set up a sequence of victories, as they have speed and jumping techniques which put rivals in the shade. Novice chases can be won (especially in very poor class events) simply by a horse surviving to complete the course.

Handicap chases

These denote the final stage in a horse's career. All specifically bred National Hunt horses are expected to graduate successfully to this level at the zenith of their racing careers. Novice chasers will usually compete in handicap races after prior success in novice chases. This will usually mean that they spend a season gaining experience competing in novice chases against similar rivals.

Handicap chases are therefore contested only by more experienced horses. The speed element, while never to be discounted, will always be tempered by jumping ability. Therefore, horses promoted to the top weights in handicap chases will be those who are the best jumpers and whose superior abilities in this sphere may not be easily thwarted by the weight burden. This is because, as a rule, handicap chases are not run at a breakneck pace from start to finish. Instead, especially in the longer-distance races (3m+) there is a gradual build-up of momentum as the race progresses, with horses reaching their peak of speed in the final third of a race. It is at this point, as the pace dramatically quickens, that the poor jumpers can ruin their chances with fencing errors, as the better jumpers and consequently top-weighted horses may be able to maximize their abilities.

HANDICAP FORM

The basic approach for someone contemplating making a selection in a handicap is to realize that most of the work in assessing the varying abilities of the competitors has already been done by the handicapper (who is constantly in the closest contact with racing, carefully watching how horses perform and assessing them accordingly). On all known form the fastest horses will be those at the top of the handicap and the slowest ones those at the bottom. From this simplistic viewpoint and by using the judgement of a truly expert professional – the handicapper – selection in handicaps can be made much less complex.

The best horses in a race will be in the upper part of a handicap and usually they will be the ones which have previously won at least one race. That means they will have the vital power of acceleration in the final stages of a race that winners usually possess. Although the better horses in a handicap will be burdened with greater weight, in middle-distance races (7f–1m 2f) their winning speed of acceleration will not be countered easily. This is the case on tight-turning racetracks (i.e. Chester, Catterick, Folkestone, Kempton, etc.) for the speed horses can travel round bends is less than on unrelenting straight courses. Therefore, races develop into a competition essentially decided by final acceleration, in which they are proven superior.

Therefore, when making a selection in a handicap, the selector will best be served by beginning at the top of the list of runners, eliminating those thought not to have the right credentials, and working down through the handicap until the one is reached which appears to have winning prospects. Sometimes the selection choice will be made very quickly, and stop at the very top weight or second or third top-weighted horse. However, once the suitable selection candidate has been arrived at by eliminating horses in weight order the selection process can stop, because the handicapper has already done the rest of the work, rating the horses beneath the selection choice as inferior. This simple approach is an effective yet uncomplicated method by which to tackle the problems posed when making a selection in handicaps. However, if you cannot find a confident selection within six horses from the top weight (the size of the field permitting) you must stop searching, because any lower than this shows that you are delving in the basement of the handicap, and rather than skillfully using the handicapper's expert rating you are opposing it. In practice this generally means that selection is being attempted in a competitive handicap where almost any horse may win.

It applies on the Flat or National Hunt – the more favoured Flat races have been explained, National Hunt races are similar although jumping obstacles safely and quickly is an added factor for horses reaching the upper part of handicaps.

COLLATERAL FORM

If there is no immediately obvious comparison of form (i.e. horses have either not run against each other and there is no disparity in class), form evaluation may be made by comparison through *collateral form*. This is form of two horses (A and B) which have not competed against each other, but have commonly raced against a third horse (C). It is by comparison of their separate performances with the third horse (C) that the abilities of A *and* B can be assessed.

To be reliable collateral form requires that:

1. The third horse is a consistent performer;
2. The conditions of the two races are similar (i.e. distance, going, jockey, course);
3. The conditions of weight can be clearly calculated.

Collateral form is most reliable when applied to top-class horses and cannot be confidently applied to moderate horses. If after the examination of collateral form the differences between horses appear indefinably balanced it is suggested (except in the case of the very top-class horses)* that no evaluation be undertaken and the selector refrains from betting.

TIME FORM

Time. This means race time and is the time taken to run a race. As a general rule, the faster the time of a race, the better the value of form. It can be expected that race times will be faster on firmer going and slower on softer going – this consideration, and weather conditions, must always be fully taken into account.

* Top-class horses usually produce extremely consistent performances and it may therefore be possible to conclude an evaluation from a careful balancing of the pertaining modifying factors (fitness and conditions).

A fast time invariably represents form of value – a race in such a time will have been a true and searching test; the winner will have had to provide a noteworthy performance, as would other horses who finished within close proximity.

A slow time usually represents form of little or no value – it does not require a noteworthy performance to win and may suggest that the race was falsely run and not a true test over the distance, and therefore any margins between horses are likely to be misleading.

The actual time of the race. (*NB.* Only the times of Flat races are official times.) In reading of form, the actual time of the race is recorded, next to which will be its comparison to the average or standard time for the race: (b0.0) represents below average time in seconds and tenths of a second; (a0.0) represents above average time in seconds and tenths of a second; (eq) indicates equalling average time.

Below average time is always a fast time – and of the highest value in assessing form.

Equal average time is a good time, but its exact value can only be ascertained by comparison with other times on the day and consideration of the going (i.e. it is not of much value when the going is firm/ hard and the times of other races at the meeting are below average).

Above average time is of least value; however, the degree of such time must be considered, as well as comparison with other race times on the day and the state of the going.

Race time applies both to Flat and National Hunt racing – good form in both codes is usually in faster comparable times. Time has been thought to be more applicable to Flat racing where the emphasis is purely on speed, there are no obstacles to contend with and ground conditions tend to be more consistent during the summer. A fast time, however, is a fast time, and the merits of a fast-run race cannot be disputed under either code of racing.

Race time is a most reliable guide to assessing the value of recent unproven form. This applies especially to 2 y.o. races of whatever class and value, for unless they are run in 'good' (fast) times the value of form is likely to be suspect. GOOD 2 y.o. form demands fast, truly run races, placing emphasis on race fitness and a horse being in a forward physical condition to compete throughout the race. On the Flat, where times are most important, the last furlong of true run races is completed in around 12 seconds, thus in 1 second a horse travels approximately 18yd or 6 lengths. Time can therefore be translated into weight using the following scales:

5–6f	1 sec =	18 lb =	6 lengths
7–8f	1 sec =	15 lb =	6 lengths
9–11f	1 sec =	12 lb =	6 lengths
12–14f	1 sec =	9 lb =	6 lengths
15f+	1 sec =	6 lb =	6 lengths

A comparison of race times for horses of different ages over the same distance on the same day (similarly handicaps with non-handicaps, etc.) give a reliable indication in the assessment of form.

A major factor affecting time is the going. A selling plater can run a faster time on firm ground than a top-class horse can return when the going is heavy. Before the value of a time can be assessed the nature of the going must be known and the time adjusted accordingly. As a rough guide the following can be used:

Firm   Add 0.2 sec per furlong to recorded time
Good   Subtract 0.2 sec per furlong from recorded time
Soft   Subtract 0.8 sec per furlong to recorded time
Heavy   Subtract 1.2 secs per furlong from recorded time

For example, a horse that runs 6f in 70 seconds on firm ground may take 76 seconds on soft ground and 72.4 seconds on good ground. Really firm ground does not make for faster times because few horses stride out freely when the ground becomes hard.

Horses racing on the same race programme but in different races can be compared from their finishing positions in the race and the corresponding race time. In novice hurdles, which usually open and end the programme at a race meeting, in heavy/soft going the earlier divisions are likely to be faster than the later divisions, as the course becomes more ploughed-up with horses racing on it. This consideration is of paramount importance in the comparison of time.

Other points to consider in respect of time. Shorter races, i.e. sprints 5–6f and races up to 1m (Flat) and 2m hurdles (National Hunt), are invariably run in faster comparable times (i.e. to standard) than longer races. Shorter races are less contests of race tactics (i.e. making sure a horse gets the trip) and more tests of pure speed. Longer races are often subject to smaller fields, muddled pace, 'cat and mouse' tactics and the resulting slower times.

The more fiercely contested races (conditions and 'going' allowing) produce fast times. This can be observed by examination of the times of top-class races (i.e. the Classics, group races), races at Royal Ascot and other top meetings and the Aintree Festival (going usually good) which produce races of below-average times.

SPEED

SPEED is the factor responsible for producing winning form, particularly in the latter stages of a race. Here the main challenge is shown by rivals and a horse has to produce that something extra to win.

This speed is a horse's ability to 'quicken' or accelerate in the final 2f of a Flat race, or from the final two obstacles in a National Hunt race.

It is the speed when a horse finds an 'extra gear' in the closing stages of a race which separates winners from losers and applies to all classes of races and distances.

All great horses of the past have possessed this quality of speed to a marked degree, having an electric burst of pace that left rivals trailing in their wake, demonstrated in the Classic successes of SIR IVOR (1968), NIJINSKY (1970), MILL REEF (1971) and more recently TROY (1979), SHERGAR (1981) and fillies ALL ALONG (1983 – Prix de l'Arc de Triomphe), PEBBLES (1985 – Champion Stakes), the triple crown success of OH SO SHARP (1985) and the triumphs of DANCING BRAVE (1986) and MTOTO (1988). Champion hurdlers such as BULA, SEA PIGEON, MONKS-FIELD and SEE YOU THEN also exemplified this quality of speed.

In contrast, horses without the ability to 'quicken' consistently end up losing, and can be seen regularly among the beaten horses in the Form Book with the ominous race commentary 'one paced'. Only in stamina-sapping long-distance Flat races (i.e. 2m and further) and long-distance hurdles and chases (3m+), especially when the ground conditions become extremely testing (soft to heavy), may the merely one-paced horse succeed over rivals with a greater turn of speed as the contest becomes essentially one of tenacity, courage and endurance.

FORM RATINGS

It is sought throughout this guide to give the enthusiast the necessary information to make reasoned independent selection decisions. Yet it is also realized that some racing fans will shy from this daunting task because of the time and skill demanded. For those without these necessary qualities it is advisable to seek some protection by following the ratings of a racing expert. Ratings information is regularly found in the racing pages of newspapers, or more private ratings can be obtainable from reputable tipping services.

It is recommended that whichever rating service the backer chooses to follow (and this has to be a personal choice) they do so consistently. Otherwise what will, and does frequently happen, by flitting from one to another they miss any purple patches of success that may be enjoyed, and end up catching losers. Each daily newspaper has its experts providing ratings, some using up-to-date computer technology to reach their findings, while others follow more traditional methods. Each tries their best but are faced with an almost impossible task of trying to pick winners for every race on the card to fulfil the whims of the ever capricious punter. It will be therefore necessary for the racing fan to concentrate on the less competitive races and gain more reliable guidance and the prospect of winning by following their mentor only on these occasions.

The most desirable ratings will be when one horse is rated well ahead of its rivals, for when the ratings of horses are similar then the value of the top-rated horse is likely to be more problematic. Ratings are private handicapping by the expert with emphasis on different aspects of form. Some focus on weight, some on time (the latter usually identified as speed ratings).

Any 'nap' rating demands close inspection as it will be considered the best advice and to have received special considerations. Ratings give the selector easy access to a well-informed viewpoint that can still be subjected to objective appraisal by the other elements contained in the selection formula.

FAVOURITES' FORM

Although not in the strictest sense within the bounds of assessment of form, a very helpful aid in the form selection process is for a careful note to be taken of the statistical record of favourites in a certain race over a number of seasons. It is more within the realms of betting than selection, but is a meeting-point of the two which will show the selector how the expectations of form (usually reflected by the market) have been upheld over a period of time.

Two examples which vividly demonstrate these extremes:
Doncaster Cup (Group III) 2¼m Doncaster.
from 1975 to 1989 was won by eleven favourites, two 2nd fav., one 3rd fav. and one outsider.
While in contrast:
Cambridgeshire Handicap 1m 1f, Newmarket
from 1975 to 1989 was won by 14 outsiders whose prices ranged from 10–1 to 50–1 and one 3rd fav.

The first example shows how more predictable form elements held sway while the second demonstrates a race of an unpredictable nature. The selector acquainted with such information can often focus form assessment into more fruitful pastures and avoid races of a more incomprehensible character.

SUMMARY OF FORM

1. Form is the record of past performance; it is the most reliable indication of ability.

2. Recent winning form is the most positive guide to assessing current ability.
3. Good top-class form is extremely reliable.
   Form of lower class is generally unreliable.

7 THE SELECTION FORMULA ANALYSED: FITNESS

Fitness is the second element in the selection formula and the major modifying factor to form. Unless a horse is fully race fit it is unlikely to produce its true or best race form.

Fitness can never be absolutely assured – a degree of fitness has to be left to trust (i.e. to the good judgement of the trainer) yet it must not be assumed just because a horse is declared to race that it is fully fit to reproduce its best form. The fact that a horse is competing in a race is not alone proof of its race fitness, and must not ever be arbitrarily accepted as such.

A horse competing in a race should have no physical ailments, be sound of eye, wind, heart and limb, but if it has not raced for a time its race fitness is not assured and cannot be assumed. This applies particularly to inexperienced horses (2 y.o., 3 y.o., maiden novice hurdlers, novice chasers), for until they have proved themselves on the racecourse, the trainer has little information upon which to assess what constitutes fitness in an individual horse, and off-course preparation is problematic.

Physical and race fitness, although closely related and dependent upon one another must not be regarded as the same. A horse's fitness on the day of the race will depend on its natural health (well-being) and the training preparation it has received prior to the race. Race fitness may be defined as peak physical fitness which gives a horse (if good enough) a positive chance of winning, as opposed to fitness which enables a horse merely to complete the race without physical injury.

The general term 'race fitness' from the selector's viewpoint should be understood as *peak race fitness*.

Although there can be many imponderables surrounding the race fitness of a horse, surprisingly, much unquestioning trust is placed on a horse being in peak physical condition when there is no evidence to support this assumption (a horse making its racecourse début, or reappearance after a lengthy absence, are in fact indications to the contrary – though some horses do show their best form on these occasions when 'fresh').

A horse will usually have to be at peak race fitness if it is to have a real chance of winning a race. The most reliable indication of a horse's fitness is a recent race performance.

A 'fit looking' horse.

This horse, photographed in the paddock prior to winning a race is instantly recognizable as being fit by the well-defined and developed lines of muscle running down its hindquarters and the lack of fatness around its girth and ribs. The skin is clear and healthy and this is borne out by the diamond pattern that is glowing across the top of its hindquarters, evidence that the horse has been well groomed as part of its pre-race preparation.

An 'unfit looking' horse.

This horse, photographed prior to finishing well beaten in its race, can be instantly recognized as still having to reach peak fitness. While appearing as a strong robust horse, there is a lack of well-defined and developed muscle on its hindquarters and an excess condition around its girth and ribs. The markings on the coat, however, are where the horse has been trace clipped, a common feature on many National Hunt horses once they have grown their winter coats.

103

The most reliable evidence of a horse being 'race fit' is proof from a recent race performance. 'Recent' is the operative word – within the previous 7 days is most favourable.

In this recent race performance a horse must have figured prominently at some stage. This will indicate that peak fitness has, or is about to be, reached. Applying the above stipulations can almost guarantee that a horse is at or will have gained peak race fitness. This is not private or inspired information but public to anyone prepared to examine recent form.

SEVEN-DAY RACE FITNESS

A horse racing twice within seven days is the fine tuning that can put a very keen edge on a horse's performance. It is a most reliable confirmation of peak race fitness. It applies where a winner, or narrowly beaten horse, races quickly again, ready to exploit proven form; or where an unfit horse is given a 'pipe-opener' to put it right for its next immediate engagement.

Whilst many of the highly successful and leading stables seldom practise this method of getting their horses fit, having their horses generally well prepared and in good race condition when they run, even their horses can be defeated by the peak race fitness of horses from less well known yards which have raced more recently (i.e. within the last 7 days).

Seven-day race fitness has a particularly dominating influence upon:
(a) all horses that have just struck the top of their form;
(b) all horses who stand up well to racing;
(c) National Hunt in the first and last month of the season, where peak fitness holds the key over less prepared rivals.

Seven days may appear an arbitrary time. It is, however, a well-tried and tested indicator of race fitness.

The essential quality of race fitness is that it is the peak of physical condition and therefore it allows the full expression of racing ability. It is, however, a transitory state which can only be maintained for a short time – 7 days is that approximate time. In practice, this means a horse will remain (without further training preparation) in physical peak condition for about a week.

An obvious qualifying factor with regard to racing again within 7 days is that the horse must have suffered no injury during its previous race. This factor can only be left to trust on the reasonable assumption that a trainer would not race a horse again so quickly if it had suffered any injury.

Similarly, races in quick succession may not be suitable for (i) horses of a weak constitution or wayward temperament who require a longer interval between races, (ii) those who have suffered from the effects of long-distance travel (travelling can blunt a horse's vitality as much as hard races).

In all of these instances, after paying due regard to the facts available, the selector must trust that the trainer's judgement to race the horse is the correct decision.

The general guiding rule to race fitness is the more recently a horse has run, the more likely it is to be race fit. The longer the time since a horse last raced, the less likely it is to be in peak condition.

On a time-scale:

1–7 days – is that special fine tuning sometimes necesssary for less than top-class horses to succeed in keenly matched contests, where peak form and fitness just 'carries the day'. It is appropriate to Flat and National Hunt. In the 1988–89 National Hunt season 32.2 per cent of hurdle race and 33.3 per cent of chase winners who raced again within a 7-day period won. Similarly in the 1988 Flat season 27 per cent of 2 y.o. winners and 24.2 per cent of 3-year-olds + winners also won their subsequent race.

8–14 days – up to 14 days is a most assured confirmation of a horse's race fitness, and this slightly longer time is appropriate to all types of horses, but particularly any who benefit from a less than immediate return to racing. (This is most appropriate for chasers who need, while maintaining their peak form and fitness, a little longer to recover from their race exertions.)

In the 1988–89 National Hunt season 28.9 per cent of chaser winners won again when subsequently raced within 8–14 days, as did 23.7 per cent of 2 y.o. 1988 Flat winners.

15–21 days – although shedding some uncertainty on peak fitness this is a most suitable time-span for horses less able to withstand frequent races. Therefore it is most appropriate for 2-year-olds whose lack of physical maturity often demands a longer recovery between races.

In the 1988 Flat season 23.0 per cent of 2 y.o. winners won again when subsequently raced within 15–21 days.

22–28 days – a length of time that sheds doubt on a horse's peak fitness, and in many instances may be a signal that a horse has just gone 'off the boil'. Appropriate, however, to all top-class horses whose next most appropriate racing engagement may fit into this time-scale.

29 days + – in most instances this is too long a period, and a horse's fitness cannot be accepted without an acquaintance with a trainer's methods or the special requirements of a particular horse.

It appears that only chase winners can be expected to retain a fair degree of fitness over an absence from racing of longer than 28 days.

In the 1988–89 National Hunt season 22.1 per cent of chase winners won again after an absence of 29 days + from racing. In 1985–86, 9.4 per cent of chasers won on their seasonal reappearance on a racecourse as opposed to 5.3 per cent of hurdlers and 6.7 per cent of Flat horses. This is further reinforced by the statistics given for both the Flat and National Hunt winners in Table 7.1.

The statistics of recent winners in Tables 7.2–7.5 suggest that the shorter the time-span in which a winner races again, the greater its winning chances.

The exceptions to this rule are the particular methods employed by certain trainers (the leading ones especially) who have the staff, the skill and facilities to prepare horses off-course, on home gallops. It applies particularly in the cases of top-class horses of experience (Flat and National Hunt) which may have an advance programme of races marked out for them at the beginning of a season, and time and effort will not be spared in these preparations.

In cases of inexperienced horses and of trainers without the staff, facilities or abilities, recent race fitness is the determining factor in the consideration of a horse's fitness and must never be lightly overlooked.

Proven fitness is the most dominating factor when considering a horse's chances of winning – and in this sphere there can be no substitute for 7-day race fitness which may finely tune a horse's performance to give it a winning edge.

While a short time between races is the ideal proof of a horse's fitness, there is often a factor which subjects a horse's next racecourse appearance to be of a longer time-span. This is the programming of race meetings and the accommodation of a suitable race for a horse. Early and late season, under both codes of racing, meetings are less frequent and so allow fewer opportunities for a horse to reappear and contest a similar type of race. Only at the height of the summer and winter seasons do race meetings abound, giving horses a greater chance of races, and the opportunity to race again within a short time – their fitness proven. So at many times during the season the selector may be presented with the dilemma of a horse having worthy form credentials, yet less than the desired guarantee of peak fitness. The most important consideration in this instance is to remember that **form** is the major element in the selection formula. Good form can beat everything and fitness is the factor which can only modify form. (A slow horse, however fit it is, is still unlikely to beat a faster one that is less fit.) Another factor in these instances is that similar conditions often apply to every horse in the race, placing none at a particular disadvantage.

The value of form can also be more satisfactorily established when

TABLE 7.1   Winners (horses with proven form and fitness) racing again

Days elapsed since the horse last ran	1988 Flat				
	2 y.o.		3 y.o.		
	Winners – Runners	%	Winners – Runners	%	
1– 7	20 – 74	= 27.0	90 – 372	= 24.2	
8–14	46 – 194	= 23.7	128 – 687	= 18.6	
15–21	45 – 195	= 23.0	91 – 585	= 15.6	
22–28	39 – 162	= 24.0	65 – 374	= 17.4	
29+	37 – 230	= 16.1	60 – 466	= 12.9	

Days elapsed since the horse last ran	1988–89 National Hunt				
	Hurdles		Chases		
	Winners – Runners	%	Winners – Runners	%	
1– 7	81 – 251	= 32.3	65 – 195	= 33.3	
8–14	123 – 564	= 21.8	144 – 499	= 28.9	
15–21	92 – 436	= 21.1	95 – 367	= 25.9	
22–28	60 – 257	= 23.3	57 – 207	= 27.5	
29+	54 – 347	= 15.6	56 – 253	= 22.1	

the time-span between races is longer and other horses who competed in the race will have contested other prizes to endorse or deny their worth.

Races such as group races are the most obvious examples of the programming of similar races of a longer rather than a shorter time-scale, being placed at strategic points throughout the season.

Of the 105 pattern or group races during the 1988 Flat season only one winner ran within the previous 7 days.

Sixty-two per cent of the races were won by winners who last raced 8–28 days previously.

Races (Flat and National Hunt) early in the season will, due to their position in the fixture calendar, be won by horses making their seasonal/racecourse débuts, underlining the problematic fitness considerations facing selection on these occasions. A trainer's record for producing horses 'fit' early in the season must be the main guide here. Some National Hunt horses are given a 'pipe-opener' on the Flat before re-embarking on a career over obstacles – especially hurdlers suited by firm 'going', which usually prevails in the opening weeks of the season.

Some horses excel early in the season, running their best races while fresh, and their later performance tails off as the season progresses. The fitness aspect in these instances does not readily submit to statistical analysis, and can be assessed only by the racing fan who goes to the race-track judging a horse's fitness by how it looks.

'FITNESS' BY LOOKS

Assessing a horse's fitness by how it looks, although outside the realms of the 'stay-at-home' racing fan and not subject to strict objective appraisal of statistics, is one of the best ways for an experienced judge to gauge a horse's fitness. Television helps to convey some of the correct impressions, but nothing beats being at the racecourse and the close presence of the horses, when a paddock inspection of the runners will quickly reveal the state of their fitness. The visual signs to notice denoting both a very 'fit looking' and an 'unfit looking' horse may be seen from the two photographs on pages 102 and 103.

A fit horse will have its muscle well defined, have little or no loose flesh, with a hint of its ribs being able to be seen. Its coat is likely to be shiny, having a gleam of well-being. (Darker coloured horses, black, brown or dark bays stand out prominently in this aspect, while grey-coloured horses are the most difficult to assess confidently from the look of their coats.)

A horse's behaviour in the paddock before a race can range from being very calm, as is common with older horses who may be experienced campaigners, to quite nervously excited, highly strung individuals, as often is the case with younger inexperienced horses. The calmer horses are likely to liven up and the more excitable ones calm down once they have been mounted and led out onto the racecourse to canter to the start.

A horse sweating up badly before a race (i.e. sweat pouring from its body and/or neck) is not a good sign as it shows signs of distress, for whatever reason, and it has wasted some of its energy before the race even starts. Weather conditions have to be taken into account as even the most placid horse may sweat at the height of summer when the temperature is high. Also it is not unusual to see a horse break out in a mild sweat between the hind legs (this is called a kidney sweat) and usually merely indicates that it is just winding up ready to spring into action once the race begins.

While not wishing to see a horse over-excited in the pre-race formalities, it is not encouraging either to see a horse so calm or disinterested that it looks half asleep and completely lacking energy. This latter impression may be dispelled once the horse leaves the parade paddocks and canters to the start, and many older horses only come to life then.

The most encouraging signs to see from a horse cantering to the post is one taking a firm hold of its bit (without pulling the jockey's arms 'out') and having a co-ordinated stride, an athletic action exuding power and energy. This is particularly important for inexperienced horses, especially 2-year-olds, who may as yet not know how to physically 'use themselves'.

This last observation is a most subjective one, yet is most important, as it quickly identifies the latent power within a horse, and therefore available to be used, sometimes with devastating effect in the race.

The racing fan who regularly goes racing will become acquainted with these illuminating insights as to a horse's fitness and then may be able to adopt, as the situation demands, a more liberal interpretation of the fitness factor than is laid down by the strict statistical terms of the selection formula.

Date of last run tables

Tables show the days since a horse last ran; the finishing position (whether first, second, third, fourth or unplaced) and the record of winners to runners on a time-scale.

TABLE 7.2   1988 Flat – Horse's previous finishing position/date of last run comparison – 2-year-olds

Days since last ran	Total W – R	1st W – R	2nd W – R	3rd W – R	4th W – R	O W – R
1–7	91 – 976 (9.3%)	20 – 74 (27.0%)	19 – 102 (18.6%)	19 – 118 (16.1%)	6 – 99 (6.6%)	27 – 583 (4.6%)
8–14	237 – 2,407 (9.9%)	46 – 194 (23.7%)	61 – 294 (20.7%)	40 – 245 (16.3%)	21 – 257 (8.2%)	69 – 1,417 (4.9%)
15–21	202 – 1,838 (11.2%)	45 – 195 (23.1%)	37 – 212 (17.5%)	30 – 195 (15.4%)	19 – 170 (11.2%)	71 – 1,066 (6.7%)
22–28	143 – 1,194 (12.0%)	39 – 162 (24.1%)	29 – 122 (23.8%)	18 – 125 (14.4%)	9 – 110 (8.2%)	48 – 675 (7.1%)
29–42	106 – 1,161 (9.1%)	23 – 135 (17.0%)	17 – 88 (19.3%)	9 – 109 (8.3%)	14 – 108 (13.0%)	43 – 721 (6.0%)
43–70	58 – 808 (7.6%)	11 – 67 (16.4%)	5 – 62 (8.1%)	7 – 63 (11.1%)	7 – 84 (8.3%)	28 – 532 (5.3%)
71–99	12 – 260 (4.7%)	2 – 18 (11.1%)	1 – 8 (12.5%)	1 – 15 (6.7%)	1 – 26 (3.8%)	7 – 193 (3.6%)
100+	4 – 131 (3.1%)	1 – 10 (10.0%)	0 – 4	0 – 2	1 – 12 (8.3%)	2 – 103 (1.9%)
1–28	673 – 6,415 (10.5%)	150 – 625 (24.0%)	146 – 730 (20.0%)	107 – 683 (15.7%)	55 – 636 (8.6%)	215 – 3,741 (5.7%)
29+	180 – 2,360 (7.6%)	37 – 230 (16.1%)	23 – 162 (14.2%)	17 – 189 (9.0%)	23 – 230 (4.3%)	80 – 1,549 (5.2%)

TABLE 7.3   1988 Flat – Horse's previous finishing position/date of last run comparison – 3-year-olds+

Days since last ran	Total W – R	1st W – R	2nd W – R	3rd W – R	4th W – R	O W – R
1–7	378 – 3,720 (10.2%)	90 – 372 (24.2%)	58 – 466 (12.4%)	64 – 367 (17.4%)	40 – 307 (13.0%)	126 – 2,208 (5.7%)
8–14	671 – 7,370 (9.1%)	128 – 687 (18.6%)	131 – 811 (16.2%)	84 – 789 (10.6%)	80 – 711 (11.3%)	248 – 4,372 (5.7%)
15–21	509 – 5,659 (9.0%)	91 – 585 (15.6%)	101 – 610 (16.6%)	75 – 547 (13.7)	40 – 532 (7.5%)	202 – 3,385 (6.0%)
22–28	336 – 3,623 (9.3%)	65 – 374 (17.4%)	46 – 287 (16.0%)	41 – 313 (13.1%)	32 – 338 (9.5%)	152 – 2,311 (6.6%)
29–42	274 – 3,117 (8.8%)	37 – 269 (13.8%)	36 – 266 (13.5%)	34 – 247 (13.8%)	27 – 243 (11.1%)	140 – 2,092 (6.7%)
43–70	125 – 1,698 (7.4%)	16 – 133 (12.0%)	17 – 116 (14.7%)	17 – 123 (13.8%)	10 – 122 (8.1%)	65 – 1,204 (5.4%)
71–99	42 – 544 (7.7%)	4 – 38 (10.5%)	3 – 39 (7.7%)	4 – 31 (12.9%)	6 – 39 (15.4%)	25 – 397 (6.3%)
100+	23 – 466 (4.9%)	3 – 26 (11.5%)	2 – 23 (8.7%)	1 – 24 (4.2%)	2 – 33 (6.1%)	15 – 360 (4.2%)
1–28	1,894 – 20,372 (9.4%)	374 – 2,018 (18.5%)	336 – 2,174 (15.5%)	264 – 2,016 (13.1%)	192 – 1,888 (10.2%)	728 – 12,276 (5.9%)
29+	464 – 5,825 (8.0%)	60 – 466 (12.9%)	58 – 444 (13.1%)	56 – 425 (13.2%)	45 – 437 (10.3%)	245 – 4,053 (6.0%)

TABLE 7.4 1988–89 National Hunt horse's previous finishing position/date of last run comparison (hurdles)

Days since last ran	Total	1st	2nd	3rd	4th	O
	W – R	W – R	W – R	W – R	W – R	W – R
1–7	284 – 2,382 (11.9%)	81 – 251 (32.2%)	72 – 262 (27.5%)	30 – 212 (14.2%)	26 – 210 (12.4%)	75 – 1,447 (5.2%)
8–14	518 – 5,427 (9.5%)	123 – 564 (21.8%)	116 – 579 (20.0%)	63 – 547 (11.5%)	60 – 476 (12.6%)	156 – 3,261 (4.8%)
15–21	383 – 4,094 (9.4%)	92 – 436 (21.1%)	76 – 395 (19.0%)	52 – 412 (12.6%)	49 – 423 (11.6%)	114 – 2,428 (4.7%)
22–28	222 – 2,356 (9.4%)	60 – 257 (23.3%)	37 – 219 (16.9%)	18 – 207 (8.7%)	17 – 208 (8.2%)	90 – 1,465 (6.1%)
29–42	166 – 2,182 (7.6%)	34 – 202 (16.8%)	28 – 189 (14.8%)	22 – 191 (11.5%)	16 – 176 (9.1%)	66 – 1,424 (4.6%)
43–70	116 – 1,482 (7.8%)	15 – 98 (15.3%)	13 – 100 (13.0%)	15 – 99 (15.2%)	16 – 106 (15.1%)	57 – 1,079 (5.2%)
71–99	32 – 570 (5.6%)	2 – 24 (8.3%)	3 – 29 (10.3%)	1 – 35 (2.9%)	4 – 44 (9.1%)	22 – 438 (5.0%)
100+	49 – 688 (7.1%)	3 – 23 (13.0%)	7 – 33 (21.2%)	7 – 46 (15.2%)	1 – 39 (2.6%)	31 – 547 (5.7%)
1–28	1,407 – 14,259 (9.9%)	356 – 1,508 (23.6%)	301 – 1,455 (20.7%)	163 – 1,378 (11.8%)	152 – 1,317 (11.5%)	435 – 8,601 (5.1%)
29+	363 – 4,922 (7.4%)	54 – 347 (15.6%)	61 – 351 (17.4%)	45 – 371 (12.2%)	37 – 365 (10.1%)	176 – 3,488 (5.0%)

TABLE 7.5   1988–89 National Hunt horse's previous finishing position/date of last run comparison (chases)

Days since last ran	Total W – R	1st W – R	2nd W – R	3rd W – R	4th W – R	O W – R
1–7	210 – 1,458 (14.4%)	65 – 195 (33.3%)	38 – 176 (21.6%)	30 – 168 (17.9%)	19 – 173 (11.0%)	58 – 746 (7.8%)
8–14	475 – 3,597 (13.2%)	144 – 499 (28.9%)	96 – 550 (17.5%)	72 – 486 (14.8%)	43 – 419 (10.3%)	120 – 1,643 (7.3%)
15–21	328 – 2,527 (13.0%)	95 – 367 (25.9%)	65 – 348 (18.7%)	39 – 347 (11.2%)	29 – 282 (10.3%)	100 – 1,183 (8.5%)
22–28	174 – 1,360 (12.8%)	57 – 207 (27.5%)	23 – 164 (14.0%)	24 – 177 (13.6%)	11 – 169 (6.5%)	59 – 643 (9.2%)
29–42	156 – 1,250 (12.5%)	37 – 171 (21.6%)	27 – 147 (18.4%)	22 – 139 (15.8%)	18 – 148 (12.2%)	52 – 645 (8.1%)
43–70	87 – 751 (11.6%)	17 – 60 (28.3%)	15 – 71 (21.1%)	14 – 74 (18.4%)	11 – 105 (10.3%)	30 – 441 (6.8%)
71–99	23 – 250 (9.2%)	1 – 10 (10.0%)	5 – 23 (21.7%)	5 – 29 (17.2%)	2 – 23 (8.7%)	10 – 165 (6.1%)
100+	18 – 336 (5.4%)	1 – 12 (8.3%)	2 – 27 (7.4%)	0 – 29	3 – 32 (6.3%)	12 – 236 (5.1%)
1–28	1,187 – 8,942 (13.2%)	361 – 1,268 (28.5%)	222 – 1,238 (17.9%)	165 – 1,178 (14.0%)	102 – 1,043 (9.8%)	337 – 4,215 (8.0%)
29+	284 – 2,587 (11.0%)	56 – 253 (22.1%)	49 – 268 (18.3%)	41 – 271 (15.1%)	34 – 308 (16.3%)	104 – 1,487 (7.0%)

8 THE SELECTION FORMULA ANALYSED: CLASS

Class is the third element in the selection formula and an important modifying factor.

Class in the racing sense means the quality of opposition a horse has competed against. In respect of quality this can range from the very best – 'top class', the Classics, Group Races (Flat) and the National Hunt equivalent – Champion Hurdle, Gold Cup – down to selling races which have been designed for the worst horses.

A 'class' horse, or 'class' in the colloquial sense accurately used means the very best horses (type and age applying).

A horse can be raised or lowered in class or compete in the same (similar) class.

A horse raised in class must improve to have a winning chance.

A horse lowered in class has only to reproduce its known form to win.

A horse in the same class may have either to improve upon or simply reproduce its best run form, depending on the evaluation of that form.

The most favourable situation, for consideration in selection is when a horse with consistent proven ability is lowered (dropped) in class.

A horse must never be considered to have a winning chance just because it has been dropped in class. It must have discernible positive ability in the higher class.

The extreme example is when a horse raced initially well above its class (e.g. maiden 3 y.o. competes in the Derby to fulfil the wishes of an ever-optimistic owner and finishes tailed off behind the rest of the field) fails or struggles when dropped in class to a modest maiden race later in the season. It is therefore necessary to examine carefully all the facts of form before making any judgements.

The evaluation of class plays a dominating role in the evaluation of form, and while differences are easily definable at the extreme ends, differences are less distinguishable in the middle range of class. Prize-money and the grade of course (Group I, II, III or IV according to previous Jockey Club ruling) provide the obvious indications of class.

One of the easiest and perhaps obvious methods of defining the class

Class is the quality or type of race contested by a horse. Top-class horses usually have the conformation and looks to match their ability while slower, moderate horses are correspondingly lacking in these features.

Champion sprinter LOCHNAGER who can be clearly seen as a strong imposing horse with a muscular athletic appearance – he is well proportioned and of good conformation.

A very fit and top class horse in action. DANCING BRAVE at Ascot, European champion 1986.

of races, horses and their form is by identification and comparison of racecourses. A graded list of racecourses is given in Table 8.1. It has been compiled in respect of the quality value of the form of most of the races contested in accord with the level of allocated prize-money (i.e. the greater the level of prize-money, the more competitive are the races, the better are the horses and therefore the higher the value of form). This list is closely based on the Jockey Club's own grading of racecourses in regard to the amount of prize-money and subsidies allotted to each course, but also with special consideration placed on experience of form selection.

The Flat racecourses have been divided into five grades and the National Hunt courses into four grades. It may be seen that while there is a clear-cut distinction between the top and bottom grades of courses, this distinction can become much less clear in assessing the value of form between two of the lower grades of courses. It will, however, serve as a basic and most reliable guide.

The most valuable races, fiercely competitive on the most testing courses, can be considered top class. The lowest prized races on the smaller, easier racecourses which attract the same regular group of contestants can be considered the lowest class. Class plays an important role in the selection formula as it is the factor which may require form improvement as a necessity or in other cases no more than a reproducing of known ability.

The old adage suggested to racehorse owners: 'Run your horse in the worst company and keep yourself in the best company', applies with equal wisdom to those seeking selections from horses lowered in class.

TABLE 8.1   Grading of racecourses

	Flat
Grade I	Ascot, Goodwood, Newbury, Newmarket, Sandown, York
Grade II	Ayr, Chester, Doncaster, Epsom, Haydock, Kempton, Newcastle
Grade III	Bath, Brighton, Leicester, Lingfield, Nottingham, Redcar, Ripon, Salisbury, Yarmouth
Grade IV	Beverley, Chepstow, Pontefract, Thirsk, Windsor, Wolverhampton
Grade V	Carlisle, Catterick, Edinburgh, Folkestone, Hamilton, Warwick

	National Hunt
Grade I	Ascot, Cheltenham, Doncaster, Haydock, Kempton, Liverpool, Newbury, Sandown
Grade II	Ayr, Chepstow, Lingfield, Newcastle, Nottingham, Wetherby, Wincanton
Grade III	Carlisle, Catterick, Folkestone, Huntingdon, Leicester, Market Rasen, Newton Abbot, Stratford, Towcester, Warwick, Windsor, Wolverhampton, Worcester
Grade IV	Bangor, Cartmel, Devon and Exeter, Fakenham, Fontwell, Hereford, Hexham, Kelso, Ludlow, Perth, Plumpton, Sedgefield, Southwell, Uttoxeter, Taunton

9 THE SELECTION FORMULA ANALYSED: CONDITIONS

Conditions are the fourth element in the selection formula, they are modifying factors which may act as the vital balancing role in forming the selection decision.

If these modifying factors are of proven positive value, they can only act as an endorsement to a decision. If they contain the negative aspect, they may serve as the eliminating element in the balance of decision-making. Occasionally these modifying elements may assume the role of the salient factor in the forming of a selection decision.

The conditions affecting the reproducing of form are in order of importance:

1. Distance (the distance of a race).
2. Going (the ground conditions on which the horse must race).
3. Weight (the weight carried, and whether it involves penalties or allowances).
4. Courses/draw (the variation of courses, and the fixed starting positions in Flat racing).
5. Jockeyship (the quality).
6. Sundry factors (i.e. blinkers – breeding – trainer – owner).

DISTANCE

Distance is the distance of a race in which a horse competes. A horse can only be considered *proven* over the distance by winning at that distance, or showing form of proven value at the distance. A change of a horse's distance from its proven distance(s) places it in the area of the unknown – for the horse is unproven at that distance.

Most horses specialize and perform best at only one distance (i.e. sprinters may be only 5f horses or be equally proficient at 5f and 6f). Milers may only act best at 1m or may act equally well between 7f and 1m 1f. Middle-distance horses, similarly, may only race well at 1¼m or

Most horses, whether Flat or National Hunt, produce their best form over one particular distance. A change in distance often produces a change in form.

These two photographs, looking up the July Course at Newmarket, illustrate the difference in distance between 1f and 2f. In the top picture the disc on the rails to the right is the 2f marker from the winning-post while in the bottom picture the disc to the right is the 1f marker from the winning-post.

be versatile between 1m 1f and 1m 4f. Stayers also may need 1½m, 1¾m, 2m or 2m+ or may act over a range of extreme distances. National Hunt horses have equal speed and stamina restrictions, ranging from 2m hurdlers to 3½m+ chasers.

Distance can and does alter performances. This may apply particularly to maiden horses (Flat) and novices (National Hunt) who may suddenly improve when they find their best distance. Change of distance is one of the fundamental reasons for reversals in form, and improvement of form when the correct one is found.

NB. All maiden 2-year-olds and 3-year-olds – novice hurdlers and chasers who show considerable improvement when raced over a different distance (normally a longer one).

Experienced racehorses are often given a 'pipe-opener' over a shorter distance than they need to bring them to peak race fitness with a race to obscure the value of their form. The oldest and easiest ploy to disguise a horse's true form and ability is to race it over its wrong distance. In the case of many maidens, however, often to the frustration of a trainer, and to confound all laws of breeding, a horse's best distance is only discovered by trial and error from racing it over various distances.

Breeding is likely to be the strongest indication of a horse's most suitable distance, but is only an assumption that cannot be accepted as fact. Breeding is not an exact science, but by examining the records of leading sires given in Table 10.1 (pages 162–3) it is possible to identify the characteristics and influences inherited by a sire's racing stock.

Distance is a most important factor in the consideration of form.

GOING

Going, on a level par with distance, is often the culprit responsible for reversals in form. A horse can only be considered to act on going if proven from the racecourse test. Similar going or slight variations are unlikely to affect a horse, but extreme changes which have not been previously encountered can have devastating effects (e.g. changes from good to heavy or good to hard).

It has been said that a 'good horse' will act on any going, and while there is a certain truth in this remark, it must strongly be stated that most horses have strong preferences and act best on particular ground. A horse's action and physique will allow it to perform better and with greater ease on certain going, and this allows some horses to display specialist capabilities on extremes of going (e.g. the soft ground specialist who revels in the mud in heavy ground and cannot act and may even get jarred up on other going; or the other type of specialist who only acts on ground when hoofs can be heard to rattle). Breeding often

Variations in going can have a vital influence on form.

Typical going that is encountered during the summer months – officially described as firm.

Going officially described as soft with clods of turf being visibly kicked up.

produces characteristics such as these passed down from one generation to the next (i.e. some sires, themselves soft ground specialists produce stock of similar tendency, other sires who preferred good or firm ground pass on this characteristic and have offspring only able to act on this type of surface). Although breeding will give strong indications of a horse's likely preferences, each horse is an individual, whose requirements can only be confirmed by test on the racecourse.

In extremes of going – going can be the salient factor to affect form.

WEIGHT

Weight is the weight a horse has been set to carry in the entry conditions of a race. This weight includes a fully clothed jockey plus the saddle and number cloth. A jockey is weighed out before the race and weighed in after the race by the clerk of the scales in the weighing-room. If the jockey and equipment are too light to make the prescribed weight the difference is made up by thin pieces of lead which are placed in pockets in the saddlecloth. A jockey must weigh in at the same weight as he weighed out, and anyone failing to make the correct weight at the weigh-in will be disqualified.

A comparison between a 1 lb saddle (left) and a 5 lb saddle (right) to illustrate part of the dead weight which a horse has to carry.

Weight is a major factor which can produce a reversal of form and can defeat even the best horse. Burdened with enough weight even a fast horse can be beaten by a normally slower rival who is carrying less weight.

Weight is a great leveller of ability. It applies to all types of horse and in all classes of race. Enough weight given to even the very best horses will stop them from winning. At level weights a race is a contest only of comparative ability and fitness, but as differences occur (weight penalties or concessions) a more involved consideration begins to dominate the assessment process.

The changes in conditions of the weight carried bring about changes in form, as revealed by handicaps and the myriad questions posed by the unequal distribution of weight. The effect weight has is exemplified in the principle of handicapping by weight, where the best horse, in the opinion of the handicapper, is given the most weight and the worst horse the least. The object is to burden the faster horses with enough weight to bring them down to the speed of the slower horses. Herein lies the key to understanding the effect of weight:

A burden of **weight** can make a **fast horse** run **slower** but even a very light **weight cannot** make a **slow horse** run **faster**!

The consideration of weight always creates certain imponderables and it is necessary as part of the selection analysis to be acquainted with the conditions of weight and their influence in the outcome of a race.

Races where horses carry level weight (within certain prescribed limits) are more readily assessed. The weight variations within this basic criterion are as follows:

1. Sex allowances (Flat racing) colts, horses and geldings giving a weight concession of 5 lb★ to fillies and mares. (National Hunt) colts, horses and geldings giving a weight concession of 5 lb to fillies and mares in all chases, hurdles and National Hunt Flat races.
2. Weight-for-age (Flat and National Hunt). Horses of different ages giving or receiving weight according to an official scale. (See Tables 9.1 and 9.2.)
3. Weight penalties (incurred for winning and/or differing according to the value of the race won).
4. Weight allowances (Flat and National Hunt for maidens at starting). A special allowance (Flat only) for horses which have previously not run.

Sex allowance

A weight allowance of 3/5 lb is given by colts and geldings to fillies; this was introduced to counterbalance the basic differences of physical strength and development between the sexes. Colts and geldings are normally more robust and faster maturing than fillies, and would without this compulsory weight concession hold initially an unfair advantage in races.

★ *but* 3 lb for 3 y.o. + in Group races.

The effect of the sex allowance in practice is therefore to resolve the physical imbalance and give equal opportunity to colts, geldings and fillies racing against each other.

NB. The sex weight allowance at certain times may, however, not represent the true differences between colts and fillies and therefore be to the positive advantage of one or the other:

1. Early in the season 2 y.o. colts with racing experience may have a distinct physical advantage over fillies which is likely to be more than 5 lb sex allowance.
2. In the late summer of their 3 y.o. careers (September to November) fillies tend to develop considerably physically, to the extent that suddenly they reach a par with colts. The 3/5 lb weight concession then is to their advantage and it is noticeable at these times how the rapidly improving fillies defeat colts in maiden races and condition races.

Weight for age (Flat and National Hunt)

Weight for age is an official scale of weights formulated by the Jockey Club to give horses of different ages racing against each other equal opportunity, by apportioning them varying weights. On the Flat it applies to 2–5-year-olds (older horses considered equal), and in National Hunt to 3–5-year-olds (older horses considered equal) and pays due regard to the varying distances (5f–2½m Flat, 2m–3m National Hunt). The scale changes throughout the season to accommodate the normal rate of maturity of younger horses (i.e. in March Flat racing a 4 y.o. would be expected over 5f to give a 3 y.o. 14–13 lb and a 3 y.o. to give a 2 y.o. 47 lb, but by October the scale would have fallen – the 4 y.o. gives a 3 y.o. 1 lb and the 3 y.o. gives a 2 y.o. 19–18 lb – similarly weight changes apply to National Hunt racing). Tables 9.1 and 9.2 give the scale of weight for age for Flat and National Hunt respectively.

Although the Jockey Club have an official weight-for-age (WFA) Scale this serves only as a guide to the clerks of courses who can frame the conditions of their races differently. It is therefore advisable to examine the conditions of WFA races and note whether conditions would seem to favour one age rather than another or if the race conforms strictly to the Jockey Club Scale.

Note well the conditions of all races where WFA applies, particularly *novice* hurdlers, where, especially in heavy going, a weight concession can be a decisive factor.

Weight penalties (Flat and National Hunt)

Weight penalties are incurred by all horses that win except if the conditions of the race preclude them.

TABLE 9.1 Scale of weight-for-age for Flat races (most recently amended 1990)

Distance (furlongs)	Age	JAN 1–15	JAN 16–31	FEB 1–14	FEB 15–28	MARCH 1–15	MARCH 16–31	APRIL 1–15	APRIL 16–30	MAY 1–15	MAY 16–31	JUNE 1–15	JUNE 16–30	JULY 1–15	JULY 16–31	AUGUST 1–15	AUGUST 16–31	SEP 1–15	SEP 16–30	OCT 1–15	OCT 16–31	NOV 1–15	NOV 16–30	DEC 1–15	DEC 16–31
5	2	—	—	—	—	—	47	44	41	38	36	34	32	30	28	26	24	22	20	19	18	17	17	16	16
	3	15	15	15	15	14	13	12	11	10	9	8	7	6	5	4	3	2	2	1	1	—	—	—	—
6	2	—	—	—	—	—	—	—	—	44	41	38	36	33	31	28	26	24	22	21	20	19	18	17	17
	3	16	16	16	16	15	14	13	12	11	10	9	8	7	6	5	4	3	3	2	2	1	1	—	—
7	2	—	—	—	—	—	—	—	—	—	—	—	—	38	35	32	30	27	25	23	22	21	20	19	19
	3	18	18	18	18	17	16	15	14	12	11	10	9	8	7	6	5	4	4	3	3	2	2	1	1
8	2	—	—	—	—	—	—	—	—	—	—	—	—	—	—	37	34	31	28	26	24	23	22	21	20
	3	20	20	19	19	18	17	16	15	13	12	11	10	9	8	7	6	5	4	4	3	3	2	2	1
	4	1	1	1	1	—	—	—	—	—	—	—	—	—	—	—	—	—	—	—	—	—	—	—	—
9	3	22	22	21	21	20	19	18	17	16	15	14	13	12	11	10	9	8	7	6	5	4	3	3	2
	4	2	2	2	2	1	1	—	—	—	—	—	—	—	—	—	—	—	—	—	—	—	—	—	—
10	3	23	23	22	22	21	20	19	18	17	16	15	14	13	12	11	10	9	8	7	6	5	4	4	3
	4	3	3	3	2	2	1	1	—	—	—	—	—	—	—	—	—	—	—	—	—	—	—	—	—
11	3	—	—	—	—	23	22	21	20	18	17	16	15	14	13	12	11	10	9	8	7	6	5	5	4
	4	4	4	3	3	2	1	1	—	—	—	—	—	—	—	—	—	—	—	—	—	—	—	—	—
12	3	—	—	—	—	24	23	22	21	19	18	17	16	15	14	13	12	11	10	9	8	7	6	6	5
	4	5	5	4	4	3	2	2	1	1	—	—	—	—	—	—	—	—	—	—	—	—	—	—	—
13	3	—	—	—	—	25	24	23	22	20	19	17	16	15	14	13	12	11	10	9	8	7	6	6	5
	4	5	5	4	4	3	2	2	1	1	—	—	—	—	—	—	—	—	—	—	—	—	—	—	—
14	3	—	—	—	—	26	25	24	23	21	20	18	17	16	15	14	13	12	11	10	9	8	7	7	6
	4	6	6	5	5	4	3	3	2	2	1	1	—	—	—	—	—	—	—	—	—	—	—	—	—
15	3	—	—	—	—	28	27	26	25	23	21	20	19	18	16	15	14	13	11	10	9	8	7	7	6
	4	6	6	5	5	4	3	3	2	2	1	1	—	—	—	—	—	—	—	—	—	—	—	—	—
16	3	—	—	—	—	29	28	27	26	24	22	21	20	19	17	16	15	13	12	11	10	9	8	8	7
	4	7	7	6	6	5	4	4	3	3	2	2	1	1	—	—	—	—	—	—	—	—	—	—	—
18	3	—	—	—	—	31	30	29	28	26	24	22	21	19	18	17	16	14	13	12	11	10	9	9	8
	4	8	8	7	7	6	5	5	4	4	3	3	2	2	1	1	—	—	—	—	—	—	—	—	—
20	3	—	—	—	—	33	32	31	30	28	26	24	22	20	19	18	17	16	15	14	13	12	11	10	9
	4	9	9	8	8	7	6	6	5	5	4	3	2	1	—	—	—	—	—	—	—	—	—	—	—

Note: allowance assessed in lb which: 4 y.o. will receive from 5 y.o., 3 y.o. will receive from 4 y.o., 2 y.o. will receive from 3 y.o.

TABLE 9.2 Scale of weight-for-age (jumping)

The Stewards of the Jockey Club recommend the following revised scale of weight-for-age should, on and after 1st January 1985, be used as a guide.

Hurdle races

Allowance, assessed in lb, which 3 years old and 4 years old will receive from 5 years old and upwards

Distance	Age	Jan	Feb	Mar	Apr	May	June	July	Aug	Sept	Oct	Nov	Dec
2m	3	12	10	8	6	5	5	20	20	18	17	16	14
	4							3	3	2	1	—	—
2½m	3	13	11	9	7	6	6	21	21	19	18	17	15
	4							3	3	2	1	—	—
3m	3	14	12	10	8	7	7	23	23	21	19	18	16
	4							4	4	3	2	1	—

Steeplechases

Allowance, assessed in lb, which 4 years old and 5 years old will receive from 6 years old and upwards

Distance	Age	Jan	Feb	Mar	Apr	May	June	July	Aug	Sept	Oct	Nov	Dec
2m	4	10	9	8	7	6	6	15	15	14	13	12	11
	5							3	3	2	1	—	—
2½m	4	11	10	9	8	7	7	16	16	15	14	13	12
	5							4	4	3	2	1	—
3m	4	12	11	10	9	8	8	17	17	16	15	14	13
	5							5	5	5	3	2	1

Weight penalties apply particularly to graduation stakes races, (formerly maidens at closing) (Flat) and all novice hurdles and novice chases (National Hunt). A horse with a penalty must be considered handicapped by this extra burden of weight – it will mean that whatever performance has been achieved, the horse is likely to have to improve further to overcome this new handicap of weight.

Individual penalties range from 3 lb to 10 lb (Flat) and 5 lb–10 lb (National Hunt). These are often cumulative in novice hurdlers and chasers or may be 7 lb for one race and 10 lb for two races won; similarly, the conditions of some races (both National Hunt and Flat) require varying weight penalties according to the value of the races won.

Weight scale

TABLE 9.3   The weight scale applied to the handicapping of horses

Flat		National Hunt	
5–6f	3 lb per length	2m	2 lb per length
7–8f	2½ lb per length	2½m	1½ lb per length
9–11f	2 lb per length	3m	1 lb per length
12–14f	1½ lb per length	3m+	½ lb per length
15f+	1 lb per length		

The weight scales given in Table 9.3 are those most widely applied.

On fast ground the allowances need to be increased, and on soft ground decreased. For example, some judges believe that 4 lb represents a length over 5f on firm ground, and ½ lb a length may be the best yardstick over 2m on soft going. The selector should use his own judgement within the broad guidelines. While weight seeks to eliminate the advantage of a faster horse it can do nothing to help a slow horse run faster than it can run already. On testing courses, especially over long distances, the burden of carrying weight can wear a faster horse down to the level of inferior rivals. However, on easy, tight-turning courses where horses cannot really race at top speed until they enter the straight (especially middle-distance races 7f–1m 2f) the weight concession by faster horses (who are the ones with that vital acceleration in the final stages of a race) will not be of any great disadvantage.

Flat racing handicaps
In flat racing handicaps the weight penalty for previous winners is usually set according to the distance of the race. A smaller penalty

(usually up to 5 lb) in longer distance races (14 furlongs+), where the burden of weight is greatest; and a larger penalty (e.g. 6 lb+) in shorter distance races (sprints 5f/6f), where the burden of weight is felt least.

In the 1985 flat racing season the record of horses defying a penalty in handicaps over sprints and longer distances was:

	5/6 furlongs			mile 6 furlongs+		
	Winners	Runners		Winners	Runners	
up to 5 lb	2	25	= 8.0%	9	70	= 12.9%
6 lb+	34	173	= 19.7%	2	16	= 12.5%
	36	198	= 17.2%	11	86	= 12.8%

These findings show that the longer the distance of a race the greater is the effect of weight. A horse can more easily defy a large penalty over a short distance.

Many situations demand the practical consideration of penalties and the likelihood of a horse defying a penalty can be said to depend on:
1. The form of a winner;
2. The size of penalty;
3. The scope it has to make the necessary improvement.

1. Form;

The form of some winners in non-handicap races is so superior to rivals that a penalty of the largest size is no inconvenience. The form of other winners may be less superior and ability to defy a penalty will depend on its size.

2. The size of the penalty;

3 lb–5 lb The lowest and easiest penalties for a horse to overcome – many horses can improve the necessary amount to overcome these low penalties, for example simply by winning a race. Early season 2-year-olds would normally develop this amount from a winning experience.

7 lb This requires a greater improvement and is likely to defeat less than better class horses, or those dropped in class.

10 lb and 10 lb+ This requires considerable improvement and will defeat all but the very best or rapidly improving horses.

3. Scope for improvement;

This is essentially bound to the horse's physical constitution and scope for development; this information can hardly be gleaned from examination of form but requires experienced observation of the horse.

Scope for improvement will also be indicated from the manner of the horse's winning performance (i.e. the ease or difficulty of winning). A horse that wins easily can hardly do more and is likely to improve upon that performance, while a horse that wins 'all out' suggests that it is less likely to improve.

Weight allowances

Weight allowances are normally framed in the conditions of race as a concession to lack of achievement (due to inability or inexperience), i.e. maiden allowance for horses that have not won a race; a weight allowance for horses which have not run previously; a weight allowance for horses that have not won a race since a certain date or a race of a prescribed value.

COURSES

There are over 50 racecourses spread throughout Britain, some specializing in Flat or National Hunt racing while others can accommodate both types. These courses can vary as much in size, shape and gradient as they do in location.

Courses range in extremes from a sharp flat track at Chester which is approximately 1m in circumference to the wide-open galloping expanses at Newmarket where there is a course a straight mile long. This variation of courses can and does strongly influence a racehorse's performance, so that some horses become course specialists. These horses only seem able to produce their best form under the conditions prevailing on a certain course, and at other tracks produce below-par performances.

The variation of courses is as wide for National Hunt racing as for Flat racing. Extremes exemplified at one end of the spectrum by figure-of-eight-shape circuits at Fontwell and Windsor and at the other by wide galloping tracks at Aintree and Haydock. The former two tracks have easy fences while the latter have large awesome fences which, having a drop on the landing side of the fences, are negotiated only by the safest of jumpers.

These differences combine to endorse the maxim 'horses for courses' especially where the course is of extreme character. *Flat*: Chester – small circuit with tight bends; Epsom, Brighton – rolling gradients; Newmarket – straightness and openness; Windsor – figure-of-eight shape. *National Hunt*: Fontwell, Windsor – figure of eights; Newton Abbot – tight flat track 1m circumference; Haydock, Aintree – big fences, galloping courses; Cheltenham – tough fences, large circuit, stamina-sapping gradients.

The different characteristics on race-tracks can have an effect on a horse's performance. British racecourses vary as much in their shape, size and undulation as they do in location.

These photographs illustrate the two extremes. The top one is looking down the July Course at Newmarket – a wide, straight galloping track, while the bottom one shows Chester which is a tight round track of approximately 1m circumference.

Some courses are right-handed, others left-handed, some suit front runners, others benefit long-striding horses who need a galloping course to be seen to best advantage. The variety of racecourses in Britain is one of the intriguing and attractive features of British racing, allowing a horse to keep its own characteristic individuality and not necessarily have to conform to the stereotyped conditions of racing that exist elsewhere. Therefore it is always necessary when assessing a horse's chances to pay attention to the special features and requirements of the course. The characteristics of both Flat and National Hunt racecourses in the UK are given below.

FLAT RACING

ASCOT (RH)	Round course 1m 6f with a run-in 2½f. It is a galloping-type course. Straight course 1m is undulating with a stiff 3f, uphill finish.
AYR (LH)	Round course 1m 4f with a run-in 4f. Straight course 6f.
BATH (LH)	Round course 1m 4f with a run-in 4f. It is a galloping-type course. Straight course 5f 167yd and uphill.
BEVERLEY (RH)	Round course 1m 4f with a run-in 3½f and stiff uphill finish. Straight course 5f.
BRIGHTON (LH)	U-shaped course 1m 4f with a run-in 3½f. It is an undulating course.
CARLISLE (RH)	Pear-shaped course 1m 5f that is undulating with a run-in 3½f uphill. Straight course 6f.
CATTERICK (LH)	Oval course 1m 2f with a run-in 3f. It is a sharp course. Straight course 5f that is downhill most of the way.
CHEPSTOW (LH)	Oval course 2m with a run-in 5f. It is an undulating course. Straight course 1m.
CHESTER (LH)	Tight, round-shaped course of 1m with a run-in 2f. Sprint races are run on the round course.
DONCASTER (LH)	Round course almost 2m with a run-in 4½f. It is a galloping course. Straight course 1m.
EDINBURGH (RH)	Oval course 1m 2f with a run-in 4f. It is a flat, sharp course. Straight course 5f.
EPSOM (LH)	U-shaped course 1m 4f with a run-in 4f. It is an undulating course. Straight course 5f downhill and very fast.
FOLKESTONE (RH)	Pear-shaped course 1m 3f with a run-in 3f. It is a sharp course. Straight course 6f.
GOODWOOD (RH)	Is a loop-shaped course that allows races up to 2m 5f to be run, run-in 4f. Straight course 6f. It is a sharp, fast course.

HAMILTON (RH)
Loop-shaped course allowing for races up to 1m 5f, run-in approximately 5f. Straight course 6f. It is an undulating course.

HAYDOCK (LH)
Round course 1m 5f with a run-in 4f. It is a galloping course. Straight course 5f.

KEMPTON (RH)
Triangular-shaped course 1m 5f with a run-in 3½f, plus a dog-leg-shaped course 10f (Jubilee Course). Separate straight 6f across in the centre of the course. It is a flat course.

LEICESTER (RH)
Oval course 2m with a run-in 5f. It is a galloping course. Straight mile which is downhill at first.

LINGFIELD (LH)
Round course 1m 4f with a run-in 3f. It is an undulating course. Straight course 7f 140yd.

NEWBURY (LH)
Oval course 1m 7f with a run-in 5f. It is a galloping course. Straight course 1m.

NEWCASTLE (LH)
Oval course 1m 6f with a run-in 4f. It is a galloping, testing course. Straight course 7f.

NEWMARKET (RH)
Rowley Course. Long course of 2m 2f with a gentle bend into the straight in 1m 2f from finish. It is a wide, galloping course.

(RH)
July Course – is of similar shape with a gentle bend into its straight 1m from the finish. It is slightly more undulating.

NOTTINGHAM (LH)
Round course 1m 4f with a run-in 4f. It is a flat course. Straight course 7f.

PONTEFRACT (LH)
Pear-shaped course 1m 4f with a run-in 2f. It is a sharp, undulating course. There is no separate straight course.

REDCAR (LH)
Round course 1m 6f with a run-in 5f. It is galloping course. Straight course is 1m.

RIPON (RH)
Round course 1m 5f with a run-in 5f. It is a sharp course. Straight course 6f.

SALISBURY (RH)
Loop-shaped course with races up to 1m 6f with a run-in 7f. Straight course approximately 1m. Last 4f are uphill and provide a stiff test. It is a galloping course.

SANDOWN (RH)
Round course 1m 5f with a run-in 4f. Stiff galloping course. Separate straight course 5f in the centre of the course and steadily rising throughout.

THIRSK (LH)
Round course 1m 2f with a run-in 4f. It is a sharpish course. Straight course 6f.

WARWICK (LH)
Circular course 1m 6f with a run-in 3f. It is a sharp course. The 5f course bends left with the junction of the round course.

WINDSOR (RH)   Shaped as a figure of eight. Flat races bend right-handed. Has almost straight 5–6f courses.

WOLVERHAMPTON (LH)   Triangular course 1m 4f with a run-in 4½f. Straight course 5f.

YARMOUTH (LH)   Oval course 13f with a run-in 5f. It is a flat course. Straight course 1m.

YORK (LH)   U-shaped course 2m with a run-in 5f. It is a galloping course. Straight course 6f.

National Hunt

	Circumference	Run-in (from final fence) (yd)	Type of course		Fences
ASCOT (RH)	1m 6f	160 (uphill)		Testing	Stiff
AYR (LH)	1m 4f	210	Flat	Average	
BANGOR (LH)	1m 2f	325	Flat	Sharp	
CARLISLE (RH)	1m 5f	250	Undulating	Stiff	
CARTMEL (LH)	1m	800	Undulating	Easy	
CATTERICK (LH)	1m 2f	240	Undulating	Sharp	
CHELTENHAM (LH)	1m 4f	350 (uphill)		Testing	Stiff
CHEPSTOW (LH)	2m	240	Undulating		
DEVON & EXETER (RH)	2m	250	Hilly	Sharp	
DONCASTER (LH)	2m	250	Flat	Galloping	
EDINBURGH	1m 2f	150	Flat	Sharp	
FAKENHAM (LH)	1m	220	Undulating	Sharp	
FOLKESTONE (RH)	1m 3f	220	Undulating	Easy	
FONTWELL					
(Chases – figure of eight)	1m	220	Flat	Tricky	
(HURDLES) (LH)	1m	220	Flat	Easy	
HAYDOCK (LH)	1m 5f	440	Flat	Testing	Stiff
HEREFORD (RH)	1m 4f	300	Flat	Easy	
HEXHAM (LH)	1m 4f	250 (uphill)	Undulating	Stiff finish	
HUNTINGDON (RH)	1m 4f	200	Flat	Galloping	
KELSO (LH)	1m 3f	490	Flat	Average	
KEMPTON (RH)	1m 5f	200	Flat	Easy	Stiff
LEICESTER (RH)	1m 6f	250	Undulating	Sharp	
LINGFIELD (LH)	1m 2f	200	Undulating	Stiff	
LIVERPOOL (LH)					
Grand National Course	2m 2f	494	Flat	Galloping	Stiff
Mildmay Course	1m 2f	260	Flat	Sharp	
LUDLOW (RH)	1m 4f	450	Flat	Stiff	
MARKET RASEN (RH)	1m 2f	220	Flat	Sharp	
NEWCASTLE (LH)	1m 6f	220	Undulating	Stiff	
NEWBURY (LH)	2m (approx.)	255	Flat	Galloping	Stiff
NEWTON ABBOT (LH)	1m	300	Flat	Sharp	
NOTTINGHAM (LH)	1m 4f	240	Flat	Galloping	
PERTH (RH)	1m 2f	450	Flat	Average	
PLUMPTON (LH)	1m 1f	200	Undulating	Sharp	
SANDOWN (RH)	1m 5f	300 (uphill)		Stiff	Stiff
SEDGEFIELD (LH)	1m 2f	525	Undulating	Sharp	
SOUTHWELL (LH)	1m 2f	250	Flat	Sharp	
STRATFORD (LH)	1m 3f	200	Flat	Sharp	
TAUNTON (RH)	1m 2f	150	Flat	Average	
TOWCESTER (RH)	1m 6f	300	Undulating	Stiff	
UTTOXETER (LH)	1m 2f	300	Flat	Galloping	
WARWICK (LH)	1m 6f	240	Flat	Sharp	
WETHERBY (LH)	1m 4f	190	Flat	Galloping	
WINCANTON (RH)	1m 3f	200	Flat	Galloping	
WINDSOR (figure of eight)	1m 4f	200	Flat	Average	
WOLVERHAMPTON (LH)	1m 4f	220	Flat	Average	
WORCESTER (LH)	1m 5f	220	Flat	Average	

N.B. The distances on the run-in from the final fence and final hurdle to the winning post are sometimes different.

A mammoth fence at Aintree (Liverpool).

An open ditch as Sandown Park.

The usual type of plain fence encountered on a park course.

The type of hurdle encountered on National Hunt courses.

TYPES OF OBSTACLES (FENCES AND HURDLES)

In National Hunt racing there are two types of obstacle – fences in steeplechase races (chases) and hurdles in hurdle races. In chases there are three different types of fence – plain fence, open ditch and water jump. On National Hunt steeplechase courses there is only one water jump, one or two open ditches, the remaining fences being plain fences. A water jump has a fence not more than 3 feet in height preceding it and an expanse of water not less than 12 feet in width. An open ditch consists of a fence not less than 4 feet 6 inches in height with a ditch not less than 6 feet in width on the take-off side of the fence. All fences are sturdily built non-movable structures made of firmly packed birch and trimmed gorse and plain fences are not less than 4 feet 6 inches in height. The stiffness and type of fences can vary from course to course.

Hurdles are portable structures consisting of two-bar wooden frames covered with gorse and are staked to the ground. They are not less than 3 feet 6 inches in height from the bottom to the top bar.

They are much less sturdy than fences and sometimes get kicked out of the ground.

Plastic hurdles of comparable size have been introduced to accommodate the artificial surfaces of all-weather racing.

THE DRAW (APPLIES ONLY TO FLAT RACING)

This is the position across the course from where a horse must start, whether placed in a starting stall or lining up behind a barrier (tape) or by flag.

It is really only a significant factor in races up to 1m with perhaps the Derby, Cambridgeshire Handicap (where there are large fields) and some longer races at Chester the exception. The draw is of particular importance in the shorter distance races of up to 1m where ground advantage lost at the start cannot be regained. The draw plays a more important role on some courses more than others, and in certain prevailing ground conditions more than others.

In considering the draw a number of factors must be taken into account:

1. The use or non-use of starting stalls. Stalls are used on most occasions (when stalls are not used, especially in races for 2-year-olds, it is essential that a jockey be experienced and competent).
2. The positioning of starting stalls. The position of the starting stalls may be moved from their normal position close to the rails, to a position either to the far side or middle of the course and thus the advantage of the draw can be radically affected. (The movement of stalls occurs usually only in emergency situations, but the effect can be dramatic.)

3. Change of going. While under normal going conditions certain numbers (high, low, middle) will be favoured by the draw, a change of going could nullify and/or reverse this advantage. For example, at Ayr the high numbers, on the stand side, are normally favoured in 5–6f races, but on very soft or heavy going the advantage reverses to the low numbers on the opposite side.
4. The size of the field. In a small field of 5 or 6 runners the runners will not be spread across the course so there is little advantage from the draw, but in fields of 16 or more runners with horses spread across the course, favourably drawn horses have a distinct advantage.

Form books, guides and newspapers regularly carry the information regarding the considered favoured draw positions on each course and this needs careful consideration when assessing the chances of a horse.

Course	Draw	Distance	Going
ASCOT	No advantage	(round course)	
	Low numbers	5f–1m	
		straight course	
AYR	High numbers	5f, 6f	
	Low numbers	5f, 6f	Soft
	Low numbers	7f upwards	
BATH	Low numbers	Up to 1m	
BEVERLEY	High numbers	5f and 1m	
BRIGHTON	Low numbers	5f, 6f	
CARLISLE	High numbers	Up to 1m	
CATTERICK	Low numbers	5f, 6f, 7f	
CHEPSTOW	High numbers	5f–1m	
	Low numbers	5f–1m	Soft
	(straight course)		
CHESTER	Low numbers	All distances	
DONCASTER	High numbers	5f–1m	
	(straight course)		
	Low numbers	1m	
	(round course)		
EDINBURGH	Low numbers	5f	
EPSOM	High numbers	5–6f	
	Low numbers	7–8f	
FOLKESTONE	Low numbers	5f, 6f	Soft
GOODWOOD	High numbers	5f, 6f	
HAMILTON	High numbers	5f, 6f	
HAYDOCK	High numbers	5f	
	Low numbers	6–8f	
KEMPTON	No advantage	5f, 6f	
LEICESTER	Low numbers	5f, 6f	
LINGFIELD	High numbers	5f–7f 40yd	
	Low numbers	5f–7f 40yd	Heavy
		(particularly	
		heavy)	

NEWBURY	High numbers (straight course)	5f–1m	
NEWCASTLE	High numbers	5–7f	
	Low numbers	5f–7f	Heavy
NEWMARKET (Rowley, July courses)	Variable	5f–1m	
NOTTINGHAM	High numbers (but variable as stall positions alter)	5f, 6f	
PONTEFRACT	Low numbers	5f, 6f	
REDCAR	High numbers	5–8f	
RIPON	Low numbers	5f, 6f	
	High numbers	8f	
SALISBURY	High numbers	5–8f	
SANDOWN	High numbers	5f	
	High numbers	7f, 8f	
THIRSK	High numbers	5f, 6f	
	Low numbers	7f, 8f	
WARWICK	High numbers	5f	
WINDSOR	No advantage	5f, 6f	
WOLVERHAMPTON	Low numbers	5f	Soft
YARMOUTH	High numbers	5–8f	
YORK	Low numbers	5–6f	

The draw affects only the distances stated and can be assumed to be of no advantage at other distances.

However, the most thoughtful analysis of the draw over recent seasons has been made by John Whitley in his book *Computer Racing Form*, an annual publication which diligently covers many aspects of Flat racing.

The effect of the draw can vary slightly from season to season in response to changes in the placement of the stalls across the race-track and improved drainage, etc., so it is suggested that the more dedicated refer to Whitley's latest edition for the most up-to-date information (*Computer Racing Form*, Racing Research, 21 Upper Green Lane, Hove Edge, Brighouse, West Yorkshire HD6 2NZ).

JOCKEYSHIP

'Fear runs down the reins' – this statement proclaims the importance of good jockeyship. Jockeyship can be the marginal difference between winning and losing in evenly balanced contests, and only when a horse is vastly superior will it overcome the disadvantage of poor handling. Good jockeys cannot win without a good horse underneath them, but bad jockeyship will certainly ruin a horse's chances of winning.

The draw applies only to Flat racing and the position of the draw can have a significant influence in sprint races where an advantage at the start may never be overcome at a later stage of the race.

Horses are usually started from stalls in Flat racing.

The tape barrier start used in National Hunt racing allows a jockey to pick his starting position. The horses are started as far as possible in a straight line and at a reasonable distance from the tape.

A jockey needs certain qualities:

(a) to be competent and reliable in ability and judgement;
(b) to be honest in application;
(c) to have tactical ability (independently to devise a strategy for a race, or to carry out proficiently the instructions given by the trainer, and yet be adept to improvise should the situation demand);
(d) to control and impose authority on a horse while encouraging it to give of its best.

The first two qualities mentioned can be said to be the basic requirements common to all the leading riders. It is in the varying degrees of development of the other two qualities, plus character and ambitious purpose, which determine the great from the merely good riders.

The aspect of a jockey's integrity requires close examination. It is usual to hear disgruntled punters loudly claim that a jockey's dishonesty was responsible for a horse's defeat when seldom is there anything further from the truth. A jockey, it must be understood, has his first allegiance to whoever engages him to ride (i.e. the trainer/owner) and it will be expected that the race instructions he is given be followed whether or not they comply strictly to the rules of racing. While making this declaration, it must be stated unequivocally that the advantages for winning far outweigh the considerations for deliberately losing a race.

A horse that a trainer may condone not winning a race, will usually not have on the day more than an extremely tenuous chance of winning. For example, in the case of a proposed future betting coup the horse is unlikely to be fully fit, and the conditions of the race – going, distance, weight – are likely to be equally unfavourable. And an inexperienced horse is likely to lack the physical maturity or racing 'know-how' at this stage in its career. Instances of trainers stopping a horse with a real winning chance from trying to win are most unusual, for most have learned from experience that a certain winner today (at any odds) is better than risking waiting for an uncertainty in the future.

For a jockey the financial rewards in the long term and sometimes in the short term of successful honest endeavour so outweigh the benefits of malpractice that such acts are a most unattractive proposition. The close-knit racing community demands a code of loyalty and integrity which once broken immediately deems a jockey unemployable.

The basic qualities of jockeyship apply to both Flat and National Hunt riders with, however, defined and distinct physical characteristics which reflect the particular demands of each code of racing.

Flat racing is a manifestation of speed, the maximum racing distance is 2m 6f and the maximum weight carried by a horse is normally 10st. National Hunt racing is a combination of speed, strength and endurance, the minimum distance is 2m with eight flights of hurdles to jump and the minimum allotted weight is 10st. Flat race jockeys are therefore small, of light weight (approx. 8 st) and rely on speed of thought and reflex to practise their skill. *National Hunt* jockeys are of normal average height, with a riding weight of 10 st (approx.). Strength, courage, durability and clear understanding are essential elements in their make-up.

The riding lifetime of National Hunt jockeys is a short one; while not gaining the full physical strength to fulfil their full potential until their mid-twenties, within a decade the effects of falls and the rigours of race riding will signal their retirement. Meanwhile Flat race jockeys not subject to the continuous effects from the hazards of injury improve with age and experience, often reaching a plateau of maturity in their thirties which they are able to exploit with notable effect.

Good National Hunt jockeys need the full complement of skills in horsemanship and race riding possessed by their Flat race counterparts with some additional ones as well:

1. The jockey's skill in keeping position during a race and bringing the horse with a well-timed challenge at the end of the race.
2. The horseman's skill in placing a horse well at its fences so that it may jump them in the easiest and most efficient way.
3. The physical courage to keep a horse racing even after it may have made bad errors in jumping – this confidence by example being transferred to the horse.
4. A strong physical constitution, to withstand the rigours of riding long distances, and crushing falls, with a resilience to make fast and complete recovery from injury and the health to resist normal winter ailments, such as colds and flu.

APPRENTICES AND CONDITIONAL JOCKEYS (CLAIMING RIDERS)

All riders start their careers as apprentices on the Flat or as claiming riders in National Hunt and amateur races. They receive a riding allowance according to the number of winners they have ridden.

Flat race apprentices until they are 24 years old can claim a riding allowance of:

7 lb until they have ridden 10 winners
5 lb until they have ridden 50 winners
3 lb until they have ridden 75 winners

These wins are only against senior riders; wins in apprentice races are not included (special allowances apply in apprentice races). These riders' allowances can be claimed in all handicaps and sellers and in all other races with up to £8,000 in added prize-money.

Conditional jockeys in National Hunt racing claim a rider's allowance until they are 25 years old. These are:

7 lb until they have ridden 15 winners,
    (under either Flat or National Hunt rules)
5 lb until they have ridden 25 winners
    (under either rules)
3 lb until they have ridden 40 winners
    (under either rules)

These National Hunt totals were amended in 1989 and wins in conditional jockey races, National Hunt Flat races and apprentice Flat races are not included (special allowances apply in conditional jockey races). Conditional jockeys can claim allowances in all handicaps, except the Grand National, all selling races, and all other races which have up to £5,000 in added prize-money.

Every season a champion Flat race apprentice and National Hunt conditional rider emerge; and by then they have often ridden enough winners to lose their allowance. Then their battle for acceptance begins in earnest, for while their services may have been in great demand when they retained their rider's allowance, without it they must compete for rides with senior jockeys on level terms. This makes the next stage of their riding career quite difficult for the recent apprentice.

JOCKEYS (FLAT RACING)

In the cause of brevity it is quite impractical here to analyse every good jockey riding in the British Isles. A concise list of jockeys has been compiled composed of the most popular riders who have recently ridden an English or Irish Classic winner or a race of equivalent stature. An omission of any jockey from this list is not an intended slur on his ability, but a present lack to meet the qualifying requirement.

All good jockeys are a combination of horseman and race rider:

Race riding requires the skill of judging pace, tactical awareness and ability to anticipate situations, plus the drive and power to ride a horse in a finish.
Horsemanship is command, control and empathy with a horse. Balancing a horse, enabling it to maintain its stride pattern, settling and imparting confidence in a nervous and/or free-running horse, galvanizing and/or inspiring a faint-hearted or ungenerous one.

The many skills a Flat race jockey needs to develop means that many jockeys only reach the height of their powers with maturity. A fact exemplified by the success of the more senior jockeys.

'Great riders are born not made' is a statement inspired by observing the empathy great jockeys have with a horse, a oneness in action and of purpose. Great jockeys, although not immune from making errors of judgement, make far fewer and less vital ones than the average rider. It is also an ability to extricate themselves from difficult or potentially difficult situations that separates the great jockeys from the others. The startling difference that divides great jockeys from the others is captured in the statement: 'Great jockeys win races they had no right to win, while other jockeys lose races they had no right to lose.'

Willie Carson (*riding weight 7 st 10 lb*)   As NASHWAN and Willie Carson swept all before them in the glorious summer of 1989 it was hard to believe the ever-youthful jockey rode his first winner in 1962. Five champion jockey titles later he is still at the top of his profession which shows there is no substitute for experience.

Although winning more than a dozen English Classic races the 1988 St Leger held special significance because Willie Carson holds the unique distinction of not only riding the winner, MINSTER SON, but of also breeding it. Such an achievement is evidence of the thought and planning that Willie puts into racing.

The hallmark of his style, the famous 'push-push' technique, has gained in subtlety and maturity over the years. A shrewd tactician, who always rides a horse to its strengths, Willie Carson has never abandoned the principle of doing the simple things consistently well. He likes to put a horse in the race from the outset so it is prominently placed and ready to seize the initiative, often before the whips get flying at the business end of events. Yet if the situation demands he is equally capable of coming with a late challenge to grab the spoils on the line.

One thing is for sure – he never gives up! Supporters know, with Willie Carson aboard, at some stage of the race they will get a run for their money. Like many of the great jockeys he is able to command a race, imposing his character on it to control the unfolding of events.

An engaging personality has always made him a public favourite and the cries of 'Come on Willie' resound around the race-track as they once did similarly for Gordon Richards and Lester Piggott. Everybody likes a trier and there is no more inspiring sight than the terrier-like Carson snapping at opponents' heels as he delivers his challenge ready to wrest victory from the jaws of defeat. No longer in the spring of his career, Willie Carson still remains a jockey never to dismiss lightly. Big race wins are common to him and with over a hundred winners a season many future successes are guaranteed for his supporters.

Steve Cauthen (*riding weight 8 st 7 lb*)   It is over a decade since Steve Cauthen first arrived on these shores, in the spring of 1979. Scarcely 19 years old he had already won almost 500 races on the ultra-competitive American racing circuit, and because of his winning earnings for owners, was hailed as 'the six million dollar kid''. Was this the coming of a real star to the British racing stage or just media hype? Any initial critics were soon to eat their words, as he won on his first ride and

Action photographs of the leading Flat race jockeys.

Willie Carson

Steve Cauthen

Pat Eddery

Ray Cochrane

Michael Roberts

Walter Swinburn

within a month rode his first Classic winner, TAP ON WOOD, in the 2,000 Guineas. Further successes have followed in all the other classics including a triple crown for OH SO SHARP in 1985. Pre-eminently a jockey for the big occasion, in 1989 he won both the French and Irish Derbys on OLD VIC, to become the only jockey ever to win the quartet of Blue Riband Classics having previously twice won the Epsom Derby, and the Kentucky Derby on AFFIRMED back in 1978.

Attached to Henry Cecil's powerful stable, which in 1987 had a record number of Flat race winners, Steve Cauthen also won his third champion jockey title. Achieving his personal best score of 197 winners, this was the highest total since Gordon Richards scored over 200 winners in the 1950s.

After battling with and overcoming a well-published weight problem a few years ago Steve Cauthen now rides at a more comfortable 8 st 7 lb. While this may limit his opportunity in handicaps it is ideally suited to condition races and top-class races, where he is a perfect pilot.

Steve has adapted his style well to suit European racing. While retaining his essential crouching stillness, whereby he keeps his mount beautifully balanced, he wants for nothing in a finish, adopting the driving technique of British riders. Besides being a superb horseman and a good tactician Steve's greatest attribute is his masterful judge of pace. You will never see a Steve Cauthen horse in an untenable position; he invariably has them well placed throughout a race, whether riding just off the pace which may be a bit 'too hot' or dictating affairs from the front. A throwback to his apprenticeship on the time-oriented tracks of the United States, Steve has a 'stop-watch in his head' whereby he is uncannily travelling at the right pace.

Riding a waiting race from the front is his speciality, cranking up the pace to suit his mount, keeping his rivals ever chasing him, and producing a little extra from up his sleeve to see them off should they get near enough to challenge.

Being a real thinking jockey Steve Cauthen is a bonus for any trainer to engage as they can be sure he will get the best from their horse and give an informed accurate appraisal after the race.

A bad accident at Goodwood in August 1988 was within a hair's breadth of ending Steve Cauthen's career. However, after missing the remainder of that campaign he returned the following season to ride with all his usual aplomb and gain many big race wins. Whether in victory or defeat 'Gentleman Steve' always conducts himself in the same charming manner endearing himself to the British racing public.

Pat Eddery (*riding weight 8 st 4 lb*)   Pat Eddery in 1986 after a gap of eight seasons regained the champion jockey title, a crown he still wears. It coincided with his decision to ride again regularly in Britain, for his new retainer Khalid Abdullah. The partnership saw the winning exploits of DANCING BRAVE particularly in the Prix de l'Arc de Triomphe. A year later TREMPOLINO's win in Europe's most prestigious race was Pat's third in a row. Success at this level confirms him to be a jockey of the highest international repute whose services are in great demand.

It means he is accustomed to riding the best horses. These quality animals match his riding temperament which is instinctive rather than cerebral. Characteristically assuming a prominent position in a race, Pat Eddery is supreme on a horse in a fast action where situations unfold fleetingly and his intuitive skills can flow. There is no more awesome sight for an opponent than Pat looming alongside at the furlong pole, his powerful all-action style delivering a challenge. When it comes to a tight finish there is no better jockey to have on your side. He has the strength and skill to drive a horse home and with a record of almost two out of three wins in any close-finish situation Pat Eddery is certainly not a jockey you would want to oppose.

Built in the classic mould for a present-day international rider he is the perfect weight to ride in all types of race, including leniently treated horses in handicaps, although he excels on the better-class horses. Riding at least 150 winners a season is standard for Pat Eddery and those days when he rides a treble or even four-timer can be occasions to savour for the backer, for once Pat hits form like that he can win on less fancied mounts as well, providing a nice profit for those who have followed him.

Pat Eddery is one of few jockeys to have graduated from champion apprentice to gaining the senior crown. He epitomizes all the hard work and dedication necessary to remain top of the tree. During the height of the Flat season this often entails riding seven days a week, sometimes with two meetings a day, and all the travelling this involves. Pat Eddery is completely dedicated to his calling and with all the skills to match is sure to remain for some time at the top as an international jockey.

Ray Cochrane (*riding weight 8 st 4 lb*) A breath-taking victory on KAHYASI in the 1988 Epsom Derby left no doubt that Ray Cochrane had really arrived on the jockey scene. An overnight success story after 14 years of neglect, which included a spell in National Hunt racing, Ray's win was also vindication of Luca Cumani's decision to employ him as stable jockey. A rider who has really battled his way to the top, there is no more dedicated or determined one.

Ray Cochrane's rise is due in no small measure to an ability to make the most of the opportunities which have befallen him. A successful partnership with that versatile horse CHIEF SINGER was the first indication that Ray had what it takes to compete against the best. It was followed by his double classic success on MIDWAY LADY, which demonstrated making the most of your luck, Ray only having got the ride originally due to the intended jockey Pat Eddery being suspended.

Now having achieved prominence among the leaders of his profession there is no way that Ray Cochrane is going easily to surrender it, and that is equally reflected in his riding. Strong and resourceful, once he gets down to work on a horse, he expects to win. Reputations or big occasions hold no intimidation for him as his wins in the Epsom and Irish Derbys showed, when he swept from behind to capture the spoils. Riding in this manner means being acclaimed the hero when you win but if circumstances conspire against, the jockey can be somewhat exposed to the brickbats.

However, now established high on the leading riders' list, ambitious Ray Cochrane still strives for even greater glories and one can be sure he will readily seize any opportunities on offer. Such determination backed by much skill make him a jockey not to be underestimated. His appointment as stable jockey to Guy Harwood for the 1990 season suggest greater ambitions about to be realized.

Michael Roberts (*riding weight 8 st*)   Champion jockey eleven times in South Africa, Michael Roberts first rode in Britain in the late 1970s but it is only since his return in 1986 that his talent has been fully recognized. Attached to Alec Stewart's Newmarket stable MTOTO's successes in 1988 drew attention to Michael Robert's superb jockeyship. This view was obviously held by Henry Cecil who after Steve Cauthen's injury late that season engaged him to ride the Warren Place horses in the big races. Two Group I victories on INDIAN SKIMMER and SALSE seemed perfect justification for the decision and confirmed Michael Robert's ranking as one of the top international riders.

A thinking jockey who carefully plans his strategy, one of Michael's greatest strengths must be the marvellous sense of timing his challenges. Seated just off the pace but in a good position to cover any moves by other jockeys, Michael Roberts has the ability to hold his challenge till just the right moment, so his horse's burst of acceleration carries it through to the winning line. However, should he decide to make the pace, he has the refined sense of timing where, as a rival draws up beside him he almost conjures another gear from his own mount to repel the challenge.

Compact and stylish in appearance, Michael Roberts' riding style is one of rhythmic driving, keeping a horse perfectly balanced and getting it to stretch out and give its all. He is now acknowledged by the racing establishment as one of the best of jockeys from whom we can expect future big race victories.

Walter Swinburn (*riding weight 8 st 4 lb*)   A famous victory on a brilliant horse rocketed Walter Swinburn to prominence. SHERGAR's facile win of the 1981 Epsom Derby ridden by a young jockey with choirboy looks not yet 20 years old was a fairy-tale start to any career, which in Walter Swinburn's case has continued to bloom as he has fulfilled all his early promise, although like all true stories there have been a few setbacks.

The partnership with Michael Stoute (although at times not without strain) has continued to bag a host of pattern race winners, including a second Derby for the Aga Khan on SHAHRASTANI, plus Epsom Oaks successes and wins in both Guineas. Yet suspensions on two occasions have also cost him two further Classic victories, SHERGAR's Irish Derby win and SHADEED's English 2,000 Guineas success.

Yet, as with his sudden rise to stardom, Walter Swinburn has taken these events very much in his stride, conveying a calm and collected approach which equally applies to his riding. While strong and determined in a finish (he has a good record in close encounters when the chips are down) it is his cool handling of race-riding situations that characterizes his style. From his earliest days he has always had the ability to do the right thing at the right time, often seeming to glide almost unnoticed into a challenging position at the opportune moment. Riding for such a meticulous planner as Michael Stoute is bound to have provided great guidance in devising race tactics to help this young man fully express his talents.

Son of a famous jockey, Walter Swinburn junior comes from the right background to succeed at the top level of the sport. So much experience of riding quality horses has been packed into his career that even greater rewards can be expected as his riding talents reach full maturity.

Billy Newnes (*riding weight 8 st*)   Champion apprentice of 1982, the same season Billy Newnes won the Epsom Oaks on TIME CHARTER. Such early success in a young jockey's career suggested the racing world lay at his feet but this was not to be. A year later an incident off the track which broke the rules of racing led to Billy Newnes having his licence withdrawn by the Stewards of the Jockey Club. Supported throughout his riding ban by his former governor Henry Candy, Billy Newnes regained his licence in 1986 and has since rebuilt his career.

The resolve to overcome this setback which he showed when out of racing has now been channelled into his riding. Although still riding for the Kingstone Warren stable Billy Newnes's quest for winners has also taken him to ride in Germany where he has achieved major successes in pattern races during the 1989 season. Not tempted by offers to move abroad Billy Newnes remains intent on re-establishing himself in Britain. While the glory days have yet to return, this Liverpool-born jockey has shown he still has all the talent to succeed in the top echelons of racing.

John Reid (*riding weight 8 st 5 lb*)   A contract in 1988 to ride for Vincent O'Brien's legendary Ballydoyle stable was at last full recognition of the talent of this most underrated jockey. Whatever his successes he seemed always just a step removed from the glamour side of the sport. Given the opportunities though, he has proved to be most capable.

ILE DE BOURBON's memorable King George VI and Queen Elizabeth Stakes victory was the first major win in John's career, and ON THE HOUSE in the English 1,000 Guineas his first Classic success. Many other pattern race victories have followed, but TONY BIN's in the 1988 'Arc' has been his most famous.

A skilled horseman whose style holds nothing of histrionics, it was no wonder that this Ulster-born rider should follow in a line of great jockeys to be associated with Ireland's premier yard. John Reid's calm style makes him an excellent rider of 2-year-olds who need firm but gentle handling if their racing education is to be a good experience, and Vincent O'Brien, always seeking to develop his quality juveniles into champion 3-year-olds, will find no better coach.

Now John Reid has broken into the big time with his abilities fully acknowledged, he can be expected to take full advantage of the fine opportunities bound to come his way.

Brian Rouse (*riding weight 8 st*)   Brian Rouse is one of the senior riders on the jockey circuit and also one of the most underrated, so that he lacks the regular opportunities his talents deserve. There are, however, few more reliable jockeys around and when it comes to a finish none harder to beat.

Brian Rouse's only classic victory was on QUICK AS LIGHTNING in the English 1,000 Guineas but he gained fleeting international success in the Japan Cup on the gallant Irish-trained mare STANERRA. Maintaining his riding links with a number of southern stables that are not renowned for strength at the quality end of racing, Brian's chances in the big races have been limited. Having known the highs and lows of racing this experienced rider holds no illusions about the glitz of the racing game. His views on horses and races are practical and straightforward and he is an ideal jockey to put up to give an uncomplicated honest assessment of a horse, with views that are worth consideration.

A strong stylish jockey who invariably gives his mounts every chance by putting them in the race from the outset, when it comes to a close finish he is rarely beaten. He is certainly a rider to make the most of the opportunities that come his way, so if the horse has got the form you can be sure it will not be wanting for assistance with Brian Rouse in the saddle.

NATIONAL HUNT JOCKEYS

A list of top National Hunt jockeys has been compiled covering the leading riders of recent seasons. Comments have been made as to their particular abilities, noting which jockeys have been champions yet refraining from categorizing them into degrees of excellence, but allowing their past record and current form to be sufficient testimony.

National Hunt racing is nothing if not a test of fate, and the jockey who is a hero and victor one day in one race can just as swiftly be cast in the role of an accident victim the following day or the next race. Fitness and durability are therefore two essential qualities needed by any National Hunt jockeys who hardly expect to sustain their riding career for as long as their Flat counterparts. In these circumstances it is hardly surprising that opportunities constanly present themselves to aspiring riders, and no jockey can rule absolutely supreme.

Peter Scudamore (*riding weight 10 st*)   A record 221 winners during the mild 1988–89 season brought Peter Scudamore his fourth consecutive champion jockey's title. Supported by Martin Pipe's record-breaking stable the partnership secured 158 victories at an amazing strike rate of 44 per cent. This feat helped put both at the head of their respective professions. It became almost a common sight to see a Pipe–Scudamore runner leading all the way. Dominating from the outset, superior fitness and ability regularly left rivals trailing in their wake.

Exhibitions such as this make it standard to expect Peter Scudamore always to have his mount prominently placed giving it every chance – and backers a real run for their money! Yet even on a horse without early pace Peter will not easily give up. He will keep pushing away, trying to get into the action at some stage in the race, and should he jump the last with half a chance there is not a harder man to beat on the run-in. At this final stage you need a jockey with the utmost strength, skill and determination, and Peter Scudamore demonstrates this with a one in two success ratio in a close finish.

Trainer Fred Winter's retirement has seen Peter Scudamore's allegiance to Martin Pipe's yard increase to the extent that hurdlers account for 60 per cent of his winners. There are, however, few better riders of chasers. He gets horses jumping confidently, often the result of the efforts he regularly puts into schooling on the training grounds, which brings its due rewards.

There now seems little more for Peter Scudamore to achieve, yet his dedication to riding winners remains. Although winning a Champion Hurdle on CELTIC SHOT and numerous other big race prizes, an association with a great or charismatic horse would surely put a gold seal on his already fantastic riding career. While he retains his enthusiasm for this relentless pursuit of winners he remains a good friend to the punters.

Richard Dunwoody (*riding weight 10 st 2 lb*)   Richard Dunwoody shot to prominence as a young jockey guiding WEST TIP to victory in the 1986 Grand National. The credibility of this former amateur rider grew

Peter Scudamore

Richard Dunwoody

Hywel Davies

Brendan Powell

further with CHARTER PARTY's win in the 1988 Cheltenham Gold Cup, and now he is the most sought-after National Hunt rider.

A supreme stylist, Richard Dunwoody's riding expresses grace in action. Coolly and sometimes seemingly effortlessly he presents horses so well at fences that they steal a length or two from rivals with better jumping. This good sympathetic horseman therefore often gains his victories 'out in the country' beating other horses long before they reach the last battle royal on the run-in. Not surprisingly chasers account for the majority of Richard's winners although he is just as accomplished over hurdles. His handling of top hurdler KRIBENSIS bears testimony to his superb technique over the smaller obstacles.

A rider for the big occasion, Richard Dunwoody has a very good record at both the Cheltenham and Aintree festivals. The daunting fences at Liverpool and the testing race-track and harsh fences of Richard's favourite course Cheltenham, bring out the best in him. The greater demand for his services each season is reflected in his yearly increase in winners and it can only be a matter of time before he wears the champion jockey's crown.

Mark Dwyer (*riding weight 10 st 2 lb*)   A former top flat race apprentice in his native Ireland, weight problems prompted Mark Dwyer's switch to the winter sport. A very successful move it has turned out to be as now he is one of the country's leading National Hunt riders.

A fruitful association with Jimmy Fitzgerald's Malton based stable has produced many big race successes highlighted by FORGIVE N' FORGET's Cheltenham Gold Cup win. He is certainly to be trusted for producing the goods on the day yet remains essentially a quiet rider whose style bears all the finesse of his former Flat racing background. A speciality is his skill holding a horse up before producing it with a well timed run to challenge at the last. On the run-in his smooth rhythmic finish comes to the fore most effectively. He is also adept at keeping a horse close up all the way, commanding a race from the front and leaving opponents trailing as the pace quickens. Definitely a versatile jockey, Mark Dwyer's winners are almost evenly divided between hurdles and chasers and on the latter he has a solid one in four strike rate.

The leading jockey, on a number of Northern courses Mark Dwyer has all the right credentials to be a serious contender for the champion's title, perhaps needing only a little wider support to lay down a really persistent challenge.

Hywel Davies (*riding weight 10 st 4 lb*)   Success on the enigmatic LAST SUSPECT in the 1985 Grand National brought the public spotlight shining on Hywel Davies. Coaxing the Duchess of Westminster's wily old campaigner home Hywel demonstrated the full range of his skill. This strong Welsh horseman, more readily associated with inspiring a tired horse to give its all at the end of the race, had shown his guile and more tender handling.

No longer in the first flush of his career, Hywel Davies brings a wealth of experience that has to be a benefit to any trainer. His successful close association with Tim Forster's chaser-oriented yard in the past immediately confirms Hywel as a fine rider of chasers. While these account for 60 per cent of his winners, given the opportunity he is most efficient over hurdles as well. Strong and determined in a finish, given half a chance on the run-in Hywel Davies will prove a difficult opponent to beat. While his enthusiasm continues for the often unenviable life of a National Hunt rider, we can expect Hywel Davies to still be riding hard for top honours.

Brendan Powell (*riding weight 9 st 7 lb*)   Once a jockey who in his desire to make the grade had the reputation of being 'willing to ride anything', Brendan Powell finally gained the recognition his skills deserved after his 1988 Grand National victory on RHYME 'N REASON. Almost a faller at Becher's Brook first time round, the combination clawed their way back into contention only to be headed two out, yet rallied again on racing's longest run-in to grab a brave victory. Nothing better epitomized Brendan's own career than that race. Things had never come easy but courage, effort and not a little skill finally reaped their just rewards.

Obviously perhaps, riding chasers is Brendan Powell's forte. These make up 60 per cent of his winners. In the past, riding often unreliable conveyances thoroughly tested Brendan's horsemanship and bravery to the full. Now offered better-quality rides the benefits of those experiences shine through in his performance as a mature jockey.

A rider who likes to put his horse in a race from the start, Brendan is sure to give a horse a good ride, pleasing a trainer and backer alike. Established as one of the leading National Hunt jockeys, this likeable Irishman is certain to seize any further opportunity offered to him and can expect some big race wins to come his way.

Steve Smith-Eccles (*riding weight 10 st 3 lb*)   From riding the fastest two-miler in training of the 1970s TINGLE CREEK to a triple Champion Hurdle success in the 1980s on SEE YOU THEN, Steve Smith-Eccles's career spans a couple of eras. Entering racing in perhaps more light-hearted times Steve has always brought a sense of enjoyment to the racing business and therefore gained the reputation of being the 'last of the Cavaliers'. However, let no one be fooled when it comes to the business of race riding – Steve Smith-Eccles is never less than the thorough professional. His career has seen him ride with much success for many of the very top stables. He has always scored a solid total of winners each season, peppered with a few big race successes. Hurdlers have accounted for the majority of his winners yet he remains a most persuasive partner for chasers where his record is a respectable one in five.

One of the senior National Hunt riders, Newmarket-based Steve is now selective in the rides he takes and so remains almost the perfect jockey for a trainer wanting an experienced rider for a job guaranteed well done. Always a determined battler, Steve Smith-Eccles continues to be a most difficult man to beat in a tight finish and one the backers should prefer to have on their side.

Steve Smith-Eccles

10 THE SELECTION FORMULA ANALYSED: SUNDRY POINTS TO NOTE REGARDING CONDITIONS

BLINKERS AND VISORS

Blinkers are stiffened eye screens attached to a cloth hood which restrict a horse's vision to looking forward. Visors are modified blinkers, with a hole that allows side-on vision. The overnight declaration of blinkers or visors is compulsory for Flat racing and National Hunt racing.

They are fitted to a horse for the purpose of inducing it to run faster. It is therefore of particular significance to establish when a horse wears them for the first time, as it is on this occasion that they are likely to have their most dynamic effect. When blinkers or visors are fitted to a horse its field of vision is reduced, thereby forcing it to direct its attention forward and hopefully concentrate its efforts into running faster.

In practice fitting for the first time can have three effects:

1. They may encourage a horse to concentrate its energies and run faster.
2. They may discourage a horse so much that it does not want to race at all and therefore goes slower.
3. They may over-excite a horse to run too quickly in the early part of a race and so it exhausts itself before the finish.

The effect when fitted for the first time in a race is always problematic and the outcome can never be guaranteed. An indication of the outcome may be drawn from observing a horse's behaviour after they have been fitted and the manner in which it cantered to the start. The questions to consider are as follows:

1. Did the fitting appear to markedly affect the horse's attitude and behaviour?
2. Did they appear to over-excite the horse, causing it to break out in sweat and become disturbed?
3. Did the horse canter to the post in an uncontrolled manner, was it pulling too hard or was it reluctant to canter at all?

Visor A horse fitted with a visor – showing how, as opposed to blinkers, the eye screens on a visor have a hole in them which allows a horse some side-on vision.

Blinkers restrict a horse's area of vision. They are fitted with the desire to concentrate a horse's attention forward and thereby induce it to run faster.

Those are the negative aspects. However, if the horse appears galvanized by their application (i.e. gently on its 'toes', excited without undue nervousness) and canters to the start keenly, taking a firm hold of its bit, these are the indications that it is responding favourably and likely to improve its performance.

Of nearly 32,000 runners on the Flat in a recent season, 3,306 wore blinkers. Of these only 6 per cent won their respective races compared with over 10 per cent for horses without blinkers. *Winning favourite* statistics of horses that wore blinkers is dismally only 22 per cent – a survey of horses winning who wore blinkers for the first time produced statistics that were even worse. The conclusion from this survey is to beware of all horses wearing blinkers or visors unless they have previously won when so equipped and wear them on a regular basis. Horses wearing them for the first time should be viewed with caution as an extra element has been introduced which cannot be calculated in advance.

BREEDING

Breeding is a factor to consider usually when some of the more fundamental elements in the selection process (such as form or fitness) need clarification or endorsement.

Breeding is an inexact science that often throws up quirks which seem to defy all reason, but usually it can give a fair indication of what will be a horse's best racing distance and sometimes what 'going' preferences it may have. It is information that can be used when considering previously unraced horses, and may at least eliminate the more unlikely candidates from consideration. Horses tend to pass on their particular strengths, weaknesses and preferences to their immediate offspring, and an acquaintance with the breeding record can be a helpful guide.

The successful outcome of matings can never be confidently predicted as numerous breeders have found to their cost, and the only comforting adage is 'Breed the best with the best and hope for the best'. Even if this mating does not produce the desired champion a consoling thought is that 'Blood will out' – meaning that bloodlines of proven quality often reproduce their influence in subsequent generations. Even the less successful representatives of a line, when mated themselves, often produce offspring better than themselves, thus continuing the quality of the line.

Horses who were absolute champions can seldom produce an immediate offspring as good or better than themselves. For example BRIGADIER GERARD (1968), a champion beaten only once during three seasons of racing has produced no horses to rival his achievements. In contrast

TABLE 10.1   Characteristics of leading sires of Flat horses

Year of birth	Sire	Sire's sire	Best distance for 3-y.o.	Sire's winning distance minimum–maximum
75	ABSALOM	by ABWAH	6–8f	5–7f
75	AHONOORA	by LORENZACCIO	8f	5–6f
74	ALLEGED (USA)	by HOIST THE FLAG (USA)	10–12f	7–12f
75	ALYDAR (USA)	by RAISE A NATIVE (USA)	9–10f	
80	ARAGON	by MUMMY'S PET	7f	5–8f
72	AUCTION RING	by BOLD BIDDER	8f	5–6f
71	BAY EXPRESS	by POLYFOTO	5–6f	5–6f
78	BELDALE FLUTTER (USA)	by ACCIPITER (USA)	10f	7–10½f
66	BLAKENEY	by HETHERSETT	10f+	7–13f
74	BLUSHING GROOM (Fr.)★	by RED GOD	8f+	5½–8f
71	BUSTINO	by BUSTED	10f+	10–14½f
80	CAERLEON	by NIJINSKY (Can.)	10–12f	6–12f
77	DANZIG (USA)★	by NORTHERN DANCER (Can.)	8f	—
80	DIESIS★	by SHARPEN UP	8–10f	6–7f
72	DOMINION	by DERRING-DO	8–10f	8f
76	ELA-MANA-MOU	by PITCAIRN	10–12f	6–12f
81	EL GRAN SENOR (USA)★	by NORTHERN DANCER (Can.)	—	7–12f
79	ELECTRIC	by BLAKENEY	10–12f	10–12f
77	FINAL STRAW	by THATCH	8–9f	5–7f
75	FORMIDABLE (USA)	by FORLI (Arg.)	7–10f	6–8f
80	GLENSTAL	by NORTHERN DANCER (Can.)	8–10f	6–9f
78	GLINT OF GOLD	by MILL REEF	10f+	7–15f
80	GORYTUS (USA)	by NIJINKSY (Can.)	8–9f	7f
66	HABITAT	by SIR GAYLORD	6–10f	8f
77	HARD FOUGHT	by HABITAT	8f	6–7f
69	HIGH TOP	by DERRING-DO	8–10f	5–8f
75	HOMING	by HABITAT	8–10f	6–10f
78	INDIAN KING (USA)	by RAJA BABA	6–7f	6–8f
79	JALMOOD (USA)	by BLUSHING GROOM (Fr.)	10–12f	7–12f
80	KAFU	by AFRICAN SKY	5–6f	5f
78	KALAGLOW	by KALAMOUN	10–12f	7–12f
76	KING OF SPAIN	by PHILLIP OF SPAIN	5–6f	5–6f
77	KNOWN FACT (USA)	by IN REALITY	8f+	5–8f
76	KRIS	by SHARPEN UP	8f	5–8f
72	LOCHNAGER	by DUMBARNIE	5–7f	5–6f
80	LOMOND (USA)	by NORTHERN DANCER (Can.)	10–12f	6–8f

Year of birth	Sire	Sire's sire	Best distance for 3-y.o.	Sire's winning distance minimum–maximum
69	MANSINGH (USA)	by JAIPUR	5–6f	5f
69	MARTINMAS	by SILLY SEASON	6–8f	6–8f
70	MR PROSPECTOR (USA)★	by RAISE A NATIVE	7–10f	6–7f
79	MUMMY'S GAME	by MUMMY'S PET	6–7f	5–7f
68	MUMMY'S PET	by SING SING	5–6f	5–6½f
73	MUSIC BOY	by JUKEBOX	5–6f	5–6f
67	NIJINSKY (Can.)★	by NORTHERN DANCER (Can.)	10–12f	6–14½f
76	NINISKI (USA)	by NIJINSKY (Can.)	12f+	8–15½f
77	NUREYEV (USA)★	by NORTHERN DANCER (Can.)	8f	7–8f
75	PERSIAN BOLD	by BOLD LAD (Ire.)	8–9f	6–7f
79	RED SUNSET	by RED GOD	8f	5–6f
73	RELKINO	by RELKO	10–12f	6–10½f
77	RUNNET	by MUMMY'S PET	7–8f	5–6f
81	SADLERS WELLS	by NORTHERN DANCER (Can.)	10–12f	8–10f
69	SALLUST	by PALL MALL	8f	5–8½f
80	SHAREEF DANCER (USA)	by NORTHERN DANCER (Can.)	10–12f	6–12f
69	SHARPEN UP★	by ATAN	7f	5–6f
77	SHARPO	by SHARPEN UP	5–6f	5–6f
75	SHIRLEY HEIGHTS	by MILL REEF	10–12f	7–12f
77	SONNEN GOLD	by HOME GUARD	7–8f	5–6f
70	STAR APPEAL	by APPIANI II	10–12f	6–12f
78	STORM BIRD (USA)	by NORTHERN DANCER (Can.)	7–8f	6–7f
77	TAUFAN (USA)	by STOP THE MUSIC	6–7f	5–6f
75	THATCHING	by THATCH (USA)	6–8f	6–9f
74	THE MINSTREL (Can.)★	by NORTHERN DANCER (Can.)	8–10f	6–12f
78	TINAS PET	by MUMMY'S PET	6f	5–6f
74	TOPSIDER (USA)	by NORTHERN DANCER (Can.)	7–8f	—
75	TRY MY BEST (USA)	by NORTHERN DANCER (Can.)	7–8f	5–7f
64	TUMBLEWIND (USA)	by RESTLESS WIND	6–8f	5–10f
78	TYRNAVOS	by HOTFOOT	9–10f	7–12f
75	VAIGLY GREAT	by GREAT NEPHEW	6–7f	5–6f
79	VALIYAR	by RED GOD	8–10f	6–8f
80	WASSL	by MILL REEF	8–10f	7–8f
66	WELSH PAGEANT	by TUDOR MELODY	8–10f	6½–8½f
69	WINDJAMMER (USA)	by RESTLESS WIND	8f	4½–8f
76	YOUNG GENERATION	by BALIDAR	6–8f	5f–1m

★ Stands abroad.

horses who may have competed yet failed at the very top echelons of racing, can often produce champions better than themselves. For example GREAT NEPHEW (1963) was just below the very best of his generation but has been responsible for two Derby winners, GRUNDY (1975) and SHERGAR (1981), who were champions of their generation.

It is important for breeders of mares seeking success to have them mated with tried and tested stallions whose breeding influence has been proven. It compares 'to drilling for oil where it is known to have already been found'.

National Hunt sires

While the influence of a Flat race sire will be more immediate (the worth of his progeny being apparent within 5–6 years of their conception) a sire's influence on National Hunt racing is much less dramatic. It will take a minimum of 10–12 years to gauge their worth fairly. While there are dual-purpose stallions at stud, breeders tend to choose either a noted Flat race stallion or a National Hunt one to mate with their mares. The syndication of top Flat race sires usually means they are restricted to covering around 40 mares per season but the more popular National Hunt sires will cover twice that number.

The current most influential National Hunt sires are:

CELTIC CONE – sire of CELTIC SHOT, CELTIC RYDE, COMBS DITCH and STANS PRIDE.

DEEP RUN – the most prolific sire of recent years; winners have included DAWN RUN, DARING RUN, EKBALCO, DEEP IDOL, AONOCH, RUN AND SKIP, DEEP GALE and AQUILIFIER.

LE BAVARD – a horse best suited to soft ground and sire of some of Ireland's best jumpers, BANKERS BENEFIT, BARNEY BURNETT, SHANNON SPRAY plus FAIR CHILD and KILDIMO.

OATS – a most popular sire of jumpers in England. WING AND A PRAYER, AGAINST THE GRAIN and PRIME OATS have been most notable offspring.

STRONG GALE – possibly the next DEEP RUN – in terms of his prolificity – with nearly 350 foals produced between 1985 and 1987. NOS NA GAOITHE and ALONE SUCCESS most noted winners.

THE PARSON – at stud since 1972. Sire of CHURCH WARDEN, DELIUS, THE BREENER and VERY PROMISING among numerous other winners.

The newer stallions whose stock promise to be successful are BUCKSKIN and LE MOSS, both Ascot Gold Cup winners.

Breeding, especially with National Hunt performers, is not an exact science as the emergence of RED RUM by RED GOD (a noted sire of sprinters) and DESERT ORCHID by a little-known stallion GREY MIRAGE have shown.

TRAINERS

The skill of racehorse trainers may be most fairly judged by their record of success from the resources at their disposal. While it should not be difficult for almost anyone with 150 horses in their care to win 50 races in a season, it would be a remarkable achievement for a stable having only 25 horses to win 50 races. Almost all trainers begin their training career with limited means (some of the most famous established names had quite lowly beginnings) and it is from the adept handling of moderate horses that a reputation is gained. Then they graduate to training better horses in higher-class races.

Although a proven ability to produce winners consistently should firmly establish a trainer within the top ranks of the profession, to reach the highest echelons, particularly in Flat racing, it will also be necessary to attract the patronage of the wealthiest owners. Only the richest owners can afford the quality of horse any trainer must have to challenge for the Classic races and other top-class prizes. And to attract and maintain this patronage a trainer may also need to be successful in climbing a rung or two up the social ladder. Barriers of class may have been broken in other spheres of British society, but in horse-racing a person's background and class are still of fundamental consideration. A failure by a trainer to enter, or be favoured by, the most privileged or fashionable circles will mean having to settle for less wealthy patronage, with correspondingly less expensive, and usually moderate horses.

The first stage in training racehorses is obtaining the horses to train. This is usually achieved by a trainer buying horses at public auction or privately, although occasionally an owner with a horse will send it on to a trainer. This is the vital beginning of the training process, where judgement, luck and available finance are the elements that control a trainer's fortunes for the following years. The results of this initial venture will be judged in the light of forthcoming success or failure on the racecourse. Skilful or fortunate buying will mean horses performing well and withstanding the rigours of racing and training. Less successful purchases will mean a trainer struggling with moderate and often unsound horses that are difficult to train and not good enough to win a race.

Each season trainers replenish their stock of horses. Flat race trainers with a new intake of yearlings, from the autumn or late summer sales, who will make into 2 y.o. of the following season. National Hunt trainers take in new recruits (which are always older horses) at more varied times throughout the year. (Ex-Flat-race horses in the autumn; unraced or lightly raced National Hunt bred horses probably from the spring or summer sales.) At these sales a trainer either buys a horse personally or through a bloodstock agency, either because their advice has been sought or to hide the identity of the prospective buyer during the auction. Leaving aside the trainer's method of purchase, the sales they attend will be strictly governed by the size of the budget available, and the commissions in hand. This applies both to Flat and National Hunt racing, but most particularly to Flat racing where the auction price of the most prized lots at the premier sales in the United States, England and Ireland can reach vast proportions. A trainer with a small budget would not be able to reach a fraction of this value and would in most instances hardly bother to attend such sales. All trainers have to cut their coat according to their cloth!

Even the 'wealthiest' patronized trainers have only so much to spend, and although the most expensive and choicely bred lots may leave the sale ring supreme, the real test of horses and man eventually takes place on the race-track. This is the leveller that even the richest owners in the world have to submit to, as many have found to their cost. For example, SNAFFI DANCER, the most expensively priced yearling at auction in 1983 failed even to make an appearance on the race-track. On the other hand the humbly bred filly SOBA (1983) won the Group III King George Stakes at Goodwood, to keep hope alive for the less wealthy people connected with racing. Wealth, while influential in racing, certainly cannot guarantee success, or prevent exceptional training skills or ability from making their mark.

It can often be noticed by the racing fan who attends race meetings, or even those who watch on television, how many of the leading trainers have horses in their charge which seem to conform to a certain type in appearance. An established trainer is likely to take on the training of a racehorse basically because he likes the look of it. It may be due also to pedigree, which causes a trainer to favour a certain sire's stock, or to experience with other members from the same family (i.e. brothers and sisters) or because they had trained the dam, etc. These factors coupled with a trainer's preference sometimes for certain colouring in a horse (some like browns and bays, and distrust chestnuts or horses with any flashy markings) plus actual training methods (feeding, grooming and general preparation) and especially combined with the type of racing tack used (bridles, nosebands, etc.) contrive to mark out horses as almost from a particular mould. H. Cecil's horses invariably have a similar look about them, as do G. Harwood's, W. Hern's, I. Balding's and M. Stoute's animals, while W. O'Gorman's sprinters (usually bought by his brother R. O'Gorman) also have a certain similar look.

Racing fans who acquaint themselves with the practices of the leading trainers at least, will often be in the favourable position to read and understand the form of their runners.

Training methods vary from trainer to trainer and are likely to be a reflection of the varying practices encountered by a trainer during an apprenticeship of gaining training experience.

The older trainers can be expected to be found practising the well-tried and tested methods of preparing racehorses (i.e. using only established food products and feeding habit patterns, having a prescribed amount of work and method of exercising horses in preparation and using only conventional methods of treating injuries). Newer and/or younger trainers may be more inclined to innovation and prepared to experiment in their training methods (i.e. new or different foodstuff, varying exercise in training with perhaps bouts of swimming for horses, seeking and being aware of other treatments to cure illnesses and heal injuries).

With so many possible ways of training a horse it is hardly surprising that there can be no strict uniformity of training methods. Individual methods can only be judged by the results they produce which will be subject to certain factors – but especially to the character and ability of the trainer himself (limited by the facilities and staff at his disposal and restricted by the type, quality and physical constitution of the horses in his care).

These considerations will be fundamental in establishing whether a horse will receive a careful, thorough off-course preparation to be brought to peak race fitness or whether it will only achieve its peak fitness by running in races. Some trainers are noted for having their horses always extremely well prepared before they are raced, ensuring that their horses are fully race fit for their seasonal racecourse reappearance or on their racing début.

Leading Flat race trainers

Henry Cecil, *Newmarket*. Born 11 January 1943, first licence 1969.
Retained jockey – Steve Cauthen.
Top trainer eight times between 1976 and 1988 including a record 180 wins in 1987, Henry Cecil's string of over 200 horses often shows a strike rate of a winner from every three runners. Renowned for his training of stayers he also has few equals in his handling of 2-year-olds. The first-time-out winning ratio with juveniles is slightly better than the stable's overall strike rate and means that no horse goes to the races just for the exercise, and they sometimes oblige at rewarding odds.

The high quality of the average Warren Place inmate means they tend to outclass the opposition on most minor tracks, where they record very high strike rates. However, more impressive is the stable's record at a Grade I track such as Newbury, where the win ratio stands at just below 40 per cent. Even at his home course at Newmarket Henry Cecil leads the field with the highest number of winners.

The message to backers is perhaps obvious, this is a stable to follow – every runner demands consideration.
Luca Cumani, *Newmarket*. Born 7 April 1949, first licence 1976.
Retained jockey – Frankie Dettori.

KAHYASI's victories in the 1988 English and Irish Derbys helped confirm Luca Cumani's position at the top of his profession. Patronage by the Aga Khan and Sheikh Mohammed guarantees high-quality horses and these classically bred animals benefit from the stable's long-held policy of bringing its horses along quietly. Juveniles do not usually appear on the racecourse until the autumn and then often with a view to their 3-year-old career. In fact second-season horses have long been a Bedford House speciality.

Maiden 3-year-olds often oblige at a minor course before being skilfully placed to great effect in handicaps. A strike rate of 40 per cent or higher at Brighton, Carlisle, Catterick and Redcar means that all runners there demand special attention; while the top-grade tracks Doncaster and Sandown also show respectable statistics.

An overall strike rate of one in four means the backer must employ some selectivity. Handicaps, once a bulwark of this now upwardly mobile stable, still remain a speciality and a source of profit for the backer. While 2-year-olds in September and October and 3-year-olds in May and June also merit attention.

John Dunlop, *Arundel, Sussex.* Born 10 July 1939, first licence 1966. *No retained jockey.*

John Dunlop trains one of the country's largest string of horses in the picturesque setting of historic Arundel Castle. Each season a few top-class horses are sure to emerge and ensure John Dunlop's position among the country's leading trainers. This success is not confined to Britain but includes pattern race prizes in Europe, particularly Italy and Germany, which compensates for the stable's overall strike rate of only around 13 per cent. However, the minor courses of Catterick and Redcar provide a one-in-three winning ratio. Also the top-grade York course gives a respectable average, indicating that long trips north from the South Coast are not undertaken lightly.

John Dunlop gives his horses time to develop. Two-year-olds are not rushed and seldom win first time out but characteristically improve a lot after their first race. Unexposed 3-year-olds who suddenly begin to blossom are therefore not uncommon, and improving types like this may be ahead of their official handicap rating.

Guy Harwood, *Pulborough, Sussex.* Born 10 June 1939, first licence 1966.
Retained jockey – Ray Cochrane.

Guy Harwood gained international recognition through the exploits of DANCING BRAVE, said by some to be the best horse not to have won a Derby. He was already a familiar face to British racing fans, rising from humble beginnings in National Hunt racing to a position of powerful influence on the summer sport. While still supported by owners of long association, the influence of Khalid Abdullah and Sheikh Mohammed's horses have helped raise the quality of the yard to its present standing.

An overall strike rate of about one in four means the backer has to concentrate on selective areas of the stable's operations. Two minor courses, Redcar and Folkestone, lead the way here, especially the latter where the opposition are usually easy prey. On the more competitive tracks Goodwood has produced many winners at just below a 30 per cent ratio. Two-year-olds can score early or late in the season but the stable's traditional strength, like most top yards, lies with its 3-year-olds. Once a Guy Harwood 3-year-old has won and proved itself it is likely to win again and this is certainly an area to concentrate on, especially when the stable hits one of its purple patches.

Dick Hern, *West Ilsley, Berks.* Born 20 January 1921, first licence 1957. Champion trainer four times between 1962 and 1983, in 1989 through the exploits of NASHWAN, Dick Hern showed he is no back number. The 'great survivor' would be a fitting title for a man cruelly wheelchair-bound after a riding accident and then further illness. However, these setbacks seem only to have concentrated Dick Hern's energies. Well assisted by a loyal hard-working staff at West Ilsley here is a stable that has always preferred quality to quantity as patronage from the Queen and other leading owner-breeders testifies.

Recognized as a trainer of stayers, Dick Hern brings out the best in this type of horse, regularly producing top-class classic animals.

A strike rate of below 20 per cent means that the stable representatives cannot be given blanket support. Dick Hern's horses concentrate on the top-grade courses where competition is fiercest and this accounts for the unspectacular figures. However, Doncaster and Chester have provided a level stakes profit while the rarer visits to minor courses such as Wolverhampton, with a one-in-three win ratio, are definitely worth watching.

Barry Hills, *Manton, Wiltshire.* Born 2 April 1937, first licence 1969. *Retained jockey* – Michael Hills.

Barry Hill's move in 1987 to the magnificent training complex at Manton heralded an immediate upturn in the stable's fortunes and almost a doubling of its annual winning total. Supported by Robert Sangster and also top Arab owners Barry Hills has built up a large string of horses and will send his charges anywhere in the country for success.

A strike rate of around 15 per cent, however, demands selectivity from the backer. However, Ayr, with a strike rate of one in three, means that the long 700m round trip from Manton does not go unrewarded. Similar records at Catterick and Thirsk show runners there must also be treated with respect. Of the higher-grade courses only Haydock shows a respectable strike rate and a healthy profit.

Patient with 2-year-olds, most of the stable's wins come from second-season horses who usually have plenty of scope for improvement. Also in this area Barry Hills remains highly regarded for his handling of fillies.

Having graduated in the late 1960s from stable lad to trainer on the

Leading Flat race trainers of the 1980s.

Henry Cecil

Luca Cumani

John Dunlop

Guy Harwood

Dick Hern

Barry Hills

Alec Stewart

Michael Stoute

proceeds of a successful gamble the stable and connections are not adverse to a selective 'tilt at the ring'. These occur only a few times each season, often in competitive looking handicaps, but when the money is down backers should take heed and grab a piece of the action themselves.

Alec Stewart, *Newmarket*. Born 21 June 1955, first licence 1983.
Retained jockey – Michael Roberts.
MTOTO's successes in 1988 highlighted the rapid rise of Alec Stewart in the trainers' ranks. This former assistant to H. Thomson-Jones has quietly built up a stable of quality horses. This success has not been missed by the bookmaking fraternity who now take no chances with this openly run stable. The lower starting prices now offered on a strike rate of around 20 per cent means the backer has to approach runners with selectivity.

Although a few more precocious 2-year-olds have recently emerged, most of the juveniles are treated patiently with hopes of reward in their 3-year-old careers, or, as in the case of MTOTO, even later as a 4- or 5-year-old.

Respectable strike rates at the top-grade tracks of Ascot, Goodwood and Sandown are even better on the minor courses of Brighton and Windsor, which are around 40 per cent. Very much a thinking trainer, Alec Stewart's horses are seldom run without them having a good winning chance and this alone must represent value for followers of the stable.

Michael Stoute, *Newmarket*. Born 22 October 1945, first licence 1972.
Retained jockey – Walter Swinburn.
Champion trainer in 1981, 1986 and 1989, in recent seasons Michael Stoute has produced a steady flow of pattern race winners that few can rival. This success is ample testimony to careful planning and the quality of horses in the Beech Hurst stables.

An overall strike rate of one in four is maintained at most of the top-grade tracks, which means horses have to be assessed on their individual merits. In recent seasons his visits to the minor course at Ayr have been outstanding with a strike rate exceeding 50 per cent.

While supported by the Aga Khan and the Maktoum family and their fine horses Michael Stoute still remains adept at producing a horse to win a competitive handicap should that be its appropriate class. Turning out a hundred winners a season is now regulation for Michael Stoute and with these victories spread across all the generations there should be ample opportunities for stable followers.

Leading National Hunt trainers

G. B. (Toby) Balding, *Weyhill, Hants.* Born 23 September 1938, first licence 1957.
Retained jockeys – Jimmy Frost and Richard Guest.
Winning the 1989 Grand National and the Champion Hurdle confirmed an upturn in the stable's fortunes which began a couple of seasons earlier when Toby Balding sold his stable complex to British Thoroughbred Racing and Breeding PLC and continued to train from the yard as an executive of the company. This enabled him to upgrade the quality of horse in the yard. Although experienced as a trainer of horses on the Flat as well, an overall strike rate of around 13 per cent does not recommend this stable as one to follow on any systematic basis. Course analysis reveals no particular strengths and while Toby Balding can certainly produce the goods given the horse each runner needs to be approached strictly on its merits on the day.

M. H. (Peter) Easterby, *Great Habton, Malton, Yorks.* Born 3 August 1929, first licence 1950.
Retained jockey – Lorcan Wyer.
Champion trainer three consecutive seasons between 1978 and 1980 Peter Easterby has never quite replaced the stable stars of that era – the legendary SEA PIGEON, NIGHT NURSE and ALVERTON. However, this dual-purpose yard remains one of the shrewdest in the business and consistently sends out 40 jump winners a season, and a total in excess of that on the Flat. An overall strike rate of around 20 per cent has hurdlers providing most victories, but it is the novice chasers on 30 per cent which have a better record. These have done particularly well at Catterick and Market Rasen where the scoring rate is around 40 per cent. On the hurdling front handicappers have been marginally more prolific than novices, and an improving handicapper may be skilfully placed to chalk up a sequence. Wetherby leads the way numerically for winners but only in line with the stable's overall average. More interesting are the fewer runners at Leicester with a winner ratio as high as three out of four. Trips down to the Grade I track of Ascot return around 30 per cent and rarely go unrewarded. About a third of the stable's runners start as favourite, and with as many as two out of three of them winning, this is definitely a stable to follow when the money is down.

David Elsworth, *Fordingbridge, Hants.* Born 12 December 1939, first licence 1978.
Champion National Hunt trainer 1987–88 few can match David Elsworth's versatility, winning the 1989 Cheltenham Gold Cup with DESERT ORCHID and a few months later the top sprint race at Royal Ascot.

On the jumping scene hurdlers provide most of the winners. However, with the yard's overall strike rate at around 20 per cent it is the chasers, on a 30 per cent ratio, which demand close inspection, especially first time out where they average one winner in three. The West Country tracks of Wincanton, Newton Abbott and Devon and Exeter numerically produce the most victories, the latter pair at around 30 per cent while the former is more in line with stable's overall strike rate. This average is reflected at most courses and Sandown is the only top-grade track which has provided a respectable level stakes profit. Being an all the year round operation the yard is in full swing throughout the summer months and is therefore ready for action early in the National Hunt campaign, which almost ensures a level stakes profit in September and October.

While the chasers always require special consideration, especially when making their seasonal début, any first-time runner receiving stable support can be followed with confidence.

Jimmy Fitzgerald, *Malton, Yorks*. Born 22 May 1935, first licence 1969.

Retained jockey – Mark Dwyer.

Jimmy Fitzgerald's speciality has been producing a horse at its peak to win the important occasion, and major chasing prizes are where the stable's intentions are principally directed. Essentially this is a traditional National Hunt stable whose aim is to produce chasers and therefore it has an overall strike rate of just over 20 per cent. This is improved once horses have graduated to their proper career, with chasers as a whole producing around a 30 per cent ratio and novice chasers winning one in three.

Newcastle is one of Jimmy's favourite courses where he leads the way numerically with a strike rate just below 40 per cent giving a healthy level stakes profit. Success here is shared evenly by hurdlers and chasers. Perth and Uttoxeter have an excellent win aggregate, often exceeding one in two, while Southwell constantly produces around a 30 per cent ratio. Winners are spread throughout the season, December is the most prolific, while September and May have shown healthy level stakes profits. Almost a third of the stable's runners start favourite, and with almost 60 per cent of these winning, the betting market gives a strong indication of a horse's chances.

Tim Forster, *Wantage, Oxon*. Born 27 February 1934, first licence 1962.

Retained jockey – Carl Llewellyn.

A trainer of three Grand National winners, Tim Forster is totally committed to the winter sport. This stable's aim is to develop horses for chasing careers and in this respect there are few more consistent outfits in the game. However, such ambition means the stable's overall strike rate remains modest at around 15 per cent. Young hurdlers are always given plenty of time to develop and usually need a few races to find their form. The chasers, however, have a one-in-five winning ratio.

Newbury is numerically the leading track and also shows the best average, especially the chasers who stand just below 30 per cent and

Leading National Hunt trainers of the 1980s.

G. B. (Toby) Balding

M. H. (Peter) Easterby

David Elsworth

Jimmy Fitzgerald

Tim Forster

Josh Gifford

Nicky Henderson

David Nicholson

Martin Pipe

Jenny Pitman

Gordon Richards

Arthur Stevenson

Fulke Walwyn

show a sound level stakes profit. Ludlow of the minor courses consistently returns a good strike rate, the chasers winning one in three. The stable gets in top gear when the ground is suitable for the chasers and once the stable hits form can usually be followed with confidence.

Josh Gifford, *Findon, Sussex*. Born 3 August 1941, first licence 1970.
Retained jockeys – Richard Rowe, Peter Hobbs.
Solid winning totals of 60 plus each season are standard for this popular southern stable. This is a yard steeped in National Hunt traditions, and the emphasis is placed on producing horses to jump the larger obstacles. With such ambition the overall strike rate is consequently around a modest 16 per cent while the chasers return one winner in five. Numerically strongest at the local track, Fontwell, where the strike rate is just below one in four, the top-grade Sandown course also offers a good number of winners and has produced a solid level stakes profit. However, more infrequent trips north to Wetherby have produced the best strike rate of just below 40 per cent. The general standard of horse in the yard is usually below the very top class and the stable is most successful in the months up until the end of December.

Nicky Henderson, *Lambourn, Berks*. Born 10 December 1950, first licence 1978.
Retained jockeys – John White, Richard Dunwoody (second claim).
Although a traditional National Hunt stable, hurdlers account for about

twice the number of winners than chasers and the overall strike rate hovers just below 20 per cent. Novice hurdles account for most of the victories and many are specifically National Hunt bred recruits who will eventually make up into chasers. The intermediate stage of novice chasers is also strong with a strike rate of one in four.

Campaigning at the most competitive meetings means that course statistics are not impressive. Numerically strongest at Cheltenham, the strike rate there is below the stable's overall average. Plumpton represents a drop in class for most of the stable inmates and consequently shows a one-in-three win ratio. Towcester and Stratford also give respectable strike rates, well above the stable's overall average, and have produced healthy level stake profits.

The stable does not usually come into action until November but then produces a steady flow of winners through to March, when it peaks, although operations continue until the season closes. Supported by a distinguished set of owners, Nicky Henderson seeks constantly to upgrade his horses, and with quality rather than quantity the key to success, this stable is one to consider in the better-class races.

David Nicholson, *Stow-on-the-Wold, Gloucester.* Born 19 March 1939, first licence 1968.

Retained jockey – Richard Dunwoody.

Set in the heart of farming and hunting countryside, the Condicote stables is a traditional National Hunt yard directed towards producing chasers. Its stoutly bred inmates usually need time and this helps account for the yard's modest strike rate of around 11 per cent. Chasers are responsible for about twice the number of winners as hurdlers, who can almost be ignored, with their careers directed towards the larger obstacles. David Nicholson's favourite course of Newbury, along with Cheltenham, produces the most winners but at a strike rate which can only warrant the most selective support. Local track Hereford shows a more respectable one-in-four winner ratio and Worcester around one in five.

Martin Pipe, *Wellington, Somerset.* Born 29 May 1945, first licence 1977.

Retained jockey – Peter Scudamore (second claim).

Champion trainer in 1988–89 with a record 208 winners, Martin Pipe constantly created new training landmarks on the way to this mammoth total. The man called the 'alchemist' for his ability to turn previously moderate horses into golden winners, for the eleventh consecutive season beat his previous best total. The stable's overall strike rate has averaged over the seasons around 30 per cent while in this record-breaking year it reached the heady heights of 37 per cent with a level stakes profit of 72 pts.

Traditionally hurdlers are the mainstay of the yard and they account for 80 per cent of the winners. Many are ex-Flat racehorses who campaign extensively as hurdlers and often do not have the scope to develop later into chasers. Novice hurdle wins therefore account for almost half the stable's total, and they score at the impressive rate of one in three. Martin Pipe is also adept at handling chasers, and although fewer in number, they return an impressive average of around 30 per cent. Numerically strongest on all the minor West Country courses, especially Newton Abbott and Devon and Exeter, the stable's record is more impressive at Newbury and Haydock, where the competition is fiercer.

Quantity has been the keynote of the stable operations and while getting the utmost often from unlikely material, in a yard boasting the finest modern facilities, Martin Pipe has yet to be associated with a number of quality horses to seal his greatness as a trainer. However, for the average backer who wants only a stream of winners this is no problem.

Public acclaim unfortunately does have its drawbacks and book-makers treat cautiously any runner from this yard, a third of which end up as favourite. Although half of these win, the backer is often faced with a short-priced favourite that is unattractive to back yet that dare not be opposed. The sheer intensity of Martin Pipe's winner-producing machine makes this a stable the backer can follow, although at times getting value from the bookies can prove difficult.

Jenny Pitman, *Lambourn, Berks.* First licence 1975.
Retained jockey – M. Pitman.
Jenny Pitman received the full media treatment as the first woman to train a Grand National winner with CORBIERE in 1983, winning the Cheltenham Gold Cup a year later with BURROUGH HILL LAD. Since these victories she has constantly sought to maintain a high-quality horse in her yard and in the best National Hunt traditions the stable's operations are focused on chasers. An overall strike rate of around 20 per cent is exceeded by the chasers and especially the novices who record about one in four.

The stable does not normally get into action until the ground eases in November and then runners often need an outing to reach their peak. However, once the stable hits form winners really flow and the momentum is maintained until March. Most courses show an average in line with the stable's overall record. Leicester numerically leads the way for winners at a one-in-three strike rate, and handsome level stakes profit, due principally to novice chasers who have exceeded a one-in-two ratio. Plumpton has also produced a good strike rate of better than one in three. Another popular medium for the stable has been National Hunt Flat races, where well-supported first-time-out runners usually oblige.

Gordon Richards, *Penrith, Cumbria.* Born 7 September 1930, first licence 1964.
Gordon Richards's has long been one of those reliable National Hunt yards almost taken for granted. Every season the stable produces at least

50–60 winners, and while big race victories are not uncommon most wins are gained on the bread and butter northern courses. An overall strike rate of around 20 per cent is bettered by the novice chasers who average one in four. A traditional National Hunt yard where hurdlers are expected to have a long-term future, chasers provide the most winners and are the stable's strength.

Gordon Richards's favourite course is Ayr and this leads the way numerically and also with a respectable 23 per cent strike rate; the novice chasers have a very good record here. The local Cumbrian course of Cartmel, with only Bank Holiday fixtures, has a respectable one-in-three ratio while journeys down to Market Rasen yield rather better than one winner in four. Two courses to avoid are Haydock and Newcastle where success has been minimal. Over the seasons the stable operations get under way from the opening month with the majority of victories gained by the turn of the year.

W. A. (Arthur) Stephenson, *Bishop Auckland, Co. Durham*. Born 7 April 1920, first licence 1959.
Retained jockey – Chris Grant.
Although not adverse to big race success canny Arthur Stephenson has long held the view that 'little fish taste sweet' and prefers to campaign his horses in races he knows they can win, rather than tilting at windmills in the hope that they might. Such a policy has always produced a good total of victories. While a true blue National Hunt yard, with a policy to produce chasers, hurdlers in the stable only win as a bonus, with the focus on their long-term rather than immediate career. This accounts for the stable's modest overall strike rate of around 15 per cent, although this is bettered by the chasers and particularly the handicappers. They win one in four and can set up a sequence in line with Arthur's policy of winning small races.

Stable successes start from the beginning of the season until November, then a traditional mid-season lull is followed by a burst in March till the season ends. Course statistics conform very much to the stable's overall strike rate, with Sedgefield the most prolific followed by Wetherby, Newcastle, Hexham and Kelso. Heavy level stakes losses on all these tracks mean runners can only be followed selectively but avoiding the hurdlers and directing attention to the handicap chasers can hold the prospect of a profit.

Fulke Walwyn, *Lambourn, Berks*. Born 8 November 1910, first licence 1939.
Retained jockey – Kevin Mooney.
The master of Saxon House operates on a much quieter level than in his heyday but still shows that he can compete at the highest level. Fulke Walwyn has always been a trainer in search of quality rather than quantity.

Chasers perform above average, returning more than one winner in five, and they invariably give a good account of themselves. There is no better judge in preparing a chaser to peak condition and keeping a remarkable sparkle of life in veteran fencers.

Competing against the best at the top venues means the stable's course statistics, an overall 16 per cent, are respectable rather than spectacular. Cheltenham leads the way numerically along with Sandown, at just below 20 per cent. In the past the Festival meeting was always a particular focus and often signalled the beginning of the stable's famous 'purple patches' when winners flowed. Now these may come at other times. A trainer proven for the big occasion, any horse of his with the 'form' can still be followed with confidence.

TRAINERS' RECORDS

For a racehorse trainer, producing winners can be described as a two-fold process. Firstly consisting of the art of training a horse to attain physical and peak race fitness, and secondly involving the often under-estimated skill of successfully 'placing' a horse (deciding the when and where to run it) so that it may have more than a hopeful chance of winning.

A trainer's record is a testimony of the methods employed and provides a further factor for consideration in the selection process. A trainer's record portrays how they race their horses, and it is useful to be acquainted with the training records of the leading trainers (Flat and National Hunt), establishing the following:

1. The racecourses where they are most successful (i.e. where they are the leading trainers or figure prominently as one of the leading trainers):

(a) Courses where a trainer has a high percentage of winners to runners. This may be where Newmarket-trained horses are sent by their stables for rare but successful visits to minor courses – or vice versa – northern stables visiting southern courses.

    NB This may apply particularly in National Hunt racing where the standard of racing throughout the country is more evenly balanced and some northern stables have a particularly high ratio of winners to runners at courses such as Ascot, Newbury, Kempton and Sandown.

(b) Conversely there are courses where trainers have a very high ratio of runners to winners – and no particular importance can be placed on their horses running there. For example, Newmarket-based horses racing at Newmarket; Lambourn-based horses racing at Newbury; northern (Malton)-based horses racing at York/Doncaster (invariably 2-year-olds, inexperienced 3-year-olds, novice hurdlers, etc. are given introductory races at these meetings close to their base).

2. The times of the season a trainer has most winners. Trainers often have the major proportion of their winners at a certain time in the season – early, mid-season or late.

A disposition for a trainer to produce winners at certain times in the season may be by circumstance or design or by a combination of the two. For example, southern trainers based at Epsom and on the south coast have a reputation of producing winners in the early part of the Flat season, being favoured by the supposed more clement winter weather conditions. Yet certain northern trainers not blessed with the supposed milder weather conditions of their southern counterparts, have a reputation for similarly producing early season winners.

Design then appears to have an equal role with circumstance, a fact which is borne out by the number of trainers who are mid-season specialists focusing their training schedule to have their horses in top condition in mid-season (Flat – July and August; National Hunt – January, February and March) when the racing fixtures are heaviest and prizes on average more valuable.

Similarly, some trainers avoid the strong competition of mid-season and concentrate early or late in the campaign. For example National Hunt trainers with the more moderate horses are seen regularly to contest prizes at the lower grade courses at the seasons opening in August, September, October or at its close in April and May.

The leading trainers, however, usually manage to have winners constantly throughout the season, yet with particular months when their crop of winners reaches a height.

Circumstance and design merged when stables stricken by the virus (which has blighted a number of Flat race stables) were forced to readjust their training programmes and make the most of their opportunities whenever possible.

3. Meetings at which a trainer is consistently successful. Certain meetings hold a particular significance for some trainers. The most important of these are (Flat) Newmarket, Newbury meetings, Epsom's Derby and spring and bank holiday meetings, Royal Ascot, the Goodwood Festival, the York Festival in August. (National Hunt) the bank holiday meetings – Christmas, Easter, Whitsun, summer – Cheltenham Festival, Aintree meeting.

A trainer may have established a good winning record at these meetings, and having discovered the specific requirements for winning a race, is then often able to seasonally reproduce that success. The runners from such a stable at these meetings are therefore always especially well prepared and always give a good account of themselves, even if they fail to win.

The significance of these races to trainers may have arisen due to other than purely racing considerations. Owners who pay the bills may demand to see and be seen watching their horses run at certain meetings and the trainer is therefore forced to accede to their wishes (e.g. H. Cecil and M. Stoute are trainers with horses particularly prepared for Royal Ascot and other major meetings).

The four bank holidays provide a feast of National Hunt races – and without a generally high standard of quality opponents in so many races, allows great opportunity for the well-placed, well-prepared horse. Some trainers who realize the value of having horses 'ready' at these meetings are rewarded with multiple winners on the day – three, four or even five winners. Trainers such as M. H. Easterby, J. A. C. Edwards, J. Fitzgerald, J. Gifford, M. Pipe, O. Sherwood and W. A. Stephenson have good records on these occasions. These may be one of the few occasions when their sporting working owners have the opportunity to watch their horses run and see them win.

Other meetings may be of significance in understanding a trainer's record, not because of the initial success that is obtained but because these meetings serve as preparation races for later success. These meetings will be essentially before the trainer has his horses completely prepared, but serve as an indicator of the progress still to be made and act as introductory race for 2-year-olds (Flat) and novices (National Hunt).

All the horses of trainers which run at a meeting where he regularly has success should always be seriously considered and their form thoroughly examined. Similar consideration can be given to the runners of a trainer who has a particularly good record in a particular race; whether it is a top-class competitive race like the Derby – where M. V. O'Brien has an enviable record – or the Grand National – where T. Forster reigned supreme – or a particular handicap at a small meeting that one trainer wins regularly.

4. Significant travelling. The significance of a horse being sent a long distance to compete in a race should not be underestimated for there is little point in a trainer going to such time and effort if the horse has not got a winning chance. The strongest indications will be as follows:

(a) When the trainer sends only one horse to the meeting – engaging a top jockey who travels a similar distance for this one ride of the day.

(b) When it is unusual for a top trainer to have a horse or horses travelling such a journey to such a meeting.

When the trainer sends a team of horses it is unlikely they all have an equal chance of winning – one probably has a real chance and the rest may be there to fill up the horse-box. This is not always so, but is generally the case. Exceptions to this are leading trainers who send better-class horses to a lower-grade meeting, often with successful doubles or trebles the outcome of such ventures.

A trainer may also be just sending a horse a long way because the owner wishes to see it run there (i.e. the owner may be a steward at the meeting, live near the course or be on holiday close by). There can be many reasons why a horse is sent a long journey to race; it is a significant factor if it is solely a calculated decision by the trainer to give a horse a positive chance of winning; it assumes less importance if made for other reasons.

5. Jockey engagement. The engaging of a top jockey to ride a horse will be for two reasons:

1. If the horse has some hint of form that it can win the race, the jockey will be engaged for that purpose.
2. If the horse has no form and/or is inexperienced it is likely the jockey is being engaged to obtain a professional opinion of the horse's racing potential and to give it an education.

It is often a significant move when successful 'in form' apprentices (Flat) and claimers (National Hunt) are engaged by a trainer especially in handicaps where the reduction of a few pounds of weight gives a horse a winning edge.

The engaging of a top jockey or otherwise cannot alone make a horse win, but coupled with other factors gleaned from a trainer's record and methods is a further indication which may assist in the assessment of a horse's chances. Reference to *The Racing Post Record* publications will provide this indispensable information.

The successful training of racehorses depends upon a large percentage of work and preparation and a final ingredient of inspiration or intuition, and it is this certain element which separates the great from the merely competent trainers.

OWNERS

To complement the manner and methods employed by trainers in the way they race their horses, it will be enlightening for the selector to have some knowledge and understanding of racehorse owners.

The owner of the horse as understood from the race-card is the person(s) or business officially registered with the Jockey Club as the owner(s). The owner will have bought or leased the horse and be responsible for training fees (that include the additional variables of veterinary bills, entry and jockey fees), but have the privilege of seeing their colours worn on the race-track.

The owner with such a considerable financial commitment can be seen as the cornerstone of the racing industry, creating and maintaining employment for trainers and their staff by providing the product (i.e. horses) that enable racing to function. Owners may come from any class in society and with the advent of horse syndication (up to 12 partners are allowed to hold shares) even from modest backgrounds, but the high cost required to own and train a horse ensures that principally owners come from the wealthiest echelons. The two different types of racing tend to produce two differing breeds of owners. Flat racing with its ever increasing outlay in new young bloodstock yet with equally its amazingly high potential reward for the most successful, attracts basically the richest and most class-conscious patrons. National Hunt racing, meanwhile, which is less prestigious, without unbounded reward for the most successful and with the prospect of disaster and injury ever looming tends to attract the more sporting enthusiast and die-hard type of owner.

This being a basic classification of the types of owner it will be useful for the selector seeking a greater comprehension of racing to become familiar with the names of leading owners and to recognize their involvement in racing and motives for ownership. Such comprehension will often give the final process of selection confirmation or further indication of a horse's chance. The most influential Flat race owners in recent seasons have been:

Khalid Abdullah. Plain Mr K. Abdullah on the racecard, stands for Prince Khalid Bin Abdullah, leading member of the Saudi Arabian royal family. His self-effacing European title reflects the low profile he generally presents yet Khalid Abdullah is one of the most influential owners. He has wide breeding interests including a major holding in Juddmonte Farms Ltd, whose operations cover England, Ireland and the United States, plus his ownership of other English studs.

DANCING BRAVE, his most famous horse, and RAINBOW QUEST both won the Prix de l'Arc de Triomphe. He has also owned champion milers WARNING, ROUSILLON and KNOWN FACT.

Winning the Epsom Derby still remains a prime ambition. Pat Eddery is his internationally retained jockey, Guy Harwood and Barry Hills his principal trainers.

H. H. Aga Khan. Western-educated Prince Karim, son of Prince Aly Khan and grandson of the illustrious Aga Khan III, inherited a racing empire which he has lovingly nurtured and improved till today it stands as one of the most powerful in the world. Owner of major studs in Ireland including the famous Ballymany Stud, from where SHERGAR was kidnapped, plus others in France, he has owned and bred many good horses. His three Epsom Derby winners of the 1980s, SHERGAR, SHAHARASTANI and KAHYASI, stand out in the public memory. His pattern of naming horses is to use the same initial letter as their dam, hence KAHYASI was out of KADISSYA, DOYOUN out of DUMKA.

Paris-based 'K', as he is known by close friends, seeks every opportunity to come to England to see his horses run. While always liking to see his fillies race before they take up stud duties, he only comes to watch his colts if they have a real winning chance. Michael Stoute and Luca Cumani are his principal English trainers.

191

The Al Maktoum family. The most dominating force in British racing for generations, the Al Maktoums have spent a fortune several times over in setting up the most comprehensive racing and breeding empire. The family who come from the oil-rich state of Dubai in the Gulf, where they combine royal and political roles, have a passion for racing which knows no bounds.

The four most influential members of the family on the British racing scene have been Sheikh Mohammed (the youngest of the brothers and the most internationally successful), Maktoum Al Maktoum the eldest, Hamdan Al Maktoum the second eldest, and Sheikh Ahmed.

Sheikh Mohammed's most famous horses have all been fillies – OH SO SHARP (triple crown winner), the great PEBBLES, INDIAN SKIMMER and SONIC LADY. His maroon and white colours have graced the winner's circle so often that these are just the tip of a very large iceberg.

Maktoum Al Maktoum also bought a wonderful filly, the French-trained MA BICHE, who won the English 1,000 Guineas. He also owned Irish Derby winner SHAREEF DANCER and English 2,000 Guineas winner SHADEED, plus his first Classic winner TOUCHING WOOD who won the St Leger.

Hamdan Al Maktoum in 1989 became the first member of the family to win England's premier Classic when NASHWAN won the Epsom Derby. Previously AL BAHATHRI, winner of the Irish 1,000 Guineas and a top miler of her generation, was his most important winner.

Sheikh Ahmed, the least-known member of the family, owned MTOTO, winner of Ascot's King George VI and Queen Elizabeth Stakes plus the Eclipse Stakes in consecutive years. He previously owned the Irish 2,000 Guineas winner WASSL.

Their breeding interests include Dalham Hall Stud, Gainsborough Stud and Shadwell Studs at Newmarket plus Derrinstown Stud in Ireland and others in the United States.

A number of managers are employed to run their racing interests and their horses are distributed between all the top trainers.

Her Majesty Queen Elizabeth II. The Queen first entered race-horse ownership in the early 1950s and has maintained a consuming interest for the sport ever since. Royal racing and breeding interests have been a tradition in England since at least Charles II's reign. The Royal studs at Sandringham and Wolferton in Norfolk were founded by King Edward VII while the Queen herself was inspirational in setting up the Polhampton Lodge Stud at Kingsclere in Berkshire.

A winner of all the Classics except the Derby, the nearest she came was with AUREOLE who finished second in Coronation year. DUNFERM-LINE, her Oaks and St Leger double winner in Jubilee year, and HIGH-CLERE, winner of the English 1,000 Guineas, were both products of the Royal studs. However, in her desire to succeed in England's premier Classic, some royal mares have visited top stallions in the United

States. It is hoped they will produce Royal winners of English Classics in the 1990s.

Her three trainers are Dick Hern, Willie Hastings-Bass and Ian Balding.

The Dowager Lady Beaverbrook. A leading owner since the 1960s, Lady Beaverbrook's devotion to the sport has been rewarded with two St Leger victories, the most recent MINSTER SON, plus numerous other big race successes including a King George VI and Queen Elizabeth win and an International Stakes victory. Her famous beaver brown and green crossbelt silks have been a popular sight on the British turf in her attempt to win the top prizes. Her penchant is to give her horses seven-letter names, as she had once worked out this was a common factor of many Derby winners. She has owned numerous good horses who fulfilled this requisite: BUSTINO, PETOSKI, RELKINO and that grand old sprinter BOLDBOY. Her ambition remains to win an English Derby and Classic staying horses are always at the top of her order list.

Her principal trainers are Dick Hern and Clive Brittain.

Lord Howard de Walden. A traditional British aristocrat whose title dates back 400 years. Lord Howard de Walden is owner of two major studs, the Plantation Stud at Newmarket and Templeton Stud in Yorkshire. Racing has long been a consuming passion and he had every owner/breeder's dream fulfilled when his SLIP ANCHOR won the Epsom Derby.

A former Senior Steward of the Jockey Club, his famous all apricot colours have long graced the turf. In recent seasons besides his Blue Riband sucess he owned and bred top miler and now successful stallion KRIS and his full brother DIESIS.

His principal trainer is Henry Cecil while Willie Jarvis (also at Newmarket) trains some of his string. In the 1970s he owned and bred champion hurdler LANZAROTE who had begun his Flat race career with Lord Howard's northern trainer Ernie Weymes.

Robert Sangster. Until the recent Arab influence Robert Sangster had been the most powerful owner on the British turf. Epsom Derby winners, THE MINSTREL and GOLDEN FLEECE, are just the pinnacle of his success story. Isle of Man based Robert Sangster, founder of the Swettenham Stud in Cheshire, has a massive breeding operation centred on the Coolmore Stud in Ireland. No longer the constant purchaser of high-price bloodlines in America, Robert's British racing interests have been focused on the large Manton estate where his home-bred horses are coming on stream. Barry Hills is his principal trainer who oversees operations.

Big race winners are still the order of the day for Robert Sangster, but he is not averse to a 'tilt at the ring' on selective occasions during the season. Competitive-looking handicaps are often the medium, and when the odds start to tumble they usually oblige.

Charles St George. Charles St George has been a successful owner over the years sometimes with horses he owned outright and sometimes in partnership. A Lloyds underwriter, Charles St George had Classic successes in the 1970s with BRUNI in the St Leger and GINEVRA in the Oaks. His most recent Classic success was with MICHAELOZZO in the 1989 St Leger. Yet his most famous horse is probably that gallant and versatile stayer ARDROSS. He often names his horses after artists; GIACO-METTI and LORENZACCIO were two of the most successful.

His principal trainer is Henry Cecil.

In contrast to the Flat racing scene, the stars of National Hunt racing tend to have belonged to owners whose influence on the sport is limited almost entirely to their one champion. Richard Burridge, owner of DESERT ORCHID, is unlikely ever again to own an equal. Mr Noel Le Mare, owner of RED RUM, was associated with a unique phenomenon, as was Mrs Charmian Hill, owner of DAWN RUN. Even Anne, Duchess of Westminster, who has had a long association with famous steeple-chasers, will never own another ARKLE.

Owners, whether they be seen as misguided philanthropists ever supporting the horse-racing and betting industry, mere exhibitionists with inflated egos seeking public limelight or perhaps a peculiar mixture of these two extremes, all live with the constant hope and dream of seeing their horse in the winner's enclosure. Having a winner to any owner is vindication of their decision to become owners, it is the reward for their months or maybe years of hope, disappointment and expense. It will serve as the proof to silence the doubters, the mocking critics and act as a rebuff to personal enemies. The racecourse then becomes the place where owners may flaunt their success, respectably exhibiting their possessions and power in the guise of expensive thoroughbred horseflesh. Ownership may become a means of obtaining fame, possibly fortune and self-advancement simply by association, deriving the benefits from the effort, struggle and skills of others (i.e. horse, trainer and jockey).

Ownership with its hands tightly affixed around the purse-strings of racing can be see to hold the seat of considerable power and influence. In consideration of these observations it will assist the selector to become acquainted with the 'who's who' of racing (reference to the *Directory of the Turf* will be most informative) and acknowledge how trainers will often direct their efforts to produce winners on particular occasions for their most favoured or prestigious patrons, for instance:

1. An owner who is a racing steward will take particular pleasure from seeing his horse win at the meeting where he is an official.
2. A prospective royal winner(s) will often be indicated by the presence of members of the royal family at the racecourse when they have horses as runners.

3. An owner surrounded by a large party of friends and relatives, all especially invited to the racecourse, is usually expecting or hoping for an occasion to celebrate success.
4. A foreign owner in the country on a business or pleasure visit will without doubt find their stay enhanced at the prospect of witnessing their horse(s) win. Such pleasing memories will in their absence from British racing serve to appease for some time any past or future lack of success that they may encounter.

These examples illustrate (while no owner has the power of guaranteed success) that when trainers focus their efforts on achieving particular aims, the selector who realizes these ambitions is in a most favourable position to recognize what may be the salient factors regarding selection in that instance.

11 THE PRACTICAL APPROACH TO MAKING A SELECTION

The approach to selection must always be in a controlled, reasoned manner, with sufficient time allowed for the unprejudiced examination of the relevant facts of form before coming to a selection decision.

SELECTION OF THE RACE

1. Decide which race(s) are suitable for selection. Those easiest to assess are likely to be non-handicaps and non-selling races with a recommended maximum of 12 runners.
2. Having chosen the race(s), check the starting time(s), and be sure to allow enough time for thorough, unhurried assessment and analysis. If there is insufficient time do not even begin assessment.

ASSESSMENT OF THE RACE

1. Consider the type of race – Flat or National Hunt – the ease or stiffness of the course and/or fences and what is required for winning, e.g. speed in sprints, stamina in long-distance races and jumping ability in National Hunt racing.

2. Read the conditions that apply to the race:
(a) The prize-money (the higher the value of prize-money, the better the class of race and often the more competitive).
(b) The distance.
(c) The entry conditions (maidens, novices, etc.).
(d) The weight conditions (sex allowances, weight-for-age, allowances, etc.).

Note the 'going' – this must always be given particular attention. Due regard should be given to sudden extreme changes of going which can engineer reversals of form. Extremes of going often allow certain horses, who can only produce their best form under such conditions, to reign supreme.

3. Analyse the form of each runner. In practice form analysis consists of:

1. The systematic assessment of the form of each runner;
2. The elimination of the improbables and no-hopers;
3. The formation of a concluding short list of probables.

4. Final selection. If the form analysis should reveal only one probable, the final selection decision can be considered complete – awaiting only final verification from the modifying factors in the formula.

Should form analysis produce more than one probable, a selection is made by comparing the corresponding graded factors of each probable as revealed in the selection formula. The horse(s) with the lowest merit grade rating will be eliminated leaving the remaining probable as the selection choice.

The most desirable situation is for the selection choice to be a probable which has top merit rating in each section of the selection formula.

In practice this total positive confirmation of all factors occurs only on rare occasions.

NB. *It does occur* and the selector who is discriminating and disciplined enough to wait only for these pristine opportunities is likely to be rewarded with an extremely high success rate. The one failing of such selections is that the odds offered on them tend to be very short, and this can make betting uneconomic on these alone.

Therefore, it becomes necessary to balance skilfully all the factors in the formula to provide reliable selections.

USING THE SELECTION FORMULA

The selection formula must be realized as containing two parts, of different degrees of importance.

$$F - F : C : C$$

Form is the dominating first part – the *keynote* in importance. Proven form is the undeniable proof of what has or has not been achieved in performance.

Fitness/Class/Conditions are the modifying factors of the second part: they can only qualify the likelihood of reproducing proven form.

The selection formula is based upon the skilful analysis of form with the assessment of the value of that form the keynote to selection.

Each section of the formula should be separated, each element divided into its key factors which are graded in an order of merit.

FORM – THE KEYNOTE

Form can be divided into three categories:

Rating	Abbreviation		
★★★	P	Proven Form	This is of the highest value – it means a horse has proven form better than rivals. It 'holds them' on form.
★★	Prom	Promising Form	This is of the second highest value. It means a horse has form of value, but is not emphatically proven as the best (i.e. there may be no means of reliable comparison with other form).
★	Imp	Improving Form	This is of the least value. A horse has shown improved form (i.e. has beaten horses that it had previously been beaten by). The true merit of its form is difficult to assess positively, because once a horse improves, it is difficult to judge its further capacity for improvement.

Form is the keynote – its value cannot be stated too forcibly.

THE MODALITIES: FITNESS, CLASS, CONDITIONS

FITNESS

An element of the fitness factor always has to be taken on trust, but the best indication of a horse's race fitness is by a recent racecourse performance.

Fitness can be graded into four categories:

Rating	Days since last race	
★★★	Up to 14 days	The most assured indication of a horse being at peak fitness (a horse without further preparation can hold its peak fitness after a race for about 7 days).
★★	15–21 days	Similar to 14-day fitness – but of a slightly lower order in confirming fitness – a horse can be falling from its peak by this time – but it is appropriate for 2-year-olds to have this slightly longer period between races.
★	22–28 days	After 21 days' fitness, confirmed peak fitness is suspect – a horse is likely to be past its peak without careful preparation – it will depend on the trainer's methods. *NB.* It is often appropriate for top-class horses whose race engagements fit this pattern.
—	after 29+ days	After a month, or longer absence from racing, a horse's fitness has to be taken entirely on trust. The selector will need to be well acquainted with a trainer's methods to have confidence in the horse being race fit. A 29-day+ absence from racing indicates that a horse has met with a training set-back (illness or injury) or has been 'let down' for a rest.

NB. Whatever the value of previous form, it is most unwise to consider a 2 y.o. for selection who has had an absence from racing of 43 days (6 weeks) or more because it is likely that due to illness or injury that the horse has suffered a reversal in its training programme. As the season progresses 2 y.o. form becomes subject to constant re-evaluation.

CLASS

This means a horse is competing against better, worse or the same quality of opposition.

Abbreviation

dr   Drop in class – is the most favourable indication. A horse has less to do.

—   In the same class – requires a horse to repeat its known performances.

up   Up in class – means a horse must improve upon its best performance to have a winning chance.

CONDITIONS

The final, and the important balancing factors which sometimes hold sway in forming a selection decision.

Distance. Change of distance can be of crucial consequence. Most horses are suited to a particular distance and are not so effective over a longer or shorter trip.

Proven/suited   *Unproven and/or untried*

D√   D?   If a horse is untried or unproven at a distance, the indications on whether it will be suited can only be estimated from its breeding and the manner it has been performing over shorter or longer distances (i.e. r.o. over shorter distances, weakening over longer distances).

NB. Experienced horses of proven ability will often more readily be successful when reverting to shorter distances than when attempting longer distances where their stamina rather than their speed will be put to the test. MOORESTYLE (1981–7f) successfully reverted to sprint distances, ARDROSS (1981–2½m Gold Cup) won at 1m 5f and ARTAIUS (1977–1¼m Eclipse) won the 1m Sussex Stakes in the same year. COMMANCHE RUN (1984 St Leger – 1m 6f) the following season won races at 1m 2f. DESERT ORCHID (1989) after winning at 3m reverted to 2m for one race and won.

Going. Can the horse act on the ground conditions? Horses have varying actions and conformations which make it possible for them to produce their best form only on specific ground conditions.

Proven   *Unproven*
G√   G?   Changed but similar going (i.e. good, good to firm, good to soft, soft) are likely to prove no measurable encumbrance to a horse. It is the extremes of going that produce the ground 'specialists' (heavy, very soft, fast). Breeding and conformation (action) are the indications to how a horse will adapt to the going.

Weight. The first consideration is *weight*. Weight is the leveller of ability. Weight allowance (lb) is positively favourable; weight concession (lb) is a disadvantage. The amount of weight allowed or conceded is the issue. It is always a matter of personal opinion to judge in each instance how much will be the deciding amount. Up to 5 lb in penalties is negligible; 7 lb+ must be given thoughtful consideration. Due regard must be given to 'going' – obviously weight is a greater burden in 'heavy' going.

Course. Will the horse act on the track, especially if of an extreme character?

Proven   *Unproven*
C√   C?

Further factors that influence conditions

Jockeyship
Jockeyship essentially resolves to personal opinion. It can be stated that while there are only slight differences in competence and ability among the leading riders, there is a considerable difference in ability between the top-class jockey and the average jockey.

Draw
The draw is applicable only to Flat racing. Its significance is dependent on:
1. The race-track;
2. The distance of the race;
3. The size of the field.

Blinkers/Visors
These are mainly of importance in Flat racing. They become of particular interest when worn by a horse for the first time.

In the context of the formula, merit ratings for the form and fitness sections have been symbolized in degree by stars, a three-star rating representing the highest value and one star the lowest.

The other sections of the formula have been symbolized as positive, negative or passive value for class (by dr, up or—); and for conditions by indicating if there is a weight allowance, e.g. 4 lb pen.) and by a tick and question-mark system.

In symbols a six-star rating: ★★★form + ★★★fitness would be the top rating, the ideal and desired choice for selection.

As the ideal situation seldom presents itself, a reliable minimum standard must be established which adheres to the principles of the selection formula. *It is recommended that a four-star rating, where there are no negative or unproven factors influencing, become the minimum standard for selection.* Passive factors will only serve as neutral influences, while positive factors give endorsement to such a selection.

A four-star rating guarantees that a selection is based on reasonable proven elements of form and fitness. Less than four-star rating is below the standard necessary for reliable selection.

Final selection is made by the comparison of the merits of each probable drawn from form analysis. These merits are more easily identified and evaluated when clearly marked in visual symbols. An example is given below:

Time	**Meeting** (Course)		**Going**		
Type of race	**Value**	**Distance**	**Number of runners**		
Name of probable (A)	**Trainer**	**Age**	**Weight**	**Jockey**	

F.	**F.**	**C.**	**C.**		
P	(5)	—	10 lb pen		
★★★	★★★				

Name of probable (B)	**Trainer**	**Age**	**Weight**	**Jockey**	
F.	**F.**	**C.**	**C.**		
Imp	(14)	up	10 lb pen		
★	★★★				

NB. (Have a maximum of only three probables. If form analysis has produced more than three, a selection must not be contemplated.)

The formula credentials of each probable can be quickly compared, the one(s) with the lowest merit rating eliminated, leaving the remaining probable as the selection choice.

In the above theoretical example probable (B) would automatically be eliminated with a rating below the minimum standard, and probable (A) which has a rating above minimum standard becomes the selection.

If the final probables have identical merit ratings they are too finely balanced to allow a selection decision to be made.

SUMMARY OF STAR RATINGS

Rating			*Betting odds comment*
6 star	– with all the modifying factors favourable	THE IDEAL RATING	Normally odds on
	– with a balance of positive and negative factors	MOST DESIRABLE RATING	Normally best odds – evens
5 star	– with all modifying factors positive	GOOD practical VALUE	Likely to be viable betting odds
	– with a balance of modifying factors	GOOD practical VALUE	Viable odds
4 star	– with all modifying factors positive	The MINIMUM requirement (The most commonly encountered selection rating, lacks absolute quality, but skilful selection will be well served by selection of this merit rating)	Good economic betting

The less positive and proven factors a selection has to support it, the longer the odds should be against it winning.

For practical guidance it can be stated that a five-star selection which is not overburdened by negative condition factors is likely consistently to produce winning selections at economic odds.

12 PRACTICAL EXAMPLES OF THE SELECTION FORMULA AS APPLIED TO ACTUAL RACES

The key to successful selection is the correct interpretation of form. So often the evidence necessary to assess the value of form is non-existent, contradictory or incomplete. Therefore, however tightly structured the selection formula is, the analysis and assessment of form depends on the experience and judgement of each selector. This aspect allows selectors to bring their initiative, skill and understanding to bear while submitting the final decision to the completely objective elements of the selection formula.

The races included as examples were all analysed and a final decision made before the races were run and the *result known*. They are a sample taken from many types of race to demonstrate how the principles in the selection formula apply despite the constantly changing facets of horse-racing.

Analysis of the majority of races reveals that the most favourable factors stipulated in the selection formula and star rating system only infrequently exist. This means that the selector must discriminately wait for only the most advantageous selection opportunities or else warily lower the highest standards prescribed in the formula.

In response to these ever present practical realities, races filling both the above categories have been included as examples. Also races ranging from the premier in the calendar to more obscure races which may be seen to conform more reliably to the higher standards desired in the selection formula.

FLAT RACE SEASON 1989

Form Book No. 1746 *NEWMARKET 12 July 1989 (good)*

3.40 — ANGLIA TV JULY STAKES
(Group 3) (2YO C & G)
£30,000 (£22,059) 6f (4)

401	(1)	111 **ROCK CITY 22 (D2)** R Hannon 9-1 .... **W Carson ●78**
402	(4)	1 **BOCA LAD 25 (D)** Lord John FitzGerald 8-10 ...... **R Hills 55**
403	(3)	21111 **CHAMPAGNE GOLD 12 (D2)** Denys Smith 8-10
			Pat Eddery 65
404	(2)	12 **WADOOD 22 (DBF)** M Stoute 8-10 .... **W R Swinburn 75**

Probable SP: 5-4 Rock City, 15-8 Wadood, 7-2 Champagne Gold, 10 Boca Lad. **FAVOURITES: 1 0 1 3 0 1 3 .**

1988: Always Valiant 8 10 (W Carson) 9-1 N Callaghan 4 ran.

NEWMARKET FORM

3.40 £22,059

Gp32yo	6f

Rock City

	2-9-01
111	
R.HANNON	br c 8Mar87 50000gns
	Ballad Rock —
	Rimosa's Pet (Petingo)

Starts	1st	2nd	3rd	Win & Pl
3	3	—	—	£29,905

89 Ascot 6f 2yoGp3 FIRM	.... £23,306
89 York 6f 2yo FIRM	.... £3,623
89 Sand 5f Mdn2yo SOFT	.... £2,976
	TOTAL: £29,905

20 Jun Ascot 6f		2yoGp3 £23,306
16 ran	FIRM	TIME 1m15.02s (slw0.4s)

1 ROCK CITY 2 8-13 ...... W.Carson¹⁵ 9/1
always prominent, led 2f out, driven out [op 8/1 tchd 10/1]
2 WADOOD (USA) 2 8-13 W.R.Swinburn⁵ 2/1F
always prominent, every chance over 1f out, no impression [op 2/1 tchd 5/2]
3 Candy Glen 2 8-13 .... N.Day² 4/1
DISTANCES 3-2-4-1-nk-1½-¾-1½-2½-nk-¾

17 May York 6f		2yo £3,623
6 ran	FIRM	TIME 1m13.21s (slw2.3s)

1 ROCK CITY 2 9-03 ..... W.Carson⁶ 8/11F
tracked leaders, led 2f out, ran on strongly [op 5/4]
2 Regal Thatch 2 8-11 ..... M.Roberts⁴ 6/1
3 Shout Out 2 8-11 .... J.Reid¹ 4/1
DISTANCES 3-nk-nk-10-1½

29 Apr Sandown 5f		Mdn2yo £2,976
10 ran	SOFT	TIME 1m10.59s (slw9.3s)

1 ROCK CITY 2 9-00 .... B.Rouse³ 7/2
led over 3f out, ridden out [op 5/1 tchd 7/1 in places]
2 Brown Carpet 2 9-00 .... PatEddery⁴ 11/4F
3 Elapse (USA) 2 9-00 .... M.Hills⁷ 10/3
DISTANCES 1½-shd-10-½-3-3-nk

Wadood (USA)

	2-8-10
12	
M.R.STOUTE	b c 14Feb87 $1300000
	Danzig (USA) —
	Foreign Missile (USA)
	(Damascus (USA))

Starts	1st	2nd	3rd	Win & Pl
2	1	1	—	£12,739

89 York 6f Mdn2yo FIRM	.... £4,045

20 Jun Ascot 6f	2yoGp3 £23,306
second, see ROCK CITY	

18 May York 6f		Mdn2yo £4,045
12 ran	FIRM	TIME 1m12.84s (slw1.9s)

1 WADOOD (USA) 2 9-00
.... W.R.Swinburn¹¹ 4/6F
started slowly, behind until headway halfway, ran on well to lead well inside final furlong [tchd 4/7]
2 Elapse (USA) 2 9-00 ...... M.Hills¹² 13/2
3 Poke The Fire 2 9-00 .... J.Reid² 14/1
DISTANCES ¾-shd-4-2-hd

Probables

(1) ROCK CITY – R. Hannon 2–9.1 W. Carson

F.	F.	C.	C.
Proven	(22)	—	C√
★★★	★		D√
			G√
			5 lb pen?

(4) WADOOD – M. Stoute 2–8.10 W. R. Swinburn

F.	F.	C.	C.
Prom	(22)	—	C√
★★	★		D√
			G√

This is an example of a conditions race for 2-year-olds over a distance of 6f. Newmarket's Group III July stakes. Staged during the main summer meeting on the July Course, with a small field of four runners, all with exposed form, presented a good opportunity for selection.

Examining each runner carefully, two runners which had both already run in a pattern race, ROCK CITY and WADOOD, emerged as the probables. The other two runners, although showing very commendable form, were now raised in class to take on two poven group race class opponents. They were therefore eliminated from further consideration. ROCK CITY and WADOOD had raced each other before in Royal Ascot's Group III Coventry Stakes over 6f. WADOOD was made favourite for that race at level weights but finished second 3 lengths behind ROCK CITY. There were no obvious excuses, both horses had every chance, and ROCK CITY proved superior. Today they opposed each other with ROCK CITY carrying a 5 lb penalty for its pattern race victory.

The question raised was would the change in weights bring about a reversal in form. At 3 lb per length (the recognized weight/distance ratio over 5/6f), ROCK CITY's 3-length advantage and only 5 lb weight penalty would mean WADOOD still had something to find. As beaten horses seldom reverse form unless there is a massive turn-around in the weights it is always advisable to select winning form.

Applying the formula, ROCK CITY, with a four-star rating (the minimum demanded), emerged as the selection choice. For once, without fear of contradiction, it could be said to have the 'proven form'. Its fitness, while not confirmed to the highest standard, was appropriate to horses campaigning in pattern races, where the interval between each contest is programmed on a less frequent scale. ROCK CITY was in the same class, proven over the distance and going, and although yet to race at Newmarket, unlikely to have difficulty coping with the open 6f track. Only the 5 lb penalty was a negative factor but considered not severe enough to stop the horse reproducing its winning form.

Result: 1st ROCK CITY (7–4) won by 5 lengths.

(*NB* The bookmakers' mark-up for this race was only 9.8 per cent, offering the backer good value.)

Form Book No. 61 *KEMPTON 27 March 1989 (good to soft)*

3.05 — QUAIL STAKES £8,000 added
(£5,952.00) 6f (11)

301	(6)	006000-	DAWN'S DELIGHT 156 (D15)	K Ivory 11-9-10		—
302	(11)	4/3214/	HOMO SAPIEN 548 (D3)	D Chapman 7-9-7	S Cauthen	—
303	(1)	001211-	JOYTOTHEWORLD 233	W O'Gorman 4-9-7	T Ives	70
304	(3)		MUNJARID	G Balding 4-9-7	T Quinn	—
305	(4)	460000-	SHARP REMINDER 142 (C&DD3)	C Williams 5-9-7	G Starkey	67
306	(7)	220050-	MARBELLA SILKS 156 (D5)	M Ryan 4-9-5	W R Swinburn	71
307	(10)	360560-	INTIMIDATE 165	J Gosden 4-9-0	M Roberts	●78
308	(9)	11/0450-	KIRAM	W Brooks 4-9-0	P Lynch (7)	—
309	(2)	460000-	TOLO 142 (D) (B)	G Lewis 4-9-0	Paul Eddery	64
310	(8)		LA GRACIOSA	G Balding 4-8-11	B Rouse	—
311	(5)	3120-	KNIGHT OF MERCY 177 (BF2)	R Hannon 3-8-0	W Carson	63

Probable SP: 5-2 Intimidate, 100-30 Sharp Reminder, 4 Joytotheworld, 11-2 Dawn's Delight, 8 Homo Sapien, 12 Marbella Silks. **FAVOURITES: 2 4 2 0 1 2 0.**
1988: Lonely Street 7 8 12 (N Adams) 14-1 P J Arthur 9 ran.

HOWARD PARKER			Last	OFFICIAL RATINGS	
Last			4		To-
Season Current		Horse and Weight	Runs	Last 4 Handicaps-latest day	
3.05 Quail Stakes					**6f**
87	,,	Dawn's Delight 11- 9-10	6000-	D ....K T Ivory	
108	,,	Homo Sapien 7- 9- 7	3214/	D ....D W Chapman	
95	,,	Joytotheworld 4- 9- 7	1211-	.........W A O'Gorman	
...	,,	Munjarid 4- 9- 7	1513/	...........G B Balding	
93	,,	Sharp Reminder..........5- 9- 7	0000-	CD ....C N Williams	
91	,,	Marbella Silks 4- 9- 5	0050-	D ....M J Ryan	
S113	,,☆	Intimidate 4- 9- 0	0560-	...............J Gosden	
...	,,	Kiram(USA) 4- 9- 0	0450-	........W G A Brooks	
91	,,	Tolo 4- 9- 0	0000-	D ....G Lewis	
...	,,	La Graciosa 4- 8-11		...........G B Balding	
89	,,	Knight Of Mercy 3- 8- 0	3120-	BF ....R Hannon	

3.5

Conditions
6f
(£5,952)
11 runners

360560- INTIMIDATE (4-9-0) (J Gosden) b c Formidable (USA) [8.4f] - Zoomie by Pinza [12.4f]. 1987, 5f good to soft (Newbury). £3,603.00 (-).

Oct 13 1988, Newmarket, 7f (Group 2), good, £32,346.00: 1 Salse (USA) (3-8-10,2), 2 Reprimand (3-8-10,8), 3 Timely (3-8-7,4), 8 INTIMIDATE (3-8-10, A Bond,1), **led for over four furlongs**, soon lost place, eased when **beaten.** (50 to 1); 8 Ran. 2½l, 2l, hd, ¾l, shthd, 5l, 2½l. 1m 27.04s (a 1.94s). SR: 78/70/61/70/61/64.

Aug 27 1988, Goodwood, 1m (Group 2), good, £44,787.00: 1 Prince Rupert (Fr) (4-9-3,bl,4), 2 Then Again (5-9-3,3), 3 Doyoun (3-9-1,5), 6 INTIMIDATE (3-8-9, G Starkey,1), **effort four furlongs out, well behind final two furlongs.** (50 to 1 tchd 66 to 1); 6 Ran. 1½l, 1½l, hd, 7l, 8l. 1m 41.50s (a 2.50s). SR: 65/60/53/49/36/1.

Aug 14 1988, Deauville (Fr), 1m (Group 1), good to firm, £68,580.00: 1 Miesque (USA) (4-8-13,6), 2 Warning (3-8-9,4), 3 Gabina (USA) (3-8-6,5), 5 INTIMIDATE (3-8-9, M Roberts,3),; 6 Ran. 1l, 2l, nose, 3l, nk. 1m 38.60s.

4-YEAR RECORD   15Rn 1w 4p

Yld:	4	1	2	Gd:	7	0	2	Fst:	4	0	0
5-6f :	7	1	2					7-8f:	8	0	2
9-11f:	0	0	0					12f+:	0	0	0

Probable

(7) INTIMIDATE – J. Gosden 4–9.0 M. Roberts

F.	F.	C.	C.
Proven	(165)	dr	C√
★★★	—		D√
			G√
			Weight condition√
			Draw?
			Jockey√

This is an example of a conditions stakes race over 6f. In condition races runners are allotted basically level weights for weight-for-age and sex allowances, and penalties for a previous win, in accordance with entry conditions of the race. Therefore horses of varying abilities can meet at equal weight terms which gives a distinct advantage to the better horses.

In the Quail Stakes such a race opportunity presented itself. Apart from two horses, HOMO SAPIEN and INTIMIDATE, the remainder were basically handicap class. HOMO SAPIEN, a former inmate of H. Cecil's stable, had not raced over 18 months due to injury. It was now having its first run for David Chapman who has a fine record with sprinters, and often other trainers' write-offs. However, it would be a remarkable feat to produce this horse at peak race fitness after such a long absence.

INTIMIDATE, the other horse, had competed in the very top class as a 3 y.o., being placed third in the Irish 2,000 Guineas and running some other fine races, notably on its seasonal début in the Group III Greenham Stakes when narrowly defeated by ZELPHI, and at the Deauville Festival in the Group I Prix Jacques Le Marois. Today INTIMIDATE was dropped in class and meeting inferior horses who in some instances were conceding weight. This was truly a golden opportunity for the selector to support the inviolate nature of proven form.

Applying the formula, fitness had to be taken solely on trust, but this was the same for each runner, as no horse had run since the previous season. As stated, INTIMIDATE was experiencing a considerable drop in class and would be suited by the course, the going, and the weight conditions – which were considerably in its favour. The distance of 6f may have been considered slightly sharp for a horse which was not a specialist sprinter but in a number of races as a 3 y.o. INTIMIDATE had shown considerable early speed over longer distances. The draw could not be considered advantageous but with its early speed this was a disadvantage INTIMIDATE was likely to overcome, especially with that brilliant judge of pace Michael Roberts as its jockey.

INTIMIDATE was therefore made the selection choice.

Result: 1st INTIMIDATE (5–2 fav.) won by ¾ length.

Form Book No. 250 *THIRSK 14 April 1989 (soft)*

4.30 — SOWERBY EBF STAKES (3YO) £3,800 added (£3,074.20) 1m 4f (9)

1	(9)	00-1	**GENERAL PERSHING** 16 (D) M Morley 9-2	G Duffield	76
2	(7)	5-	**ALBAZM** 164 M Jarvis 8-11	T Ives	76
3	(3)	5-2	**ALLASDALE** 11 (BF) G Harwood 8-11	G Starkey	77
4	(2)	0-	**BALLAD RULER** 266 (B) B Hanbury 8-11	P Bloomfield	—
5	(8)		**BENZ BEST** M H Easterby 8-11	M Birch	—
6	(1)		**DANCING FALCON** M Stoute 8-11	G Carter	—
7	(6)	03-	**IBN NAAS** 213 B Hanbury 8-11	B Raymond	77
8	(4)	5	**AUNTIE GLADYS** 14 C Brittain 8-8	W Ryan	●78
9	(5)	00-	**NICOLA NICKLEBY** 214 R Hollinshead 8-8	S Perks	—

Probable SP: 7-4 Dancing Falcon, 9-4 Allasdale, 4 Ibn Naas, 6 General Pershing, 8 Albazm, 10 Auntie Gladys. **FAVOURITES: 1112221.**
1988: Kneller 9 2 (Paul Eddery) Evens Fav H Cecil 8 ran.

THIRSK FORM

4.30 £3,074

3yo **1m4f**

Allasdale (USA)

5-2 **3-8-11**
G.HARWOOD b c **Alleged** (USA) —
  Delray Dancer (USA)
  (Chateaugay)

Starts	1st	2nd	3rd	Win & Pl
2	—	1	—	£524

3 Apr Leicester 1m2f Mdn3yo £1,884
18 ran | SOFT | TIME 2m16.3s (slw12.2s)

1 Icona (USA) 3 9-00 . . . . W.R.Swinburn³ 7/2
2 ALLASDALE (USA) 3 9-00
. . . . PatEddery¹¹ 11/8F
3rd straight, every chance 3f out, soon ridden, one pace [op 6/4 tchd 7/4 and Evens]
3 Spring Hay 3 9-00 . . . . . M.Roberts¹⁹ 16/1
DISTANCES 6-nk-1½-2-2-¾-nk-3-1

9 Jul⁸⁸ Salisbury 7f Mdn2yo £3,012
13 ran | GOOD | TIME 1m28.62s (slw2.3s)

1 Al Hareb (USA) 2 9-00 . . . . W.Carson⁵ 4/5F
2 Shallow Waters 2 9-00 . . . . T.Quinn¹³ 11/2
3 Bramber 2 8-09 . . . . G.Sexton⁹ 50/1
5 ALLASDALE (USA) 2 9-00 G.Starkey¹¹ 7/2
no headway final 2f [op 5/2 tchd 5/1]
DISTANCES 8-4-1-2½-½-hd-¾-3-1-nk-nk-½

Dancing Falcon

M.R.STOUTE **3-8-11**
b c **Mill Reef** (USA) — Vielle (Ribero)

General Pershing

90-1 **3-9-02**
M.F.D.MORLEY br c **Persian Bold** — St
  Colette (So Blessed)

Starts	1st	2nd	3rd	Win & Pl
3	1	—	—	£1,324

89 Cttck 1m14f40y Mdn3yo GD-SFT £1,324

29 Mar Catterick 1m4f40y Mdn3yo £1,324
10 ran | GD-SFT | TIME 2m49.5s (slw12.9s)

1 GENERAL PERSHING 3 9-00
. . . . G.Duffield² 5/1
chased leaders, ridden and 4th straight, stayed on to lead well inside final furlong [op 4/1]
2 Fresh Line 3 8-11 . . . . M.Wigham⁸ 8/1
3 Silent Ring (USA) 3 9-00 . . . . J.Lowe⁷ 14/1
DISTANCES 2-12-hd-7-2-10-5-8-12

11 Oct⁸⁸ Redcar 7f Mdn2yo £4,161
20 ran | GD-FM | TIME 1m23.4s (fst0.5s)

1 Jungle Pioneer (USA) 2 9-00 . W.Ryan⁸ 2/5F
2 Twin Jet (USA) 2 9-00 . . . . G.Starkey¹⁷ 8/1
3 First Secretary (USA) 2 9-00
. . . . W.R.Swinburn² 9/1
14 GENERAL PERSHING 2 9-00
. . . . R.Cochrane²⁰ 26/1
outpaced from halfway [op 14/1]
DISTANCES 4-2-4-2½-1-nk-nk-2½-2-1½-1-nk-1-shd

20 Sep⁸⁸ Leicester 7f Mdn2yo £2,794
18 ran | GD-FM | TIME 1m23.9s (slw1.0s)

1 Zayyani 2 9-00 . . . . J.Reid¹⁸ 6/1
2 Top-Boot 2 9-00 . . . . R.Cochrane¹⁷ 9/2
3 Greensmith 2 9-00 . . . . . PatEddery¹⁴ 5/4F
9 GENERAL PERSHING 2 9-00
. . . . PaulEddery⁶ 33/1
with leaders 5f, weakened quickly
DISTANCES 6-1½-2½-2½-1½-¾-½-10-½-hd-1

Probables

(1) GENERAL PERSHING – M. Morley 3–9.11 G. Duffield

F.	F.	C.	C.
Prom	(16)	up	C√
★★	★★		D√
			G√
			5 lb pen?

(3) ALLASDALE – G. Harwood 3–8.11 G. Starkey

F.	F.	C.	C.
Prom	(11)	—	C√
★★	★★★		D?
			G√
			Trainer√

NB DANCING FALCON – M. Stoute 3–8.11 G. Carter

This is an example of a 3 y.o. conditions race over 1m 4f. It was a typical stakes race for staying 3-year-olds held on the Yorkshire course of Thirsk where a number of choicely bred southern trained horses travel a considerable distance to contest the spoils.

Form analysis revealed two probables, GENERAL PERSHING, a winner on its seasonal début 16 days earlier at Catterick, when made favourite. All the remaining runners, with the exception of AUNTIE GLADYS, were making their seasonal or even racecourse début, and were likely at this stage of the season to be at a disadvantage against fitter rivals. However, of these, the previously unraced DANCING FALCON was a most interesting newcomer. Trained by Michael Stoute at Newmarket, and on breeding being by MILL REEF (an English Derby winner) out of VIELLE (placed in the Epsom Oaks), it had a Classic winner's pedigree, and so deserved serious consideration for a lowly northern conditions race.

Dealing with the race in the present, however, and not on what horses may achieve as the season progresses, the issue of current form and fitness took precedent.

GENERAL PERSHING, the only previous winner in the field, had only won a poor-class race at Catterick, and although proven at 1½m distance and going, was being raised in class and penalized 5 lb for its victory.

ALLASDALE was having only its second race ever when beaten on its seasonal début, whilst in its only other race, as a 2 y.o., had met the top-class, subsequent Group I winner, AL HAREB. On each occasion it had come to the races not unfancied, from a stable not loathe to support its inmates, so it was reasonable to assume the horse had some ability. Only the 'dark' unraced rival DANCING FALCON was likely to prove superior on any known form.

Applying the formula ALLASDALE, with a five-star rating, was made the selection choice. A promising form rating, its race 11 days earlier, showed ALLASDALE to be at peak fitness and contesting a similar value race as a 2 y.o. Unlikely to be inconvenienced by Thirsk's easy but sharp track, ALLASDALE was proven on the going, and being by that champion staying sire ALLEGED was likely to appreciate the extra distance of 1½m. These factors seemed also to have been given the seal of approval by trainer Guy Harwood, who had sent just this one horse the long 272m trip from Pulborough in Sussex to contest the race. It was also ridden by stable jockey Greville Starkey, as his only mount of the day.

Result: 1st ALLASDALE (2–1 fav.) won by 8 lengths.

Form Book No. 573 *CHESTER 9 May 1989 (good to firm)*

3.15 — DALHAM CHESTER VASE
(Group 3) 3-Y-O £30,000
added (£22,275) 1m 4f 65yd (5)

301	(1)	235-3 CHILD OF THE MIST 15 (B) B Hills 8-11	M Hills	66
302	(3)	10- FUTURE GLORY 199 J Hanson 8-11	E Johnson	56
303	(2)	1 GOLDEN PHEASANT 25 C Brittain 8-11	M Roberts	65
304	(5)	61-11 OLD VIC 10 H Cecil 8-11	S Cauthen	●78
305	(4)	11- WARRSHAN 193 M Stoute 8-11	W R Swinburn	66

Probable SP: 5-4 Warrshan, 6-4 Old Vic, 4 Child of the Mist, 20 Golden Pheasant, 25 Future Glory. **FAVOURITES:** – – – – 3 1.
1988: Unfuwain 3 8 11 (W Carson) 1-3 fav (W R Hern) 4 ran

CHESTER FORM

3.15   £22,275
Gp33yo   **1m4f65y**

Old Vic
61-11   3-8-11
H.R.A.CECIL   b c Sadler's Wells (USA)
| Starts 1st 2nd 3rd Win & Pl | — Cockade (Derring-|
| 4   3   — —   £40,864 | Do) |

89 Sand 1m2f 3yoGp3 SOFT £31,264
89 Nbury 1m3f 3yo GD-SFT £6,784
88 Hdock 1m Mdn2yo SOFT £2,816
TOTAL: £40,864

| 29 Apr Sandown 1m2f | | 3yoGp3 £31,264 |
| 3 ran | SOFT | TIME 2m20.65s (slw15.9s) |

1 OLD VIC 3 8-08 .... S.Cauthen⁴ 4/9F
*2nd straight, led 2f out, ridden 1f out, ran on
well inside final furlong* [op ½ tchd 4/7 in places]
2 Spring Hay 3 8-08 ...... M.Roberts⁵ 10/1
3 Pride of Araby (USA) 3 8-08 PatEddery² 9/4
DISTANCES 4-6

| 15 Apr Newbury 1m3f | | 3yo £6,784 |
| 6 ran | GD-SFT | TIME 2m28.30s (slw10.0s) |

1 OLD VIC 3 8-09 ...... S.Cauthen² EvensF
*4th straight, led 2f out, shaken up and quick-
ened 1f out, easily* [op 6/4 tchd 13/8 in places]
2 Icona (USA) 3 8-09 ... W.R.Swinburn⁵ 15/8
3 Singular Run 3 8-13 ...... T.Quinn³ 11/1
DISTANCES 10-7-4-8-7

| 12 Oct⁸⁸ Haydock Park 1m | | Mdn2yo £2,816 |
| 12 ran | SOFT | TIME 1m52.51s |

1 OLD VIC 2 9-00 ...... W.Ryan¹² EvensF
*7th straight, headway 3f out, led over 1f out,
ran on well* [op Evens tchd 11/10 & 10/11]
2 Rendezvous Bay 2 8-09 . . R.Cochrane⁹ 20/1
3 Amoodi (USA) 2 9-00 ...... T.Ives² 12/1
DISTANCES 6-5-hd-2½-¾-2½-1½-¾-2

Warrshan (USA)

11- M.R.STOUTE	3-8-11 b c Northern Dancer — Secret Asset (USA) (Graustark)
Starts 1st 2nd 3rd Win & Pl 2 2 — — £6,617	

88 Nmkt 1m 2yo GOOD	. . . .	£4,799
88 Yarm 7f Mdn2yo GD-FM	. . . .	£1,818
		TOTAL: £6,617

28 Oct[88] Nmkt 1m	2yo £4,799
9 ran GOOD	TIME 1m40.79s (slw2.4s)

1 WARRSHAN (USA) 2 8-13
. . . . W.R.Swinburn[1] 4/11F
*made virtually all, ridden final furlong, ran
on* [op½]
2 Torjoun (USA) 2 8-10 . . . R.Cochrane[8] 12/1
3 Sultan's Son 2 8-10 . . . . T.Quinn[8] 25/1
DISTANCES hd-4-½-shd-1-½-6

14 Sep[88] Yarmouth 7f	Mdn2yo £1,818
13 ran GD-FM	TIME 1m22.2s (fst1.6s)

1 WARRSHAN (USA) 2 9-00
. . . . W.R.Swinburn[8] 13/8
*always prominent, shaken up to lead close
ome* [op 7/4 tchd 9/4 & 5/4]
2 Jungle Pioneer (USA) 2 9-00 .W.Ryan[9] 10/1
3 Vault (USA) 2 8-09 . . . . .L.Dettori [(5)13] 6/5F
DISTANCES ½-½-4-1-2-2-nk-nk-1-1-4-4

Probables

(4) OLD VIC – H. Cecil 3–8.11 S. Cauthen

F.	F.	C.	C.
Proven	(10)	—	C?
★★	★★★		D√
			G?

(5) WARRSHAN – M. Stoute 3–8.11 W. Swinburn

F.	F.	C.	C.
Prom	(193)	up	C?
★★	—		D?
			G√

This is an example of a conditions race for 3-year-olds over a distance of 1m 4f 65yds. The Group III Chester Vase is a recognized Epsom Derby trial where the real contenders are quickly distinguished from the mere pretenders around the tight Roodeye Course. SHERGAR (1981) with its memorable victory was the last horse to complete the double, following HENBIT (1980).

The 1989 event followed the trend of recent seasons in attracting a small field of five runners, four of which still held engagements for the premier English Classic. The only contestant not to hold such ambitions was GOLDEN PHEASANT, the winner of a Newbury maiden race on its racecourse début and only race so far. The form of this race, however, had not been endorsed and with other runners in this race still holding Classic aspirations GOLDEN PHEASANT was eliminated from calculations.

Similarly so was CHILD OF THE MIST, still a maiden after competing respectably in a couple of 'hot' races as a 2 y.o.; once when third behind subsequent 2,000 Guineas winner NASHWAN, and on its final race as a juvenile in Doncaster's Group I Futurity Stakes. However, CHILD OF THE MIST had failed to improve upon these efforts, being beaten in its only race at Brighton on its seasonal reappearance. Today fitted with blinkers for the first time (the record of such horses is poor) any consideration it might have received was almost completely nullified. FUTURE GLORY, winner of one of its two races as a juvenile, had finished 12 lengths behind CHILD OF THE MIST in the Futurity and was unlikely to reverse that, so was also eliminated from calculations.

This left two probables, OLD VIC and WARRSHAN, the latter making its seasonal reappearance, while OLD VIC had already run in two races, winning both. The second of these was Sandown's Classic Trial Group III over 1m 2f, and the same route taken by two recent Derby winners SHERGAR and HENBIT. OLD VIC therefore presented the strongest credentials. WARRSHAN, in contrast, was contesting a group race for the first time, but unbeaten as a 2 y.o. had been forwarded for sometime as Michael Stoute's Derby challenger. Workman-like rather than spectacular, WARRSHAN still had some way to go to live up to its $3,700,000 purchase price as a yearling.

Applying the formula, OLD VIC, with a five-star rating, was made the selection choice. Its form, although not unequivocally superior, had been achieved most recently in a group race only 10 days previously. OLD VIC was therefore proven fit, racing in the same class, and its victories over 10f and 11f suggested that stamina was its forte and it would have no problems over this slightly extended 12f trip. The only questions against its was its ability to handle Chester's tight track (a factor common to all the runners) and its ability to adapt to the faster ground, having achieved its victories on more testing going.

Result: 1st OLD VIC (6–4) won by 2½ lengths.

Form Book No. 656 *HAMILTON 15 May 1989 (good to firm)*

3.45 — EBF DRUMLOCH MAIDEN STAKES
(2-Y-O colts & geldings) £1,800 added
(£1,408.00) 5f (7)

1	(5)		CALL RACECALL	C Thornton 9-0	.............J Bleasdale	—
2	(2)	0	MR CHEEKYCHOPS 46	M Brittain 9-0	........A Munro (5)	—
3	(4)	23	ONE AT A TIME 13 (BF) (B)	J Berry 9-0	........K Darley	●78
4	(7)		PADDY CASH	J S Wilson 9-0	.........................G Duffield	—
5	(3)	3	PIQUANT 14	W Hastings-Bass 9-0	..........Dean McKeown	77
6	(6)	4	TARNSIDE CLUB 17	J Etherington 9-0	.........B Raymond	64
7	(1)	53	TOSHIBA COMET 10	W Pearce 9-0	................D Nicholls	68

Probable SP: 7-4 One At A Time, 5-2 Piquant, 5 Toshiba Comet, 7 Tarnside Club.
FAVOURITES: 2 2 3 1 2 1 1.
1988: Nightstalker 2 9 0 (G Duffield) 5-4 P C Haslam 5 ran.

HAMILTON FORM

3.45 £1,408

2yoMdn **5f**

One At A Time

23		2-9-00
J.BERRY		b c 21Mar87 20000gns
Starts 1st 2nd 3rd Win & Pl		Music Boy — Single Bid
2 — 1 1 £1,098		(Auction Ring (USA))

2 May Redcar 5f		Mdn2yo £1,590
13 ran	FIRM	TIME 0m58.4s

1 Brisas 2 9-00 . . . . S.Whitworth[2] 5/1
2 Sink The Fleet (USA) 2 9-00 B.Raymond[5] 6/1
3 **ONE AT A TIME** 2 9-00 . . . K.Darley[10] 6/4F
close up, led 2f out until over 1f out, no extra [op 11/10]
DISTANCES 1½-1½-5-1-¾-¾-2½-shd

20 Apr Nmkt 5f		Mdn2yo £2,976
12 ran	GD-SFT	TIME 1m03.83s (slw4.1s)

1 Candy Glen 2 9-00 . . . . N Day[10] 33/1
2 **ONE AT A TIME** 2 9-00 . . . . K.Darley[1] 16/1
chased leaders, every chance 2f out, kept on one pace [op 10/1]
3 Broughton Bay 2 9-00 . . . M.Wigham[11] 33/1
DISTANCES 3-¾-¾-2-2-nk-6-1½-¾-1½

Piquant

3		2-9-00
W.HASTINGS-BASS		b/br c 11Mar87 Sharpo
Starts 1st 2nd 3rd Win & Pl		— Asnoura (MOR)
1 — — 1 £306		(Asandre (FR))

1 May Kempton 5f		Mdn2yo £2,322
7 ran	SOFT	TIME 1m04.40s (slw6.0s)

1 Factuelle 2 8-09 . . . . M.Roberts[1] 16/1
2 Absolutely Perfect 2 9-00 . . . . P.Cook[6] 9/2
3 **PIQUANT** 2 9-00 . . . . . W.R.Swinburn[7] 13/2
outpaced over 2f out, rallied final furlong, ran on [op 5/2 tchd 7/1]
DISTANCES nk-3-¾-2-7-20

Probables

(3) ONE AT A TIME – J. Berry 9.0 K. Darley

F.	F.	C.	C.
Prom	(13)	—	C√
★★	★★★		D√
			G?
			BL (1st time)?

(5) PIQUANT – W. Hastings-Bass 9.0 Dean McKeown

F.	F.	C.	C.
Prom	(14)	—	C√
★★	★★★		D√
			G?
			Trainer's record√

This is an example of a 2 y.o. maiden race over 5f. As with all maiden races the selector is backing a horse to do something it has never done before, that is, to win a race. Therefore this is always a venture into the unknown, and shocks can and frequently do occur. These normally come in the shape of a previously unraced horse who upsets the sometimes fragile assumptions of the form upon which selection has been based.

Approaching this maiden race at Hamilton it was thought prudent to examine the two horses making their racecourse débuts. CALL RACECALL was by first-season sire REASONABLE, who had been a precocious 2 y.o., but like the other newcomer PADDY CASH was from a stable not renowned for winning with juvenile débutants. These two were dismissed from calculations and analysis directed to those which had already run. This readily revealed two probables, ONE AT A TIME and PIQUANT.

ONE AT A TIME from the stable of Jack Berry, an expert with fast early season 2-year-olds, already had two runs. The first was a most promising effort at Newmarket where it had finished second, beating a subsequent winner, but had followed this with a rather disappointing display as beaten favourite when lowered in grade at Redcar. This placed a question mark over its abilities, and as the form commentaries on its running read 'no extra' and 'kept on one pace' it might well lack that vital extra acceleration at the close of a race, a factor which inexorably divides winners from losers.

PIQUANT, a horse owned by the Queen and trained by Willie Hastings-Bass at Newmarket, had only one previous race, finishing third. It had been easy to back on its début, drifting in the market, suggesting it had not been trained to win first time out. Yet it had produced its best efforts in the closing stages of the race, i.e. 'rallied final furlong, ran on'. A most encouraging commentary for any horse, but particularly for a juvenile.

On the star ratings of the formula both were equal and it would be imprudent to say which had the better form, and both had proven fitness. Therefore the conditions element of the formula gave the determining factors as to selection choice.

Neither horse seemed likely to be inconvenienced by the course or distance, but the going for each might pose a problem. ONE AT A TIME had shown its better form on good to soft ground and had disappointed on firm going; while PIQUANT's one race had been on soft going and its sire SHARPO was better on testing ground.

ONE AT A TIME was also fitted with blinkers for the first time (a factor giving poor winning statistics) and that almost automatically barred it from consideration. PIQUANT's chances also seemed increased by trainer Hasting-Bass's record at Hamilton for 1985–88, a 27.8 per cent overall strike rate, but with three winners from five runners for his 2-year-olds. This seemed a most salient factor especially as, being from Newmarket, it had seemed worth while to travel no less than 360m to the Scottish track. These two factors balanced the selection decision in PIQUANT's favour.

Result: 1st PIQUANT (9–4) won by 2 lengths.

Form Book No. 2086 *GOODWOOD 25 July 1989 (firm)*

5.20 — EBF NEW HAM MAIDEN FILLIES STAKES (2-Y-O) £7,000 added (£5,208.00) 7f (7)

601	(5)	**CLARE COURT** I Balding 8-11 ....J Matthias	—
602	(2)	64 **MERBAYEH GIRL** 33 K Brassey 8-11 ....N Adams	—
603	(7)	5 **PLATINUM DANCER** 13 P Kelleway 8-11 ......S Cauthen	73
604	(4)	0 **SANDFORD SPRINGS** 28 I Balding 8-11 ...W R Swinburn	—
605	(6)	**SINGING** B Hills 8-11 ....Pat Eddery	—
606	(1)	2 **ZAWAHIR** 11 J Dunlop 8-11 ....W Carson	●78
607	(3)	00 **ZIZANIA** 28 C Brittain 8-11...........................M Roberts	—

Probable SP: 13-8 Zawahir, 3 Singing, 4 Clare Court, 6 Platinum Dancer, 10 Zizania, 12 Merbayeh Girl. **FAVOURITES: 1 2 3 2 1 1 2.**
1988: Babiana 2 8 11 (Pat Eddery) 3-1 B W Hills 8 ran.

GOODWOOD FORM

5.20   £5,208

2yoMdn	7f

Platinum Dancer

5   **2-8-11**
P.A.KELLEWAY   b f 1Feb87 11000gns
                                      Petorius — National
Starts 1st 2nd 3rd Win & Pl	Dress (Welsh Pageant)
1 — — —	£—

12 Jul Nmkt 6f	Mdn2yo £5,436
13 ran	GOOD	TIME 1m12.41s (slw0.3s)

1 Ozone Friendly (USA) 2 8-11 PatEddery[1] 5/2
2 Moon Cactus 2 8-11e[1] ... S.Cauthen[6] 15/8F
3 Line of Thunder (USA) 2 8-11
....R.Cochrane[5] 6/1
5 PLATINUM DANCER 2 8-11
.........................G.Bardwell[2] 33/1
prominent, lost place 3f out, ran green below distance, stayed on final furlong
DISTANCES shd-nk-5-2½-1½

Zawahir (USA)

2   **2-8-11**
J.L.DUNLOP   ch f 11May87 Nureyev
                                      (USA) — Solariat (USA)
Starts 1st 2nd 3rd Win & Pl	(Secretariat (USA))
1 — 1 — £1,230	

14 Jul Newbury 6f	Mdn2yo £4,110
16 ran	GD-FM	TIME 1m14.13s (slw1.6s)

1 Curia Regis (USA) 2 9-00 .... W.Carson[10] 8/1
2 **ZAWAHIR (USA)** 2 8-09 .. PatEddery[9] 8/1
always prominent, led 1f out until inside final furlong, unable to quicken [op 10/1 tchd 12/1]
3 Tirol 2 9-00 ....B.Rouse[15] 9/4F
DISTANCES 2-2-2-hd-1½-2½-¾-1½-nk-1-hd

Singing (USA)

B.W.HILLS   **2-8-11**
b f 22Feb87 The Minstrel (CAN) — Social
Column (USA) (Swoon's Son)

Probables

(3) PLATINUM DANCER – P. Kellaway 2–8.11 S. Cauthen

F.	F.	C. C.
Prom	(13)	— C?
★★	★★★	D√
		G√

(6) ZAWAHIR – J. Dunlop 2–8.11 W. Carson

F.	F.	C. C.
Prom	(11)	— C√
		D√
★★	★★★	G√

NB SINGING – B. Hills 2–8.11 Pat Eddery

This is an example of a 2 y.o. maiden race for fillies over a distance of 7f.

Analysis resolved to two probables, PLATINUM DANCER and ZAWAHIR, the two most recently raced fillies. Both had run within the previous 14 days in maiden races over 6f. PLATINUM DANCER (in what usually turns out to be quite a hot maiden race) at Newmarket, where the winner OZONE FRIENDLY had subsequently franked the form, winning the Group II Prix Robert Papin at Maison Laffitte; while ZAWAHIR had run in good-class maiden company at Newbury against colts, where the third horse and beaten favourite TIROL had been unable to endorse the form, subsequently being defeated in a maiden race at Newmarket. The issue therefore rested on which of those two performances represented the best form. PLATINUM DANCER, beaten at level weights by almost 8 lengths by a subsequent Group II race winner; or ZAWAHIR beaten 2 lengths by a colt CURIA REGIS from Major Hern's powerful yard.

PLATINUM DANCER, an unfancied 33–1 shot on her racecourse début, after taking a prominent position in the early stage of her race, had shown her lack of fitness and forward training by running 'green' at the 'business' end of the race, when the main contenders accelerated. She only started to get her 'racing act' together in the final furlong when the leaders had won.

In contrast, ZAWAHIR had contested throughout to lead a furlong out, until unable to quicken inside the final furlong. This posed the question, was this merely a weaker filly beaten by a stronger colt, or was it yet another instance of the dreaded 'one-paced' syndrome which constantly divides winners from losers. In this case it seemed likely to be the first explanation because in a field of 16 runners, made up of only 2 fillies, ZAWAHIR had 13 colts behind her. Now she was tackling just her own sex there was reason to believe her task would be easier, especially with the benefit of that learning experience on her début and coming from the local stable of John Dunlop whose juveniles invariably improve from their first race. So of the two form probables ZAWAHIR was preferred.

But one question remained: could an unraced horse on its début defeat either or both form candidates? Two of the runners, CLARE COURT and SINGING, were débutants. CLARE COURT was from Ian Balding's stable, which had a poor record for producing first-time 2 y.o. winners, and so she was disregarded. However, SINGING from Barry Hills's stable, demanded closer scrutiny being predicted as a possible favourite in the national racing papers' SP forecast. A well-bred filly who had been entered for later in the season top-class races over 6f, she was surprisingly making her début at 7f, suggesting that she was possibly not forward enough to beat a tough experienced rival. So with Hills's Manton yard also having no particularly strong record in producing first-time juvenile winners SINGING was also passed over.

Applying the formula, both PLATINUM DANCER and ZAWAHIR received a five-star rating for form and fitness. Both were in a similar class of race, and both proven on the going, and likely to be suited by the distance. Although both had raced over long straight courses on their début, this downland course might be more suited to the locally trained ZAWAHIR than to Newmarket-based PLATINUM DANCER.

Almost inseparable by the ratings of the formula, the author chose ZAWAHIR, as trainer John Dunlop's 2-year-olds had the reputation for considerable improvement after their first race.

Result: 1st ZAWAHIR (9–4 jt fav.) won by 2½ lengths.

Form Book No. 160 *HAMILTON 6 April 1989 (heavy)*

4.30 — **DECHMONT MAIDEN STAKES (3YO) £1,800 added (£1,394) 6f (7)**

1	(5)		2 A LITTLE PRECIOUS 10 , N Callaghan 9-0	L Dettori (5)	●78
2	(1)	352260-	FULHAM TRADER 215 (B) J Berry 9-0	J Carroll	72
3	(2)	40	SQUARE DATA DYNAMO 1 M Brittain 9-0	M Wigham	60
4	(4)	00-	TRAVELLING LIGHT 184 Mrs J Ramsden 9-0	Dean McKeown	—
5	(6)	65200-5	KNOWETOP 10 S Muldoon 8-11	J H Brown	60
6	(7)	0-	KOO 202 N Tinkler 8-11	Kim Tinkler	—
7	(3)	26-	PUSSY FOOT 155 Sir Mark Prescott 8-11	G Duffield	77

Probable SP: 7-4 A Little Precious, 9-4 Pussy Foot, 5 Fulham Trader, 7 Square Data Dynamo, 8 Knowetop. **FAVOURITES: 2 2 2 3 1 1 3 .**
1988: Majority Holding 9 0 (P Bloomfield) 5-1 A Bailey 10 ran.

4.30 🏇🏇🏇 3-y-o Maiden 6f (£1,394) 7 runners

-2 A LITTLE PRECIOUS (9-0) (N A Callaghan) b c Precocious - The Silver Darling by John Splendid [7.5f]

March 27, Nottingham, 6f (3-y-o) mdn, good to soft, £1,710.00: 1 Langtry Lady (8-4,7*,10), 2 A LITTLE PRECIOUS (8-9, L Dettori,5*,9), **never far away, driven to nose ahead final furlong, caught last stride,** (20 to 1 op 14 to 1) 3 Spoilt Son (9-0,3),: 13 Ran. Nk, ½sl, 3l, 1l, ½l, 3l, ½l, ½l, nk. 1m 19.00s (a 7.20s). SR: 31/33/31/19/12/10.

Probable

(1) A LITTLE PRECIOUS – N. Callaghan –9.0 L. Dettori (5)

F.	F.	C.	C.
Prom	(10)	—	C√
★★	★★★		D√
			G?

This is an example of a 3 y.o. maiden race over 6f.

Analysis of this compact field of six runners (horse 3 was a non-runner), quickly revealed only one probable, A LITTLE PRECIOUS, beaten only by a very narrow margin on its racecourse début 10 days earlier. This was the obvious current form choice, being superior to the only other rival with the benefit of run in the present season. The issue therefore resolved on whether this form was superior to that of a more experienced rival who had raced as a 2 y.o. yet whose fitness was unproven.

FULHAM TRADER was the obvious danger, having shown commendable form as a juvenile, yet only over 5f. Today's extra furlong might be its undoing, compounded by the heavy going, which places a premium on fitness and a horse seeing out the distance. Also FULHAM TRADER was fitted with blinkers for the first time and the record of Flat race horses sporting the 'blinds' is so poor as to eliminate them from calculations.

The only other runner with any semblance of form as a 2 y.o. was PUSSY FOOT, placed second on her début over 5f on similar going here at Hamilton, only to disappoint on the second and final race of her juvenile season. This disappointing second race placed a question mark over her ability and whether as a 3 y.o. she could produce her initial promise. Fillies at this stage of their second season are at a considerable disadvantage with colts, receiving just 3 lb sex allowance.

Applying the formula, A LITTLE PRECIOUS with proven current form, fitness, competing in similar class and distance, was made the selection choice.

Result: 1st A LITTLE PRECIOUS (Evens fav.) won by 15 lengths.

Form Book No. 1861 *AYR 15 July 1989 (good to firm)*

4.15 — RUSSIAN WINTER TROPHY (HANDICAP) £3,000 (£2,448) 5f (9)

1	(1)	40-6006	**NORTH OF WATFORD 49** (D) J Wilson 4-9-11.P D'Arcy	70
2	(7)	422-	**SPANISH HARLEM 386** W Pearce 3-9-8	D Nicholls	60
3	(4)	004653	**HONOUR'S DEGREE 11** D Chapman 4-9-8	G Starkey	70
4	(6)	052211	†**KABCAST (7lbex)**5(D4)(B) D Chapman 4-9-2	M Hills	●78
5	(8)	000303	**PHILIP 12 (D6)** N Tinkler 7-9-0	Kim Tinkler	76
6	(3)	006-531	†**KING CHARLEMAGNE 12 (D12)** Mrs Reveley 10-8-10		
					— 77
7	(2)	500000-	**SUM MUSIC 277** J Wainwright 4-8-0	L Charnock	—
8	(9)	60-4020	**BUNNYLOCH 9** J Etherington 5-7-7	P Burke (5)	75
9	(5)	000000	**CAPEABILITY POUND 5 (V)(C&D3D)** A Jones 6-7-7		

† Declared to run in the 9.15 Hamilton last night M Fry —

Probable SP: 15-8 King Charlemagne, 3 Kabcast, 4 Philip, 7 Spanish Harlem, Capeability Pound, Honour's Degree. **FAVOURITES: 2 0 2 2 2 1 1.**
1988: Impala Lass 5-9-0 (M Lynch) 2-1 Fav B A McMahon 7 ran.

LAST SIX OUTINGS – LATEST ON RIGHT						4.15 HANDICAP	TODAY	FUTURE
68⁴	72⁰	69⁶	67⁰	67⁷	64⁶	North of Watford	61	
		—	—	—	—	Spanish Harlem	65	
—	65⁸	62⁴	62⁶	60⁵	58³	Honour's Degree	58	
44⁰	40⁵	36²	37²	37¹	44¹	Kabcast	52	−7
56⁰	56⁷	53⁸	50³	51⁸	51³	Philip	50	
54⁹	52⁹	47⁶	45⁵	45³	43¹	King Charlemagne	46	
54⁵	49⁰	49⁰	41⁸	43⁰	44⁰	Sum Music	36	
—	39⁸	—	32⁷	30²	31⁷	Bunnyloch	29	−1
46⁰	39⁸	34⁹	34⁰	30⁹	—	Capeability Pound	29	−4

AYR FORM

4.15 £2,448

Hcap(0-70)3yo +   **5f**

Kabcast ®52

90601701090008-052211   **4-9-02**
D.W.CHAPMAN   b g Kabour — Final Cast (Saulingo)

Starts 1st 2nd 3rd	Win & Pl
29 4 2 1	£10,930

89 **Edin** 5f Am(0-70)Hcp GOOD ...... ®44 £2,167
89 **Cttck** 5f (0-70)Hcp FIRM .... ®37 £2,383
88 **Bevly** 5f 3yo(0-75)Hcp GOOD .... ®48 £3,111
88 **Pfrct** 5f 3yo(0-75)Hcp GD-SFT ... ®47 £1,803
TOTAL:£9,464

● **Engaged 9.15 Hamtn yesterday**

10 Jul Edinburgh 5f	Am(0-70)Hcp £2,167
10 ran	GOOD	TIME 1m01.30s (slw3.1s)

1 **KABCAST** 4 10-08b½ 7 . MissE.Bronson⁵ 6/4F
made all, clear 2f out, ran on final furlong   [op 7/4 tchd 11/8]
2 Supreme Optimist 5 10-06b   MrsC.Peacock
       (5)⁸ 10/1
3 Mummy's Chance 5 10-06b
.... MrsJ.Goulding² 10/1
DISTANCES 4-1½-¾-2½-1½-1½-½-1½-1

6 Jul Catterick 5f	(0-70)Hcp £2,383
11 ran	FIRM	TIME 0m57.1s (fst1.8s)

1 **KABCAST** 4 8-07b .. DeanMcKeown² 3/1F
made all, soon clear, pushed out   [op 7/2]
2 Lady's Mantle (USA) 5 8-07 .. K.Fallon³ 6/1

3 Ridgiduct 5 8-13 .... N.Carlisle⁸ 25/1
7 **BUNNYLOCH** 5 8-01 ...... J.Lowe¹ 11/2
chased leaders, soon driven along, no chance
from halfway   [op 9/2 tchd 6/1 in places]
DISTANCES 2½-nk-1½-1½-nk-½-1½-1-3-5

3 Jul Edinburgh 5f	(0-70)Hcp £2,363
second, see KING CHARLEMAGNE

King Charlemagne ®46

140634259/79000996-531   **10-8-10**
MRS.G.R.REVELEY   gr g Habat — Calibina (Caliban)

Starts 1st 2nd 3rd	Win & Pl
76 13 10 6	£32,673

89 **Edin** 5f (0-70)Hcp GOOD .... ®43 £2,363
87 **Edin** 5f App(0-75)Hcp GD-FM .... ®70 £865
85 **Reder** 5f (0-50)Hcp GD-FM ...... ®84 £3,015
85 **Edin** 5f (0-50)Hcp GOOD .... ®77 £2,708
84 **Hdock** 5f (0-60)Hcp FIRM £3,501
84 **Donc** 5f 140y (0-50)Hcp GOOD £2,683
84 **Hamtn** 5f (0-35)Hcp FIRM £1,428
84 **Edin** 5f (0-50)Hcp FIRM £833
84 **York** 5f App(0-50)Hcp GD-FM £2,435
83 **Edin** 5f (0-35)Hcp GOOD £918
83 **Hamtn** 5f (0-35)Hcp FIRM £1,247
83 **Bevly** 5f (0-35)Hcp HARD £1,090
83 **Edin** 5f AmHcp FIRM £713
TOTAL: £23,799

● **Engaged 9.15 Hamtn yesterday**

3 Jul Edinburgh 5f	(0-70)Hcp £2,363
12 ran	GOOD	TIME 0m59.4s (slw1.2s)

1 **KING CHARLEMAGNE** 10 8-02 J.Lowe⁹ 4/1
chased leaders, ridden to lead well inside final
furlong   [tchd 9/2 and 7/2 in places]
2 **KABCAST** 4 7-03b .... J.Tate (7)¹² 6/1
led, soon clear, ridden over 1f out, headed well
inside final furlong, kept on   [op 5/1]
3 **PHILIP** 7 8-10 .... KimTinkler² 8/1
behind until headway over 1f out, ran on
well   [tchd 10/1 in places]
DISTANCES nk-1½-hd-hd-3-1-2½-1-hd-2½-6

Probable

(4) KABCAST – D. Chapman 4–9.2 M. Hills

F.	F.	C.	C.
Proven	(1)	—	C√
★★★	★★★		D√
			G√
			BL√
			7 lb pen√

This is an example of a 5f handicap for 3-year-olds and upwards rated 0–70.

It is an example of using the official handicapper's rating of a horse to pin-point the winner. In this instance there emerges a horse in top form which has suddenly made such dramatic improvement that it remains ahead of the handicapper's assessment.

However, using the elimination technique we start at the top of the handicap with NORTH OF WATFORD, a horse not placed in its past six races. Although now lowered in class it appears to need a still lower rating by the handicapper to be given a winning chance.

Next in the weights is SPANISH HARLEM, a 3 y.o. maiden making its début in a handicap on its seasonal reappearance. The handicapper had certainly taken no chances with this horse's rating and it would be a big surprise if it were able to recapture its best 2 y.o. form after over a year's absence.

HONOURS DEGREE is a 4 y.o. maiden after eight races and only once in the frame, being placed third in its previous race. The horse may at last be ready to fulfil its potential but it seems still strongly in the handicapper's clutches, and may need a further lowering in the ratings before it can win a race.

With the fourth horse we reach KABCAST, at the peak of its form, and attempting a third victory in the past 5 days and a fourth consecutive win. KABCAST was twice a winner as a 3 y.o. without wearing blinkers and yet finished its season with the 'blinds' fitted unsuccessfully in three races. Its fortunes had however been transformed with their reintroduction in the current campaign. Although the handicapper had raised its rating, from 37 after its first victory, now to 52 (including a 7 lb penalty for a victory since its last assessment) this still appeared to be an inadequate assessment of its true ability, for only the evening before at Hamilton it had won easily by 6 lengths. In the words of the form commentary 'made all, quickened clear halfway, eased final furlong' – a very comprehensive victory. Yet the handicapper was unable to assess this performance and revise the rating, which was based on the 6 July race, and KABCAST received only a 7 lb penalty for two easy successes since.

Form assessment under the handicap selection method stopped with KABCAST. Applying the formula KABCAST, with a six-star rating for form and fitness, racing in similar class as before, over the same distance and going, and wearing blinkers, was made the choice.

Result: 1st KABCAST (Evens fav.) won by 2½ lengths.

Form Book No. 337 *ASCOT 22 April 1989 (good to soft)*

3.40 — INSULPAK VICTORIA CUP
(Handicap) £20,000 added (£17,090.00)
7f (25)

401 (24)	2130-21 **OTTERGAYLE 7 (D)** P Walwyn 4-9-10	N Howe
402 (6)	001040- **GOVERNORSHIP 247 (C) (B)** C Nelson 5-9-8	P Cook
403 (18)	301010- **GOLD PROSPECT 182 (C&DD2)** G Balding 7-9-6	S Cauthen
404 (13)	20002-2 **GOLDEN ANCONA 10** M H Easterby 6-9-3	J Bleasdale
405 (15)	022000- **BARCLAY STREET 210 (D2)** I Matthews 6-9-2	B Rouse
406 (23)	31511-0 **TOP DREAM 21 (D)** M Jarvis 4-9-1	W R Swinburn
407 (20)	2101/5- **VAGUE DISCRETION 385 (D)** R Williams 4-9-1	T Ives
408 (16)	0015-62 **SILVER HAZE 8 (D4BF)** Miss S Hall 5-9-0	A Culhane (3)
409 (7)	15030-2 **PENULTIMATION 19 (DBF)** G Harwood 4-8-12	G Starkey
410 (25)	40140-0 **FAG IN HAND 21 (D)** W Haggas 4-8-9	M Hills
411 (2)	5530-10 **PINCTADA 21 (D10)** R Simpson 7-8-8	N Gwilliams (7)
412 (14)	.03100- **SEE NOW 311 (D)** J Shaw 4-8-7	R Cochrane
413 (8)	360131- B LDOMERO 252 (D2) (B) W Jarvis 4-8-6	T Quinn
414 (12)	006420- **BERTIE WOOSTER 182 (C)** R Holder 6-8-5	— —
415 (4)	31000-6 **HIGHEST PRAISE 14 (D4)** I Balding 5-9-0	M Marshall (5)
416 (17)	0000-00 **SHARP ROMANCE 7** J Hudson 7-8-5	DOUBTFUL
417 (10)	24100-3 **WINKING WINNER 28** N Callaghan 4-8-3	L Dettori (5)
418 (19)	5/0000-0 **RUMBOOGIE 7** C Austin 5-8-2	M Fry
419 (5)	0350-02 **VICEROY JESTER 14** R Holder 4-7-13	M L Thomas
420 (3)	30010-0 **FOOLISH TOUCH 15** W Musson 7-7-11	E Johnson
421 (22)	046/34-0 **COMPLEAT 14** R Akehurst 6-7-11	T Williams
422 (21)	411103- **TAKENHALL 218** M Fetherston-Godley 4-7-10	R Fox
423 (9)	3205-11 **NORTHERN COMMANDER 10 (D)** J Berry 3-7-7	J Carroll
424 (11)	00001-0 **SERGEANT MERYLL 14 (D3)** P Howling 5-7-7	N Adams
425 (1)	3000-50 **FABLED ORATOR 14** R Hannon 4-7-7	Dana Mellor (5)

Probable SP: 4 Ottergayle, 9-2 Silver Haze, 13-2 See Now, 8 Golden Ancona, 10 Gold Prospect, 12 Highest Praise, Northern Commander, 14 Pinctada, Penultimation, Viceroy Jester, 16 Fag In Hand.
FAVOURITES: — — 0 2 2 0 2
1988: Wing Park 4 9 1 (Pat Eddery) 7-1 A Bailey 16 ran.

ASCOT RATINGS

HANDICAPS: The figures on the left are the official handicap marks the horse ran off on its last six outings, adjusted for penalties, overweight and long handicap. The superior figure shows the finishing position. A dash shows the race was not a handicap.
The TODAY figure is the Jockey Club rating for today, adjusted for penalties and long handicap. Its significance is in the comparison with past and future marks.
The FUTURE figure highlights horses on a higher (+) or lower (−) mark for future handicaps. Look for plus figures, which show horses well-treated today, and be wary of horses with minus figures, other than those caused by penalties.

LAST SIX OUTINGS – LATEST ON RIGHT						**3.40 HANDICAP**	TODAY	FUTURE
—	—	—	87[8]	86[2]	91[1]	Ottergayle	99	
94[0]	—	93[1]	100[9]	99[4]	99[0]	Governorship	97	
—	95[0]	95[1]	102[7]	99[9]	98[0]	Gold Prospect	95	
91[2]	98[7]	91[0]	91[7]	89[2]	90[2]	Golden Ancona	92	
—	95[2]	93[2]	96[7]	96[8]	96[0]	Barclay Street (USA)	91	
77[3]	77[1]	81[5]	80[1]	83[1]	90[0]	Top Dream	90	
—	—	—	—	—	—	Vague Discretion	90	
88[7]	88[0]	85[1]	85[5]	87[6]	87[2]	Silver Haze	89	
—	92[5]	92[0]	89[3]	89[9]	—	Penultimation	87	
88[4]	89[0]	—	90[4]	89[0]	85[8]	Fag In Hand	84	
79[5]	79[5]	79[3]	79[0]	78[1]	85[0]	Pinctada	83	
—	—	—	—	100[0]	—	See Now	82	
—	—	78[9]	—	75[3]	75[1]	Baldomero	81	
80[0]	80[7]	80[6]	80[4]	78[2]	78[9]	Bertie Wooster	80	
82[3]	81[1]	87[0]	84[7]	84[0]	81[8]	Highest Praise (USA)	80	
—	—	—	90[0]	86[0]	84[0]	Sharp Romance (USA)	80	
74[2]	74[4]	74[1]	78[8]	80[7]	78[3]	Winking Winner	78	
—	—	99[9]	95[9]	95[0]	83[0]	Rumboogie	77	
76[9]	72[3]	72[5]	74[9]	71[2]	73[2]	Viceroy Jester	74	
72[3]	70[7]	73[0]	72[1]	75[0]	75[0]	Foolish Touch	72	

82[0]	80[4]	80[6]	75[3]	75[4]	73[8]	**Compleat**	72	
–	56[1]	63[1]	60[1]	78[0]	71[3]	**Takenhall**	71	
–	–	–	–	–	–	**Northern Commander**	83	
69[7]	69[0]	67[9]	65[0]	62[1]	67[0]	**Sergeant Meryll**	68	–2
70[3]	70[9]	70[0]	70[0]	68[5]	67[0]	**Fabled Orator**	68	–4

Ottergayle ®99

232615/025632138-21   **4-9-10**
P.T.WALWYN   br c Lord Gayle (USA)
                                       — Otterhill (Brigadier
| Starts | 1st | 2nd | 3rd | Win & Pl | Gerard) |
| 17 | 3 | 5 | 3 | £34,332 | |

89 Nbury 1m (0-110)Hcp GD-SFT .... ®91 £7,876
88 Donc 7f Ladies GOOD £4,500
87 Lingf 6f 2yo HEAVY £1,724
                              TOTAL:£14,100

| 15 Apr Newbury 1m | (0-110)Hcp £7,876 |
| 21 ran | GD-SFT | TIME 1m42.18s (slw4.8s) |

1 OTTERGAYLE 4 8-11 ... PatEddery[5] 9/2F
  headway over 3f out, ridden over 2f out, led inside final furlong, comfortably [op 5/1 tchd 6/1 and
  4/1]
2 Beau Sher 6 10-00 ..... B.Raymond[3] 10/1
3 Joveworth 6 8-02 ..... G.Baxter[17] 20/1
0 SHARP ROMANCE (USA) 7 8-04[2]1
  .... P.Cook[21] 33/1
  always behind   {tchd 40/1}
0 RUMBOOGIE 5 8-03[2]1 ..... B.Rouse[14] 50/1
  tailed off
DISTANCES 3-¾-1½-hd-2-nk-4-shd-1-nk-¾-
nk-½

| 1 Apr Doncaster 1m | Hcp £49,453 |
| 25 ran | GOOD | TIME 1m37.48s (fst0.6s) |

1 Fact Finder 5 7-09 ...... T.Williams[8] 20/1
2 OTTERGAYLE 4 8-00 ..... N.Howe[25] 25/1
  outpaced and behind, headway under pressure
  stands side 3f out, ran on very well final furlong,
  just failed   [op 20/1 tchd 28/1 in places]
3 Eradicate 4 8-09 .... T.Ives[9] 11/1
6 SILVER HAZE 5 8-01 ..... W.Carson[7] 7/1
  tracked leaders far side, challenged 2f out, unable to quicken final furlong   [tchd 8/1]
8 FAG IN HAND 4 7-10[2]1 A.Shoults[(3)11] 33/1
  chased leaders far side, not quicken final 2f
13 PINCTADA 7 7-06[2]7 N.Gwilliams[(7)20] 16/1
  behind stands side, effort over 3f out, no
  impression   [op 14/1]

14 TOP DREAM 4 8-01 ..... J.Quinn[(3)2] 20/1
  headway far side, prominent 3f out, weakened
  over 1f out   [op 16/1]
DISTANCES nk-½-1½-nk-shd-hd-1-shd-hd-½-
hd-½-nk-1½-½

| 13 Oct[88] Nmkt 7f | (0-110)Hcp £7,387 |
| eighth, see PINCTADA | |

Top Dream ®90

36903/231511-0   **4-9-01**
M.A.JARVIS   br c High Top —
                                       Pleasant Dream
| Starts | 1st | 2nd | 3rd | Win & Pl | (Sharpen Up) |
| 12 | 3 | 1 | 3 | £14,376 | |

88 Lingf 7f 140y (0-100)Hcp GOOD ... ®83 £4,162
88 Warwk 7f 3yo(0-90)Hcp GD-FM ... ®80 £3,095
88 Lingf 7f 140y 3yo(0-90)Hcp GOOD ®77 £3,517
                              TOTAL:£10,774

| 1 Apr Doncaster 1m | Hcp £49,453 |
| fourteenth, see OTTERGAYLE | |

| 8 Jul[88] Lingfield Park 7f 140y | (0-100)Hcp £4,162 |
| 10 ran | GOOD | TIME 1m30.56s (slw2.3s) |

1 TOP DREAM 3 8-06 .... B.Raymond[3] 2/1F
  field up, led inside final furlong, led last stride [op
  9/4 tchd 11/4 in places]
2 Father Time 4 8-07b .... P.Robinson[6] 12/1
3 Aitch N'Bee 5 7-13 .... M.Marshall[(7)2 5/1]
DISTANCES shd-5-1½-½-2½

| 18 Jun[88] Warwick 7f | 3yo(0-90)Hcp £3,095 |
| 15 ran | GD-FM | TIME 1m26.5s (slw1.6s) |

1 TOP DREAM 3 9-03 ..... B.Raymond[4] 3/1F
  chased leaders, 5th straight, led inside final furlong, hard ridden, held on   [op 7/2 tchd 5/1]
2 Spanish Heart 3 7-13 ..... S.Dawson[3] 4/1
3 Ballad Dancer 3 9-07 ..... J.Williams[8] 20/1
DISTANCES nk-1½-½-hd-2½-1-1½-1½

This is a second example of the elimination approach applied to handicaps and shows how the skilful selector can employ the ratings of the
official handicapper to considerable advantage. Beginning at the top of
the handicap the selector examines the credentials of each horse in the
light of the demands of the race, and stops when he considers these
demands are fulfilled. Whether this be with the first horse at the head of
the handicap or with a horse further down in the weights, analysis can
stop immediately because all the horses below have been rated inferior
by the handicapper.

The highly competitive Insulpak Victoria Cup, a 7f handicap rated 0–115 over Ascot's straight Royal Hunt Cup course, may seem rather a daunting challenge, yet demonstrates how the method can be successfully applied even to a tough handicap.

The top weight in this 23-runner field is OTTERGAYLE, a narrowly beaten second in Flat racing's first important race of the season 'The Lincoln' run at Doncaster 21 days earlier. OTTERGAYLE subsequently gained compensation for that defeat, winning Newbury's mile Spring Cup, just 7 days earlier, demonstrating its current fine form. However, now set to carry 9 st 10 lb, it would be attempting to carry the highest winning weight in the past 15 seasons (except for 9 st 13 lb carried by COLUMNIST in 1981).

The new five-day entry system introduced in 1989 for Flat racing meant that the official handicapper has had the opportunity to reassess OTTERGAYLE's most recent performance, and has raised it 8 lb in the handicap, which will almost certainly negate its chances. Coupled with this, the recent record of horses (especially favourites, as OTTERGAYLE was) after a good performance in Newbury's Spring Cup has been so dismal as to disqualify them from consideration in the Victoria Cup. OTTERGAYLE was therefore eliminated.

GOVERNORSHIP, the second top weight in the handicap, was a 5 y.o. carrying 9 st 8 lb. A winner of last season's Royal Hunt Cup, on the same course but over a furlong further, GOVERNORSHIP was today making its seasonal reappearance. With the record of such débutants being quite poor, this deemed its elimination.

GOLD PROSPECT, the third weight from the top, carrying 9 st 6 lb, was an inmate of Toby Balding's currently in-form, all-conquering stable. GOLD PROSPECT thus demanded respect but was also making its seasonal début. Not having won its opening race in any season for 2 years it seemed unlikely to do so now, especially as a 7 y.o.. Furthermore, no horse older than a 5 y.o. had won this race for 14 seasons, so GOLD PROSPECT was also eliminated.

GOLDEN ANCONA, the fourth in weight, was a 6 y.o. carrying 9 st 3 lb and a confirmed 6f sprinter who had never won over a longer distance. GOLDEN ANCONA was beaten in last season's Victoria Cup carrying 8 st 3 lb and seemed hardly likely to have improved 14 lb as a 6 y.o. It was therefore dismissed from consideration.

BARCLAY STREET was the fifth in the weights, also a 6 y.o. set to carry 9 st 2 lb, 5 lb less than when third in the race last season. The handicapper certainly seemed to have given BARCLAY STREET a good chance on its best form. However, although a consistent performer, BARCLAY STREET had not won since the 1986 season and had never won a handicap. These two factors plus the fact that it was also making its seasonal début lead to it being eliminated from consideration.

TOP DREAM, the next horse in the handicap, was a 4 y.o. carrying 9 st 1 lb. It won three of its six races last season including its final one, when it received an injury which unfortunately meant its season ended in early July. TOP DREAM was one runner ideally suited by Ascot's 7f course, having gained its three victories at this distance or over an extended 7f. Strictly on the Form Book, TOP DREAM in its seasonal reappearance in 'The Lincoln' was held by some other runners also in today's race. However, that was over a distance of 1m, and TOP DREAM had been in contention until beaten at the furlong marker. It therefore seemed that the extra distance, possibly combined with a lengthy absence after injury, was responsible for this defeat, and a better showing might be expected over this specialist 7f trip. TOP DREAM seemed to have the important credentials necessary for a horse to win the Victoria Cup. Namely, a horse coming into form rather than one which had already peaked at this early stage in the season, a horse exposed in the handicap to show its abilities, and one suited to this in-between distance of 7f which is neither a sprint nor a real stamina test.

Analysis stopped here and TOP DREAM was made the probable.

Probable

(6) TOP DREAM – M. Jarvis 4–9.1 W. Swinburn

F.	F.	C.	C.
Proven (21)		—	C√
★★	★★		D√
			G√
			Draw√

TOP DREAM had five-star rating of proven form, and 21-day fitness. In similar class, it was likely to be suited by the course, having won over a straight course twice. Proven at the distance and on the going, and drawn not unfavourably (winners in the Victoria Cup come from high or low in the draw but not the middle), it received the formula's seal of approval and became the selection choice.

Result: 1st TOP DREAM (14–1) won by 2 lengths.

Form Book No. 1749 *NEWMARKET 12 July 1989 (good)*

5.15 — REG DAY MEMORIAL TROPHY
H'CAP £10,000 (£6,985) 2m 24yds (7)

1	(3)	311-124	**NOMADIC WAY 20 (B)(D)** B Hills 4-10-0	M Hills	75
2	(1)	1-2P5	**WINNING GALLERY 11** N Callaghan 4-8-11		
				Pat Eddery ●78
3	(5)	010-514	**THE FRESHES 37 (BF)** W Jarvis 4-8-8	M Roberts	77
4	(6)	0-22	**YAMASHITA 12** Mrs N Macauley 4-8-3	N Day	75
5	(7)	316-53	**UPTON PARK 32 (D)** J Watts 4-8-1	W Carson	71
6	(2)	000126	**SWEET ENOUGH 22 (D)** C Brittain 4-7-10	G Bardwell	71
7	(4)	212405-	**CAIRNCASTLE 250 (D)** R Williams 4-7-9	D Biggs (7)	60

Probable SP: 5-2 Winning Gallery, 3 Upton Park, 5 The Freshes, 6 Sweet Enough, 13-2 Nomadic Way, 9 Cairncastle. **FAVOURITES: 0031333.**
1988: Sudden Victory 4 9 10 (M Hills) 9-2 B Hills 4 ran.

ST SIX OUTINGS – LATEST ON RIGHT						**5.15 HANDICAP**	TODAY	FUTURE	POSTMARK
80³	81¹	91¹	90¹	94²	–	Nomadic Way (USA) 103			F109
		–	88²	91⁰	88⁵	Winning Gallery 86			111◄
89⁷	–	88⁰	85⁵	82¹	85⁴	The Freshes 83			110
			–	–	–	Yamashita (USA) 78			·
			–	78⁵	75³	Upton Park 76			106
70⁷	70⁰	67⁸	65¹	72²	72⁶	Sweet Enough 71			F106
–	–	–	75⁴	75⁹	75⁵	Cairncastle 70			107

NEWMARKET FORM

5.15 £6,985

Hcap(0-110)4yo +   2m24y

Winning Gallery ®86

1-2P5   **4-8-11**
N.A.CALLAGHAN   b c Giacometti —
                                                  Balnespick
Starts 1st 2nd 3rd	Win & Pl	**(Charlottown)**
4	1 1 —	£5,333

88 Nmkt 1m6f Mdn3yo GD-FM £4,013

1 Jul Newcastle 2m		Hcp £43,798
12 ran	GD-FM	TIME 3m29.68s.(slw3.9s)

1 Orpheus (USA) 3 7-07 .... R.Fox³ 4/1J
2 Ala Hounak 5 9-02‡8 .... W.Newnes² 11/2
3 Misrule 7 7-07 .... J.Carter¹⁰ 20/1
5 WINNING GALLERY 4 8-01 ..... A.Munro
                                                    (5)⁸ 15/2
*chased leaders, 4th straight, kept on same pace
final 2f* [op 7/1 tchd 8/1]
DISTANCES 3-nk-¾-1½-nk-5-8-¾-7

24 Jun Ascot 2m		(0-110)Hcp £9,240
9 ran	FIRM	TIME 3m25.02s (fst1.2s)

1 Thethingaboutitis (USA) 4 8-11
 .... PaulEddery⁸ 7/2
2 Nebulatis (USA) 3 7-10 .. W.Carson⁶ 10/3F
3 Raahin (USA) 4 8-01 ..... T.Williams³ 9/2
P WINNING GALLERY 4 9-10 PatEddery⁷ 7/2
*whipped round start, tailed off until pulled after
2f* [op 9/4]
DISTANCES 2-2-2½-6-nk-2

14 Jun Newbury 1m5f60y		(0-90)Hcp £4,425
8 ran	GD-FM	TIME 2m53.18s (slw4.4s)

1 Nashid 4 10-00 ....M.Roberts³ 6/5F
2 WINNING GALLERY 4 10-00
 .... PatEddery⁷ 11/2
*2nd straight, led over 3f out until inside final
furlong, hard ridden, ran on well* [op 9/2 tchd 6/1]
3 Beau Ideal 4 9-06 .... W.R.Swinburn⁶ 12/1
DISTANCES hd-8-2-2-½-¾-1½

Probable

(2) WINNING GALLERY – N. Callaghan 4–8.11 Pat Eddery

F.	F.	C.	C.
Proven	(11)	—	C√
★★	★★★		D?
			G√

This is an example of a handicap for 4-year-olds and upwards rated 0–110 over a distance of 2m 24yds, and as before in handicaps, the recommended approach is to use the ratings of the official handicapper to pin-point the winner.

Starting at the head of the handicap NOMADIC WAY was the first horse under scrutiny. Last time out this tough proven stayer had finished

226

fourth in the Group I Ascot Gold Cup over 2½m. So impressed was the handicapper by that performance that NOMADIC WAY was raised 9 lb from its previous rating, so now it was rated at 103 and set to carry 10 st in today's race. Previously its best winning performance had been when rated 91. This season it had won first time, when fit from a hurdling campaign, off a rating of 90. It had then been beaten off a rating of 94. Now it was asked to win off a rating of 103, an impossible task unless it had dramatically improved, which is most unlikely in 4 y.o. stayers.

A good performance in a group race often results in over-reaction by the official handicapper and this seemed to have been NOMADIC WAY's unfortunate fate, and it was therefore eliminated. The second from the top of the weights was WINNING GALLERY, a very lightly raced horse due to training problems. It had won its only race as a 3 y.o. when making its racecourse début but since then had only three other races. Rated 88 by the handicapper, WINNING GALLERY had put up a tremendous performance on its reappearance as a 4 y.o., (over a year after its only other race). At Newbury in a 0.90 Handicap over 1m 5f 60yds, carrying 10 st and at level weights it had been beaten by only a head with the third horse (receiving 8 lb) 8 lengths behind. This form was endorsed when that third horse won its next race. This resulted in WINNING GALLERY's rating being increased 3 lb by the handicapper when on its next race a strange incident occurred; in a race started by flag the horse jinxed, got left behind by the rest of the field, and was eventually pulled up.

Its last race was in the Northumberland where it was fifth, beaten approximately 5½ lengths by the well-handicapped 3 y.o. ORPHEUS. However, the handicapper had relented after that performance and lowered WINNING GALLERY's rating by 2 lb to 86. Having only been narrowly beaten off 88 on its seasonal reappearance this certainly appeared to give a winning opportunity.

Analysis stopped here and WINNING GALLERY was made the probable and subjected to the scrutiny of the selection formula. It merited a six-star marking for its form and proven fitness, and was running in similar class, proven over the course and on the going. Although yet unproven by winning over 2m, none the less the form commentary 'kept on same pace final 2 furlongs' in its last race, indicated that stamina was not likely to be a problem.

WINNING GALLERY was made the selection choice.

Result: 1st WINNING GALLERY (10–3) won by 2 lengths.

NATIONAL HUNT SEASON 1988–89

Form Book No. 2174 *TAUNTON 16 February 1989 (good)*

1.45 — FLAIRPARK JUVENILE NOVICES' HURDLE (4-Y-O) (Div I) £1,200 added (£1,044) 2m 1f (11) [Formcast]

1	1	DOMINION TREASURE 2 (D)	J Baker 11-10	W Irvine (4)	●78
2	0	ARCTICFLOW 91	N Thomson 11-0	D Tegg	—
3	0P1403	CLASSICAL QUARTET 2	C Popham 11-0	M Jones (7)	75
4	00P0	HAWORTH 15	D R Tucker 11-0	N Coleman	—
5	00002	JADE STAR 10	A Leighton 11-0	C Llewellyn	—
6	0	LORD LAMMAS 15	D Elsworth 11-0	B Powell	—
7	P05346	SHELLY'S FOLLY 12	Mrs G Jones 11-0	C Mowen (7)	66
8	5P0	TOAD ALONG 20	L Cottrell 11-0	R Millman	67
9	00002	ANHAAR 23	G Yardley 10-9	W McFarland (7)	63
10		COBUSINO	J Roberts 10-9	DOUBTFUL	
11	F0	LA GRACIOSA 7	G Balding 10-9	J Frost	—

Probable SP: 6-4 Dominion Treasure, 3 Classical Quartet, 9-2 Jade Star, 6 Lord Lammas, 8 Shelly's Folly, 10 Anhaar, 12 Haworth. **FAVOURITES: — — — — — 0.**
1988: Fairthorne Lad 4-11-0 (M Perrett) 33-1 M Madgwick 11 ran.

1.45 Novice Hurdle 2m 1f £1,044 11 runners

-1 DOMINION TREASURE (11-10) (J H Baker) b or br c Dominion - Chrysicabana by Home Guard (USA) **1988-89, 2m 150yds h soft** (Newton Abbot). £1,072.00 (£1,072.00).

Feb 14, Newton Abbot, 2m 150yds (4-y-o) nov hdle, soft, £1,072.00: 1 DOMINION TREASURE (10-6, W Irvine,4*), **behind, headway fifth, staying on when leader blundered last, led run-in, driven out.** (25 to 1 op 14 to 1 tchd 33 to 1) 2 Torkabar (USA) (10-8, inc 5lb ow,7*), 3 CLASSICAL QUARTET (10-10, B Powell), **always chasing leaders, one pace from sixth.** (12 to 1 op 10 to 1 tchd 25 to 1); 13 Ran. 6l, 15l, 1½l, 10l, 1l, sht-hd, 3l, 10l. 4m 23.30s (a 27.30s). SR: 26/20/5/13/-/-.

-0 LORD LAMMAS (11-0) (D R C Elsworth) gr c Tap On Wood - Seriema by Petingo

Feb 1, Windsor, 2m 30yds nov hdle, good, £1,068.00: 1 Nice Dynasty (Fr) (5-11-10), 2 Teenage Scribbler (4-11-0), 3 Devil's Valley (6-11-3), 7 LORD LAMMAS (4-10-7, B Powell), **prominent to halfway.** (12 to 1 op 10 to 1 tchd 14 to 1); 21 Ran. 10l, 3l, 5l, hd, 2l, 2½l, hd, 7l. 4m 2.40s (a 15.40s).

LATEST FLAT FORM
Official ratings in brackets

ARCTICFLOW (USA) (85)

Oct 12 1988, Haydock, 2m h'cap (0-100), soft, £4,807.20: 1 Enemy Action (3-8-9,7), 2 Path's Sister (7-7-13,bl,10), 3 Panienka (Pol) (4-9-1,4), 10 ARCTICFLOW (USA) (3-9-6, G Starkey,9),**fifth into straight, soon beaten, tailed off.** (9 to 1 op 7 to 1 tchd 10 to 1); 11 Ran. Sht-hd, 12l, 2l, 1l, 8l, 8l, 20l, 2½l, sht-hd, 15l. 3m 49.34s (a 22.54s). SR: 46/35/39/15/24/17.
4-YEAR RECORD
6Rn 0w 4p

DOMINION TREASURE (64)
Wins : 1987, 6f good (Goodwood). £1,030.40 (-).

Sept 16 1988, Ayr, 1¼m (3-y-o) h'cap (0-100), good to soft, £5,173.80: 1 Own Free Will (7-9,9), 2 Queens Tour (7-7,5*,13), 3 Whipp's Cross (8-1, inc 1lb ow,11), 13 DOMINION TREASURE (7-6, inc 3lb ow, J Quinn,5*,4),**outpaced halfway, soon behind.** (33 to 1); 16 Ran. 2½l, 1l, 5l, 3l, ½l, 1½l, 1l, nk, ¾l. 2m 10.90s (a 5.90s).(After a stewards' inquiry, the placings remained unaltered.) SR: 47/45/46/41/40/33.
4-YEAR RECORD
8Rn 1w 1p

LORD LAMMAS (58)

Sept 19 1988, Leicester, 1½m (3-y-o) h'cap (0-75), good to firm, £2,827.50: 1 Proud Patriot (7-9,13), 2 Tikrara (USA) (9-9,19), 3 Ann Du Feu (7-7, inc 4lb ow,7*,16), 5 LORD LAMMAS (8-4, M Roberts,bl,11),**closed on leaders three out, every chance approaching final furlong, no extra.** (15 to 2 op 7 to 1 tchd 8 to 1); 21 Ran. Nk, ¾l, 1½l, nk, 6l, 2½l, sht-hd, 2l, 4l, dd-ht. 2m 30.10s (b 0.40s). SR: 31/58/29/42/33/29.
4-YEAR RECORD
8Rn 0w 1p

Probables

(1) DOMINION TREASURE – J. H. Baker   –11.0 W. Irvine (4)

F.	F.	C.	C.
Proven	(2)	—	C√
★★★	★★★		D√
			G?
			10 lb pen?

(6) LORD LAMMAS – D. Elsworth   –11.0 B. Powell

F.	F.	C.	C.
Prom	(15)	—	C?
★★	★★		D√
			G√
			Trainer's course record

This is an example of a juvenile novice hurdle although for 4-year-olds over 2m 1f. It was for first-season or juvenile novice hurdlers and therefore each horse will still be relatively inexperienced at the National Hunt game. There is thus little form to go on and so analysis resolved to immediate issues.

Only two horses in the field had previously won a hurdle race; DOMINION TREASURE a winner of its only race and début in the winter sport where it had comprehensively defeated the other previous winner CLASSICAL QUARTET (who had in any case only won a seller). While DOMINION TREASURE was an obvious probable CLASSICAL QUARTET, beaten by 21 lengths, could be disregarded.

Of the remainder all, with the exception of LORD LAMMAS, had shown themselves to be lacking ability. LORD LAMMAS, a maiden Flat race horse, had made an encouraging début in its only National Hunt race, but would need to improve.

Where there is so little evidence on which to assess a horse's ability it is often necessary to consider Flat race form.

DOMINION TREASURE (rated 64) was considered 6 lb superior to LORD LAMMAS (rated 58). While ARCTICFLOW, a fairly expensive acquisition from G. Harwood's Flat stable, was rated 85, and 21 lb superior on the Flat, yet was still a maiden. On the Flat it had campaigned at around 2m and might need a further distance than this over hurdles. Its début in a National Hunt race 91 days earlier had not been very encouraging and it could not be considered on that form.

Applying the formula, DOMINION TREASURE, with the six-star rating of best proven National Hunt form and fitness, was made the selection choice. The factors against DOMINION TREASURE were its unproven ability to a 10 lb penalty, and to handle the going.

Result: 1st DOMINION TREASURE (5–2) won by 2 lengths.

229

Form Book No. 1286 *AYR 16 December 1988 (good to soft)*

2.30 — GATEHEAD NOVICES' HURDLE £1,000 added (£895) 2m 4f (10)

1	F12	KING'S HARVEST 15 (D)	G Moore 5-11-4	L Wyer	70
2	2-1	REGARDLESS 15	J Blundell 6-11-4	M Brennan	70
3	2-12332	THIRD IN LINE 14 (DBF)	J FitzGerald 5-11-4	M Dwyer	●78
4	F5	BALLYDALY EXPRESS 23	G Richards 5-10-12	N Doughty	—
5	'0	CANEY RIVER 11	J S Wilson 5-10-12	J J Quinn	—
6	52	LEON 7	N Tinkler 6-10-12	G McCourt	77
7	5	RIEN NE VA PLUS 3S	R Fisher 5-10-12	R Beggan	54
8	0050-0	SCANDALOUS RUMOUR 18	Miss M Milligan 5-10-12	B Storey	56
9	0	SMILES BETTER 18	R Fisher 6-10-12	P Niven	—
10	250056	PRETTY GAYLE 9	Denys Smith 6-10-7	A G Smith (7)	62

Probable SP: 11-4 Leon, 7-2 Regardless, 9-2 King's Harvest, 6 Third In Line, 8 Ballydaly Express, 10 Rien Ne Va Plus, 12 Smiles Better.

FAVOURITES: 3 1 0 3 2 2 1.

1987: Arctic Call 4 11 4 (G Bradley) 11-8 fav Mrs M Dickinson 19 ran.

```
 2.30   Nov Hurdle
        2½m (£895)
        10 runners
 🏇🏇 🏇🏇 .
```

0/0404-1F12 KING'S HARVEST (5-11-4) (G M Moore) ch g Oats - Sovereign Court by Sovereign Path 1988-89, 2m firm (Tralee (Ire)), 2½m h good (Hexham). £2,019.00 (£2,019.00).

Dec 1, Carlisle, 2m 1f 110yds nov hdle, heavy, £680.00: 1 Homme D'Affaire (5-10-10), 2 KING'S HARVEST (5-11-4, M Hammond), *patiently ridden, headway to lead two out, driven flat, just worn down*. (13 to 8 op 2 to 1 tchd 6 to 4) 3 West Ender (5-10-10),; 18 Ran. Hd, 2½l, 4l, 5l, 10l. 4m 41.80s (a 28.80s). SR: 30/37/26/22/17/7.

Nov 11, Hexham, 2½m nov hdle, good, £685.00: 1 KING'S HARVEST (5-11-0, M Hammond), *led to four out, led two out, ran-in*. (6 to 4 on op 5 to 4 on) 2 Copeland Lad (6-11-0), 3 West Ender (5-11-0), 4 RIEN NE VA PLUS (5-10-7, R Hodge,7*), *covered up in midfield, niggled along three out, no impression after*. (6 to 1 op 3 to 1 tchd 7 to 1); 13 Ran. 7l, 1½l, 10l, 1½l, 4l, ¾l, 1l, 1l. 5m 4.00s (a 10.00s). SR: 36/29/27/20/15/11.

Oct 15, Kelso, 2m nov hdle, good, £1,004.20: 1 Interlok Divider (5-11-0), 2 Boynton (5-11-0), 3 Fell Mist (5-11-0), F KING'S HARVEST (5-11-0, M Hammond), *disputed lead to fourth, led next till fell two out*. (6 to 4 fav tchd 7 to 4); 11 Ran. ¾l, 12l, 3l, 1l, 7l, 4l. 4m 1.00s (a 12.50s).

3-YEAR RECORD	9Rn 2w 2p
Yld: 3 0 1	Gd: 3 1 0	Fst: 3 1 0
2m-2m3f: 8 1 1	2m4f-2m7f: 1 1 0
3m-3m3f: 0 0 0	3m4f+ : 0 0 0

2-1 REGARDLESS (6-11-4) (J W Blundell) b g Quayside - Bel Arbre 1988-89, 2m 5f h soft (Warwick). £1,264.80 (£1,264.80).

Dec 1, Warwick, 2m 5f nov hdle, soft, £1,264.80: 1 REGARDLESS (6-10-10, M Brennan), *good headway from sixth, led three out, hit next, blundered last and soon headed, driven to lead near finish*. (10 to 1 op 8 to 1) 2 Lyns Magic (6-10-3,7*), 3 Adams Imprint (5-10-10),; 22 Ran. 1l, 2l, ½l, 10l, 3l, 12l, 1½l. 5m 22.70s (a 32.70s).

April 16 1988, Fairyhouse (Ire), 2¼m inh flat, good, £1,380.00: 1 Hey Boss (4-11-6), 2 REGARDLESS (6-11-9, Mr T Lombard,5*),(25 to 1) 3 Silverhills (5-11-13),; 25 Ran. 3l, hd, 2l, 1l. 3m 59.70s.

Probables

(1) KING'S HARVEST – G. Moore 5–11.4 L. Wyer

F.	F.	C.	C.
Prom	(15)	—	C?
★★	★★		D√
			G√
			6 lb pen?
			Trainer's record√

(2) REGARDLESS – J. Blundell 6–11.4 M. Brennan

F.	F.	C.	C.
Prom	(15)	—	C?
★★	★★		D√
			G√
			6 lb pen?

This is an example of a novice hurdle for older horses over 2½m.

Analysis of this compact field of 10 runners revealed just two probables, KING'S HARVEST and REGARDLESS. Perhaps surprisingly THIRD IN LINE was eliminated from calculations at an early stage. Since winning its seasonal début it had continued to disappoint, getting beaten in races where the form subsequently proved to be poor. Now in this race it was being fitted for the first time with a visor in an attempt to sharpen its performance – a most discouraging sign.

Both probables KING'S HARVEST and REGARDLESS had competed in 'bumpers' (National Hunt Flat races) before being purchased by their present connections. KING'S HARVEST had won a race at Tralee while REGARDLESS had finished second in a similar race at Fairyhouse.

The more experienced KING'S HARVEST had three previous races, falling on his hurdle début in England, winning comfortably next time out over this distance, and finally just getting beaten on its next race when the final hurdle was omitted because of the state of the ground, making the run-in a tortuous 2f. REGARDLESS, in contrast, had one previous race in England, winning its hurdle début but showing signs of inexperience with a number of blunders.

Applying the formula, both horses had almost identical ratings. On form there were no collateral lines to make a choice between them, KING'S HARVEST was the more experienced and in novice races this can be a telling factor. On fitness both earned two-star ratings having run 15 days previously. Both were unproven over the course, but the galloping Ayr course would not disadvantage either. Both were proven adaptable to the going and suited to the distance, and carried the same 6 lb penalty. The one condition to separate the two runners was the trainer's record. George Moore, trainer of KING'S HARVEST, had a most impressive record at Ayr with an up-to-date 36.1 per cent ratio of winners to runners and 7 winners from 18 runners in novice hurdles. This appeared as a most telling factor with KING'S HARVEST having this race as a well-considered engagement.

Applying the formula, with both horses most evenly balanced, KING'S HARVEST's trainer's record at Ayr served as the determining factor to make it the selection choice.

Result: 1st KING'S HARVEST (7–2) won by 7 lengths.

Form Book No. 1535 *CHELTENHAM 2 January 1989 (good to firm)*

1.20 — STEEL PLATE & SECTIONS YOUNG
CHASERS QUALIFIER (NOVICES')
£5,000 added (£3,730) 2m (3)

201 140-111 **WATERLOO BOY 14 (D3)** D Nicholson 6-11-7...................... R Dunwoody **77**
202 360-46U **BEECH ROAD 7** G Balding 7-11-3...G McCourt —
203 2/24533- **DICTALINO 353** C Brooks 8-11-3...B de Haan ●**78**
Probable SP: Evens Waterloo Boy, 7-4 Beech Road, 4 Dictalino.
FAVOURITES: — — 0 1 3 1 1.
1988: Private Views 7 11 11 (K Mooney) 4-7 fav N A Gaselee 3 ran.

1.20 ✦✦ᕯᕯ **Novices'
Chase 2m
(£3,730)
3 runners**

422140-111 WATERLOO BOY (6-11-7) (D Nicholson) ch g Deep Run - Sapphire Red by Red Alert 1987-88, 2m 100yds h heavy (Newbury) 1988-89, 2m ch good to firm (Worcester), 2m ch soft (Bangor), 2m 50yds ch good (Towcester). £8,029.50 (£5,230.00).

Dec 19, Towcester, 2m 50yds h'cap chase (0-45), good, £1,478.00: 1 WATERLOO BOY (5-11-11, R Dunwoody), **jumped well, chased leader until led approaching last, soon clear.** (Evens fav op 11 to 8 on tchd 11 to 10) 2 Nodalotte (8-11-6), 3 Betty's Girl (8-10-3),: 8 Ran. 8l, 4l, 6l, 2½l, 1l. 4m 19.90s (a 15.40s). SR: 16/3/-/-/-/-.

Dec 2, Bangor, 2m h'cap chase, soft, £1,618.00: 1 WATERLOO BOY (5-11-10, J Osborne), **led to seventh, pressed leader and every chance from next, close second and ridden when left in lead two out.** (6 to 4 fav op Evens tchd 2 to 1) 2 Jolly Mariner (8-9-7,7*), 3 Candlelight Dinner (7-10-6),: 7 Ran. 10l, 30l, ½l, 15l. 4m 33.00s (a 29.00s).

Oct 29, Worcester, 2m h'cap chase (0-45), good to firm, £2,134.00: 1 WATERLOO BOY (5-10-12, R Dunwoody), **tracked leaders, every chance from four out, ridden to lead last 50 yards.** (13 to 2 op 7 to 1 tchd 9 to 1) 2 Acclaim (8-11-4), 3 Stonehenge (11-10-2),: 13 Ran. Hd, 2½l, nk, 10l, 20l, ¾l. 4m 2.80s (a 12.80s). SR: 20/25/6/24/11/-.

March 11 1988, Sandown, 2m nov hdle, good, £2,326.90: 1 Cashcanon (6-11-0), 2 A Lad Insane (7-11-0), 3 Epitrot (5-11-4), 9 WATERLOO BOY (5-11-4, R Dunwoody), **disputed lead, took definet advantage 6th, soon headed, ridden two out, weakened quickly** (11 to 2 op 4 to 1); 15 Ran. Nk, ½l, ½l, 6l, 5l, 15l. 4m 1.80s (a 13.80s). SR: 12/11/14/17/3/2/-.

3-YEAR RECORD   11Rn 4w 3p

Yld: 8 2 3	Gd: 2 1 0	Fst: 1 1 0	
2m-2m3f: 10 4 3		2m4f-2m7f: 1 0 0	
3m-3m3f: 0 0 0		3m4f+ : 0 0 0	

24/533- DICTALINO (FR) (8-11-3) (C P E Brooks) b g Arctic Tern (USA) - Dictabya by Dicta Drake

Jan 15 1988, Ascot, 2m nov chase, heavy, £9,804.00: 1 Saffron Lord (6-11-5), 2 Neblin (9-11-5), 3 DICTALINO (FR) (7-11-5, P Scudamore), **led till headed 3 out, ran on one pace** (14 to 1 op 10 to 1 tchd 16 to 1); 6 Ran. 8l, 6l, 12l. (Time not taken).(Time not taken)

Dec 30 1987, Warwick, 2m nov chase, soft, £2,506.75: 1 Bespoke (6-11-0,4*), 2 Flag Of Truce (7-11-11,bl), 3 DICTALINO (FR) (6-11-4, P Scudamore), **progress 6th, unable to quicken from 3 out** (5 to 4 fav op 2 to 1 tchd 9 to 4); 16 Ran. 10l, ¾l, hd, ¾l, 15l. 4m 10.40s (a 14.40s). SR: 50/47/39/38/37/22.

Dec 12 1987, Lingfield, 2m nov chase, good to soft, £5,959.00: 1 Yabis (USA) (6-11-0), 2 Yeoman Broker (9-11-0), 3 Royal Stag (5-11-0), 5 DICTALINO (FR) (6-11-0, P Scudamore), **chased leaders until weakened after 8th** (7 to 1 op 8 to 1 tchd 6 to 1); 12 Ran. 4l, 10l, ½l, dist, 5l, 4l, 5l. 4m 15.60s (a 18.10s). SR: 57/57/43/42/-/-.

026360-46U BEECH ROAD (7-11-3) (G B Balding) ch g Nearly A Hand - North Bovey by Flush Royal 1985-86, 2m 1f h heavy (Taunton) 1987-88, 2m 1f h good to soft (Devon & Exeter), 2½m h soft (Cheltenham), 2½m 120yds h good (Newbury). £9,331.50 (-).

Dec 26, Newton Abbot, 2m 5f h'cap chase, good to soft, £3,127.25: 1 Sabin Du Loir (Fr) (9-11-0), 2 Hope Cove (NZ) (6-10-13), 3 Paddy O'Brien (8-10-7,7*), U BEECH ROAD (6-11-0, R Guest), **chased winner sixth, challenging when mistake and unseated rider ninth.** (4 to 1 op 3 to 1 tchd 9 to 2); 9 Ran. 30l, 6l, 30l, 10l. 5m 26.20s (a 20.20s). SR: 62/31/26/-/-.

Dec 10, Cheltenham, 2m hdle, good, £13,336.00: 1 Condor Pan (5-11-2), 2 Floyd (8-11-10), 3 Sprowston Boy (5-11-2), 6 BEECH ROAD (6-11-2, R Guest), **held up, headway three out, every chance before last, no extra run-in.** (33 to 1 op 25 to 1 tchd 50 to 1); 8 Ran. 4l, 2l, 4l, 2½l, sht-hd, 3l, 15l. 4m 3.00s (a 11.00s). SR: 58/62/52/56/45/44.

Nov 29, Newton Abbot, 2m 5f 110yds h'cap hdle, good, £3,874.50: 1 Pertemps Network (4-9-9,7*), 2 Sonny Hill Lad (5-9-8,7*), 3 Gwennap (5-9-11, inc 4lb ow,7*), 4 BEECH ROAD (6-11-11, Mr J Geake,7*), **headway sixth, went second eighth, soon left flat footed, weakened last.** (13 to 2 op 4 to 1 tchd 3 to 1 and 7 to 1); 18 Ran. 12l, 2l, 4l, ¾l, 1l, 8l, hd, 10l, 2½l, 2½l. 5m 30.20s (a 27.20s).

Feb 13 1988, Newbury, 2m 100yds h'cap hdle (Listed Race), heavy, £32,200.00: 1 Jamesmead (7-10-0), 2 Buck Up (6-10-4), 3 High Knowl (5-11-0), 18 BEECH ROAD (6-11-3, A Charlton,7*), **always in rear, well behind from 4th, tailed off** (20 to 1 tchd 33 to 1); 19 Ran. ¾l, 6l, 4l, 1½l, sht-hd, nk, 10l. 4m 20.00s (a 27.00s). SR: 73/76/80/76/64/60.

3-YEAR RECORD   21Rn 6w 4p

Yld: 14 3 3	Gd: 7 1 0	Fst: 0 0 0	
2m-2m3f: 11 2 1		2m4f-2m7f: 9 2 2	
3m-3m3f: 1 0 0		3m4f+ : 0 0 0	

Probable

(1) WATERLOO BOY – D. Nicholson 6–11.7 R. Dunwoody

F.	F.	C.	C.
Proven	(14)	up	C√
★★★	★★★		D√
			G√
			4 lb pen weight conditions

This is an example of a novice chase over 2m. Novice chases are won principally by accurate jumping and the issues presented in this field of only three runners is testimony to this principle. On the criterion that winning form over the larger obstacles is the soundest basis for selection WATERLOO BOY emerged as a probable.

BEECH ROAD as a hurdler subsequently proved to be top class but had only one experience over fences and demonstrated the difference of these larger obstacles by unseating its rider. This was at Newton Abbott where the fences have no reputation for stiffness, unlike those to be encountered today at Cheltenham. BEECH ROAD had therefore to be eliminated.

DICTALINO, an ex-French gelding, had been placed a few times over fences in America and shown ability in two of its races last season, although both times on much softer ground.

Applying the formula, WATERLOO BOY with a six-star rating had outstanding credentials, a winner of its only three chases, all of which were handicaps against much more experienced opponents. In its previous race carrying top weight it had outjumped experienced rivals and therefore showed it had the proven form. Its current fitness was also proved by this performance being just 14 days before. Although the value of today's race was greater, the competition did not appear to be more exacting or of higher class. WATERLOO BOY was proven at the distance and on the going and appeared likely to be quite well suited to Cheltenham's galloping course after a good win on Towcester's stamina-testing track. Today's weight conditions also favoured WATERLOO BOY as despite being a winner of three races it received only a 4 lb penalty.

Result: 1st WATERLOO BOY (6–4) won by a distance.
(The second horse was remounted to finish.)

(*NB*. In this small field the bookmakers' margin was restricted to 10 per cent so the odds favoured the astute backer.)

Form Book No. 1715 *ASCOT 14 January 1989 (good)*

3.05 — PETER ROSS NOVICES' CHASE (Listed Race)
£9,000 added (£6,403.50) 3m (4)

501	1F1-111	**SIR BLAKE** 19 (D)	D Elsworth 8-12-0	**B Powell** ●78
502	432-111	**SLALOM** 8 (D2)	M Robinson 8-12-0	J White 73
503	15-4F23	**CHASE THE LINE** 19 (BF)	D Nicholson 6-11-4	P Scudamore 68
504	002-011	**POLYFEMUS** 15 (D)	N Henderson 7-11-4	J Osborne 77

Probable SP: 4-5 Sir Blake, 13-8 Slalom, 7-2 Polyfemus, 8 Chase The Line.
FAVOURITES: 1 1 1 — 0 — —.

3.5 ♞♞♞♞

Nov Chase (Listed) 3m (£6,403) 4 runners

000115-4F23 CHASE THE LINE (6-11-4) (D Nicholson) ch g Celtic Cone - Miss Universe by Reverse Charge 1987-88, 2½m h good to firm (Huntingdon), 2½m h good to firm (Cheltenham). £4,053.20 (-).

Dec 26, Kempton, 2½m nov chase, good to firm, £5,921.25: 1 Star's Delight (6-11-0), 2 Hogmanay (Can) (6-11-4), 3 CHASE THE LINE (5-11-0, R Dunwoody), **in touch, ridden along three out, rallied after last, finished well.** (6 to 4 fav op Evens tchd 13 to 8); 8 Ran. Nk, hd, 3l, 25l, 3l, sht-hd. 5m 0.20s (a 10.20s).

Dec 17, Ascot, 2½m nov chase, good to firm, £6,004.00: 1 Larchwood (7-10-10), 2 CHASE THE LINE (5-10-10, R Dunwoody), **tracked leaders, good headway four out, every chance approaching last, rallied run-in, just failed.** (12 to 1 op 8 to 1 tchd 14 to 1) 3 Hogmanay (Can) (6-11-1),; 8 Ran. Sht-hd, 10l, 6l, 5l, 20l, 1l, 1l. 4m 57.50s (a 9.50s). SR: 7/6/1/-/-/-.

Nov 24, Ludlow, 2½m nov chase, good, £1,973.75: 1 Alaoui (6-11-0), 2 Twighlight Moth (10-11-0), 3 Smithy's Choice (6-11-0,bl), F CHASE THE LINE (5-11-0, R Dunwoody), **always prominent, disputing third place when fell three out.** (3 to 1 tchd 4 to 1); 14 Ran. 3l, 1l, 15l, 10l, 6l, 1l, hd. 5m 16.10s (a 18.10s).
3-YEAR RECORD   15Rn 2w 3p

Yld: 8 0 0	Gd: 2 0 0	Fst: 5 2 2	
2m-2m3f: 6 0 0		2m4f-2m7f: 9 2 2	
3m-3m3f: 0 0 0		3m4f+ : 0 0 0	

22/002-011 POLYFEMUS (7-11-4) (N J Henderson) ch g Pollerton - Bardicate by Bargello 1988-89, 2m 5f 110yds ch good (Towcester), 3m ch good to firm (Newbury). £3,474.75 (£3,474.75).

Dec 30, Newbury, 3m nov chase, good to firm, £2,038.75: 1 POLYFEMUS (6-11-4, J White), **tracked leader, led ninth, ridden and quickened clear run-in.** (6 to 1 op 6 to 1 tchd 10 to 1) 2 Stepaside Lord (USA) (6-11-4), 3 Kodiak Island (6-11-0,bl),; 6 Ran. 2½l, 15l, 2l, dist. 6m 5.90s (a 7.40s). SR: 16/13/-/-/-.

Dec 19, Towcester, 2m 5f 110yds nov chase, good, £1,436.00: 1 POLYFEMUS (6-11-4, J White), **tracked leaders, led ninth, ridden and kept on well from two out.** (4 to 1 op 5 to 2) 2 Major Match (NZ) (6-11-7), 3 Wood Singer (9-11-0),; 10 Ran. 7l, nk, 10l. 5m 51.30s (a 25.30s).

Dec 6, Leicester, 2½m chase, good; £1,203.75: 1 Mamora Bay (6-11-0), 2 Rebel Song (6-11-0), 3 Ibn Majed (6-11-8), 8 POLYFEMUS (6-11-0, J White), **well placed to 11th.** (6 to 1 op 7 to 1); 10 Ran. Hd, nk, ¾l, 10l, 3l. 5m 21.90s (a 21.90s).
3-YEAR RECORD   8Rn 2w 3p

Yld: 4 0 2	Gd: 3 1 1	Fst: 1 1 0	
2m-2m3f: 4 0 2		2m4f-2m7f: 3 1 1	
3m-3m3f: 1 1 0		3m4f+ : 0 0 0	

/141F1-111 SIR BLAKE (8-12-0) (D R C Elsworth) ch g Sexton Blake - Syrsanta (FR) by Santa Claus 1985-86, 2m good to soft (Down Royal (Ire)) 1987-88, 2m h good to soft (Kempton), 2½m h good to soft (Chepstow), 2½m h soft (Liverpool) 1988-89, 2½m 120yds h good (Newbury), 2½m ch good (Newbury), 3m ch good to firm (Kempton). £37,811.00 (£18,851.00).

Dec 26, Kempton, 3m nov chase, good to firm, £10,272.00: 1 SIR BLAKE (7-11-4, B Powell), **pulled hard, hit sixth and 11th, mistake 15th, led two out, comfortably.** (11 to 8 on tchd 6 to 4 on and 5 to 4 on) 2 Alone Success (5-11-4), 3 Vulgan Warrior (6-10-11),; 4 Ran. 2½l, 4l, dist. 5m 57.00s (a 4.00s). SR: 2/-/-/-.

Nov 26, Newbury, 2½m chase, good, £4,240.00: 1 SIR BLAKE (7-11-0, B Powell), **made all, jumped well, pushed out run in.** (6 to 4 fav op 5 to 4) 2 Brown Windsor (6-11-5), 3 Secret Rite (5-11-0),; 11 Ran. 2½l, 20l, 2l, 10l, dist, 8l. 5m 7.90s (a 11.90s).

Nov 2, Newbury, 2½m 120yds , good, £4,339.00: 1 SIR BLAKE (7-11-8, B Powell), **led to third, disputed lead till led seventh, made rest, easily.** (6 to 4 on op 5 to 4 on tchd Evens and 13 to 8 on) 2 The Hill (6-10-9), 3 The Bakewell Boy (6-11-0),; 4 Ran. 12l, 7l. 4m 59.90s (a 2.40s). SR: 60/35/33.
3-YEAR RECORD   13Rn 8w 0p

Yld: 9 4 0	Gd: 3 2 0	Fst: 1 1 0	
2m-2m3f: 7 2 0		2m4f-2m7f: 5 4 0	
3m-3m3f: 1 1 0		3m4f+ : 0 0 0	

111432-111 SLALOM (8-12-0) (M H B Robinson) ch g Deep Run - Arctic Nook by Arctic Slave 1986-87, 2½m soft (Clonmel (Ire)) 1987-88, 2½m h heavy (Wolverhampton), 2m 5f 75yds h good (Sandown), 2½m 120yds h heavy (Newbury) 1988-89, 3m ch good to soft (Haydock), 2½m ch good to soft (Haydock), 3m ch heavy (Haydock). £27,268.50 (£12,952.80).

Jan 6, Haydock, 3m chase, heavy, £2,193.00: 1 SLALOM (8-11-8, J White), **not fluent, made most, steadily drew clear two out, easily.** (5 to 1 on tchd 9 to 2 on) 2 Paddy Buck (9-11-0), 3 Rawthey Bank (7-11-0),; 5 Ran. 20l, sht-hd, dist. 7m 24.60s (a 74.10s).

Dec 10, Cheltenham, 2½m nov chase, good, £7,635.00: 1 SLALOM (7-11-10, J White), **tracked leaders, mistake eighth, went second next, challenged two out, led approaching last, ran on well.** (5 to 4 fav op 11 to 10 on tchd 11 to 8) 2 Nos Na Gaoithe (5-11-5,v), 3 Just This Once (NZ) (7-11-10),; 7 Ran. 2l, 7l, 2½l, 4l, dist. 5m 24.70s (a 17.70s).

Nov 23, Haydock, 3m chase, good to soft, £3,124.80: 1 SLALOM (7-11-6, J White), **tracked leaders, led last, driven out.** (6 to 4 fav tchd 13 to 8 and 11 to 8) 2 Bigsun (7-11-10), 3 Red Columbia (7-11-6),; 10 Ran. ¾l, 15l, 10l, 1½l, 1l. 6m 52.40s (a 41.90s).
3-YEAR RECORD   17Rn 7w 3p

Yld: 13 5 3	Gd: 4 2 0	Fst: 0 0 0	
2m-2m3f: 1 0 0		2m4f-2m7f: 14 5 3	
3m-3m3f: 2 2 0		3m4f+ : 0 0 0	

Probables

(1) SIR BLAKE – D. Elsworth 8–12.0 B. Powell

F.	F.	C.	C.
Prom	(19)	—	C√
★★	★★		D√
			G√
			10 lb pen?

(2) SLALOM – M. Robinson 8–12.0 J. White

F.	F.	C.	C.
Proven	(8)	—	C√
★★★	★★★		D√
			G√
			10 lb pen?

This is an example of a top-class novice chase over 3m. The small field of four runners, all of whom had good form, resolved to two probables, SIR BLAKE and SLALOM, both unbeaten in three races over fences. There was no immediate comparison of form between the two horses; however on a collateral form line through another horse BROWN WINDSOR, SLALOM came out the better.

SIR BLAKE, receiving 5 lb, had beaten BROWN WINDSOR by 2½ lengths at Newbury over 2½m; whereas at Cheltenham again over 2½m, BROWN WINDSOR, at level weights, had finished 11½ lengths behind SLALOM. On that basis SLALOM had a considerable advantage over SIR BLAKE. This was endorsed by a more tenuous line where SLALOM on his chase début defeated the experienced BIGSUN, who in its next race comprehensively beat ALONE SUCCESS, who was only beaten 2½ lengths by SIR BLAKE in its previous race.

Thus SLALOM had the proven form, and its recent race 8 days ago confirmed its fitness. Both horses had won similar-class events and both were now carrying 10 lb penalties for their success. Both were proven at the distance, going, and over a right-hand course like Ascot with stiff fences. Using the rating system of the formula, SLALOM, with six stars was made the selection choice.

Result: 1st SLALOM (9–4) finished alone.

Form Book No. 2914 *LIVERPOOL 6 April 1989 (soft)*

Last 4 outings	Today's rating	Horse	Official rating

2.35 Martell Chase (Feature Race) 3m 1f

91¹	105¹	105¹	91¹	101	Desert Orchid ★ 11-13	**107**
71¹	82³	82⁴	50²	97	Hungary Hur 11-9	**92**
90¹	96²	88¹	91³	93	Beau Ranger 11-5	**105**
72¹	76¹	78²	84ᴾ	93	Bishops Yarn 11-5	**93**
91⁵	98⁴	90ᶠ	91³	93	Charter Party 11-5	**99**
61¹	76ᶠ	79¹	82ᴾ	93	Delius 11-5	**91**
77ᵁ	85ᴾ	90²	84⁴	93	Weather The Storm 11-5	**93**
79⁶	79²	79³	91²	93	Yahoo 11-5	**100**

Last 4 outings				Today's rating	Horse	Official rating
91^1	105^1	105^1	91^1	101	Desert Orchid ★ 11-13	**107**
71^1	82^3	82^4	50^2	97	Hungary Hur 11-9	**92**
90^1	96^2	88^1	91^3	93	Beau Ranger 11-5	**105**
72^1	76^1	78^2	84^P	93	Bishops Yarn 11-5	**93**
91^5	98^4	90^F	91^3	93	Charter Party 11-5	**99**
61^1	76^F	79^1	82^P	93	Delius 11-5	**91**
77^U	85^P	90^2	84^4	93	Weather The Storm 11-5	**93**
79^6	79^2	79^3	91^2	93	Yahoo 11-5	**100**

2.35 — MARTELL CUP CHASE £30,000 added (£20,094.00) 3m 1f (8)

201	111111	DESERT ORCHID 21 (C&DD3) D Elsworth 10-11-13 .... S Sherwood	●78
202	411342	HUNGARY HUR 5 (BF) J Mulhern 10-11-9 .... T Carmody	43
203	31-1213	BEAU RANGER 22 (C&DC) M Pipe 11-11-5 .... P Scudamore	63
204	B6112P	BISHOPS YARN 40 (DBF) G Balding 10-11-5 .... R Guest	53
205	1-554F3	CHARTER PARTY 21 (D2) D Nicholson 11-11-5 .... R Dunwoody	68
206	111-F1P	DELIUS 40 (C&DBF) R Lee 11-11-5 .... B Dowling	59
207	22UP24	WEATHER THE STORM 22 A Moore 9-11-5 .... T Taaffe	58
208	4-26232	YAHOO 21 (D3) J Edwards 8-11-5 .... T Morgan	71

Probable SP: Evens Desert Orchid, 7-2 Yahoo, 6 Beau Ranger, 8 Charter Party, 12 Delius, 14 Bishop's Yarn. **FAVOURITES:** — — 3 0 0 0 2.

1988: Desert Orchid 9 11 5 (S Sherwood) 3-1 D R C Elsworth 4 ran

---

2.35 ♞♞♞	Conditions Chase 3m 1f £20,094 8 runners

232211-111111 DESERT ORCHID (10-11-13) (D R C Elsworth) gr g Grey Mirage - Flower Child by Brother **1983-84**, 2m h firm (Ascot), 2m h good (Ascot), 2m h good (Kempton), 2m h good (Sandown), 2m h good to soft (Wincanton), 2m h firm (Ascot) **1984-85**, 2m h soft (Sandown) **1985-86**, 2m 1f ch good to firm (Devon & Exeter), 2m ch firm (Ascot), 2m 18yds ch good (Sandown), 2½m ch good (Ascot) **1986-87**, 2½m 68yds ch good (Sandown), 2m ch good (Ascot), 3m ch soft (Kempton), 3m 118yds ch good (Sandown), 3m 1f ch soft (Wincanton), 2½m ch good to soft (Ascot) **1987-88**, 2m 5f ch good (Wincanton), 2½m ch good to soft (Kempton), 3m 1f ch good (Liverpool), 3m 5f 18yds ch good to firm (Sandown) **1988-89**, 2m 5f ch good (Wincanton), 3m ch good to firm (Kempton), 2m ch good (Ascot), 3m 118yds ch good (Sandown), 3¼m ch heavy (Cheltenham). £359,624.45 (£158,947.25).

March 16, Cheltenham, 3¼m chase, heavy, £66,635.00: 1 DESERT ORCHID (10-12-0, S Sherwood), led to 14th, left in lead three out, soon headed, quickened to lead again run-in. (5 to 2 fav op 11 to 4 tchd 7 to 2) 2 YAHOO (8-12-0, T Morgan), well in touch, led approaching two out, headed under pressure run-in, all out. (25 to 1 op 20 to 1 tchd 33 to 1) 3 CHARTER PARTY (11-12-0, R Dunwoody), always with leaders, ridden and every chance three out, kept on gamely one pace from next. (14 to 1 op 20 to 1); 13 Ran. 1½l, 8l, dist, dist. 7m 17.60s (a 37.60s). SR: 88/86/78/-/-.

Feb 4, Sandown, 3m 118yds h'cap chase, good, £19,340.00: 1 DESERT ORCHID (10-12-0, S Sherwood), led to 12th, steadied, ran on again three out, led briefly last, fought back gamely to lead near finish. (6 to 5 fav op Evens tchd 5 to 4) 2 Pegwell Bay (8-10-10), 3 Kildimo (9-10-13), 4 CHARTER PARTY (11-11-7, R Dunwoody), jumped slowly early, in last place 18th, but every chance till weakened three out. (10 to 1 op 8 to 1 tchd 12 to 1); 4 Ran. ¾l, 2½l, 25l. 6m 18.80s (a 16.30s). SR: 81/62/62/45. r , ¬

Jan 14, Ascot, 2m h'cap chase, good, £21,949.50: 1 DESERT ORCHID (10-12-0, S Sherwood), led third until headed after fifth, ridden to dispute lead last, headed run-in, fought back to lead post. (6 to 4 fav op 5 to 4 tchd 13 to 8) 2 Panto Prince (8-10-6, inc 4lb extra), 3 Ida's Delight (10-10-0, inc 4lb extra),; 5 Ran. Hd, 8l, 10l. 3m 59.90s (a 9.90s). SR: 97/74/60/52.

3-YEAR RECORD					36Rn 22w 9p	
Yld:	12	5	5	Gd:	18 11 4	Fst: 6 4 0
2m-2m3f:	13	6	5		2m4f-2m7f: 11 6 1	
3m-3m3f:	10	7	3		3m4f+ : 2 1 0	

114131-1213 BEAU RANGER (11-11-5) (M C Pipe) ch g Beau Chapeau - Sand Martin by Menelek **1981-82, 2m h good (Limerick (Ire)), 2m h good (Limerick Junction (Ire)) 1982-83, 2m h soft (Taunton), 2m 1f h soft (Devon & Exeter) 1983-84, 2m ch good to firm (Wincanton) 1984-85, 2½m ch firm (Worcester), 2½m ch good (Liverpool), 2½m ch good to soft (Cheltenham), 2½m ch good to soft (Kempton), 2½m 68yds ch good to soft (Sandown), 2m 1f ch soft (Devon & Exeter), 2m 5f ch good (Wincanton) 1985-86, 3m 1f ch good (Liverpool) 1987-88, 2½m ch soft (Cheltenham), 3m ch soft (Haydock), 2½m ch good to firm (Worcester), 2½m ch good to firm (Cheltenham) 1988-89, 3m ch good to soft (Haydock), 2½m ch heavy (Worcester).** £103,001.85 (£15,380.25).

March 15, Cheltenham, 2m chase, soft, £40,698.80: 1 Barnbrook Again (8-12-0), 2 Royal Stag (7-12-0), 3 BEAU RANGER (11-12-0, P Scudamore), **led until approaching three out, ridden and kept on one pace from two out.** (11 to 4 op 9 to 4 tchd 3 to 1); 8 Ran. 4l, 4l, ¾l, 30l. 4m 6.00s (a 8.00s). SR: 84/80/76/75/45.

March 1, Worcester, 2½m chase, heavy, £6,324.00: 1 BEAU RANGER (11-11-8, P Scudamore), **not fluent, led to third, closed tenth, hit 11th, mistake three out, ridden to lead approaching last, pushed out.** (85 to 40 on op 2 to 1 on tchd 5 to 2 on) 2 Panto Prince (8-11-4),; 2 Ran. 5l. 5m 29.90s (a 34.90s). SR: -/-.

Dec 10, Cheltenham, 2½m h'cap chase, good, £18,600.00: 1 Pegwell Bay (7-10-13), 2 BEAU RANGER (10-12-0, P Scudamore), **led to sixth, disputed lead for rest of race, ran on well run-in, no impression close home.** (100 to 30 fav op 9 to 4 tchd 7 to 2) 3 Oregon Trail (8-10-2), 6 BISHOPS YARN (9-10-11, R Guest), **held up in rear, effort four out, never near to challenge.** (16 to 1); 10 Ran. 1½l, sht-hd, 3l, 15l, 12l, 1½l, sht-hd, 1l. 5m 12.30s (a 5.30s). SR: 82/95/68/65/48/47.

3-YEAR RECORD							26Rn 8w 8p			
Yld:	15	4	3	Gd:	9	1	4	Fst:	2	2
2m-2m3f:	3	0	2		2m4f-2m7f:	12	4	2		
3m-3m3f:	11	3	3		3m4f+ :	0	0	0		

421154-26232 YAHOO (8-11-5) (J A C Edwards) b g Trombone - Coolroe Aga by Laurence O **1985-86, 2¾m h good to soft (Ayr), 3m h good to soft (Wetherby) 1986-87, 3m ch soft (Haydock), 3m ch soft (Hexham), 3m 100yds ch good to firm (Wetherby), 3m 100yds ch good to firm (Wetherby) 1987-88, 3m ch soft (Newbury), 3m 100yds ch good (Wetherby), 3m ch good to soft (Haydock).** £41,344.90 (-).

March 16, Cheltenham. See DESERT ORCHID

Feb 8. Ascot. 3m h'cap chase, good, £22,320.00: 1 Proud Pilgrim (10-10-9), 2 Ballyhane (8-11-2), 3 YAHOO (8-11-8, T Morgan), **held up, making headway when hampered by faller three out, recovered and stayed on, never nearer.** (5 to 1 op 5 to 1 tchd 6 to 1): 10 Ran. 1l, 10l, 1l. 2l, 4l. 6m 15.00s (a 18.00s).

Jan 7, Haydock, 3m h'cap chase. heavy, £4,386.00: 1 Proud Pilgrim (10-11-0), 2 YAHOO (8-12-0, Mr P Fenton), **waited with, mistake four out, slight lead last, ran on, just caught.** (5 to 1 op 9 to 2) 3 Prince Metternich (8-9-10.4*),: 7 Ran. ¾l, 15l, 5l, 20l, ½l, 7m 1.80s (a 51.30s). SR: 65/78/35/33/27/31.

3-YEAR RECORD							27Rn 10w 12p			
Yld:	18	6	6	Gd:	5	1	3	Fst:	4	2	ı
2m-2m3f:	0	0	0		2m4f-2m7f:	4	1	2		
3m-3m3f:	23	8	8		3m4f+ :	0	0	0		

Probables

(1) DESERT ORCHID – D. Elsworth 10–11.13 S. Sherwood

F.	F.	C.	C.
Prom	(21)	—	C√
★★	★★		D√
			G√
			8 lb pen?

(3) BEAU RANGER – M. Pipe 11–11.5 P. Scudamore

F.	F.	C.	C.
Prom	(22)	—	C√
★★	★		D√
			G?

(8) YAHOO – J. Edwards 8–11.5 T. Morgan

F.	F.	C.	C.
Prom	(21)	—	C√
★★	★★		D√
			G√

This is an example of a conditions chase over 3m 1f. Held at Liverpool on the first day of the three-day Grand National meeting, the Martell Cup attracted a compact field of top-class staying chasers who were not vastly disproportionate in ability. In the official handicapper's view there was only a 16 lb difference between the runners. While this gave the top-rated horses an obvious advantage (as except for two runners with penalties the rest met at level weights) such differences can often be overcome should one of the more favoured contestants prove slightly under par or put in a sluggish jumping performace.

However, using the views of the official handicapper, the race seemed to resolve to the three top-rated horses. DESERT ORCHID (rated 107), BEAU RANGER (rated 105) and YAHOO (rated 100). All three probables had last run at the Cheltenham Festival some 3 weeks before. BEAU RANGER had contested the 2m Champion Chase where it had been found wanting for a 'turn of foot' over the minimum distance.

In contrast, DESERT ORCHID and YAHOO had fought out a memorable finish in the 3¼m Gold Cup with DESERT ORCHID at level weights winning by 1½ lengths.

DESERT ORCHID had won the Martell Cup the previous year and BEAU RANGER, as an 8 y.o. in 1986, had also won. However, BEAU RANGER was probably not the force he once was although now trained and ridden by the record-breaking team of Martin Pipe and Peter Scudamore. A collateral form line through PANTO PRINCE suggested he could have the measure of DESERT ORCHID and his chances therefore deserved the utmost respect.

The form of the Gold Cup showed what a brilliant horse DESERT ORCHID was and how adept at all distances from 2 to 3¾m and over so many courses. Yet YAHOO on its favoured soft going had run the champion to a narrow margin, and now meeting on 8 lb better terms had every right to reverse that defeat.

DESERT ORCHID had shown himself to be better than ever all season, overcoming the huge burdens the handicapper had set him over a variety of distances, and eventually overcoming his Cheltenham hoodoo to win chasing's greatest prize. Although proving a law unto himself, DESERT ORCHID had some very hard races in these victories and as the National Hunt season reached its zenith could at last be feeling the effect of these exertions.

Applying the selection formula, the issue rested between DESERT ORCHID and YAHOO (BEAU RANGER being eliminated because of failure to reach the prescribed minimum star rating). On form DESERT ORCHID was officially the top-rated horse – 7 lb superior to YAHOO, but today had to concede 8 lb. This in the light of their Cheltenham running had to bring them even closer together. Could DESERT ORCHID again defy the limitations of weight? Logically no, but with this super horse the heart wondered.

DESERT ORCHID and YAHOO both received a four-star rating, on form inseparable, and of the same proven fitness. Racing again in the same or very similar class, the deciding issue would be the conditions. DESERT ORCHID was a course and distance winner having won the year before, yet common belief was that he was still a better horse on a right-handed track where 25 of his 27 previous victories had been achieved. YAHOO, in contrast, had achieved his wins on left-handed tracks as was today's.

DESERT ORCHID, like many great horses, was adept at all going; YAHOO had a marked preference for the soft ground conditions encountered today. Finally there was the 8 lb penalty DESERT ORCHID had to carry. While all season the 'grey wonder' had defied all such impositions, this might be the final straw to break the camel's back. The issue rested on this final element which swung it to YAHOO's favour.

YAHOO was the formula's selection choice.

Result: 1st YAHOO (5–1) won by 10 lengths.
(DESERT ORCHID fell at the 12th fence, both horse and jockey returned unscathed, and the grey champion was rested for the remainder of the season.)

Please note: the author in this instance defied all his own logic and reasoning and although expecting the defeat of DESERT ORCHID by YAHOO, went and backed BEAU RANGER!

Form Book No. 2226 *WINDSOR 18 February 1989 (good to soft)*

4.00 — **THAMES VALLEY HUNTERS' CHASE (AMATEURS) £1,200 added (£1,198) 2m 5f (19)**

601	33444P-	AMBER RAMBLER 264 (D) P Scouller 10-12-7 ....P Scouller (7)	070
602	P0123-F	FEARLESS IMP 9 J Truman 14-12-7 ....Mrs K Hills (7)	71
603	23513/1	HALF FREE 9 (D3) C Brooks 13-12-7 ....C Farrell (7)	63
604	6PF0-UB	KINGSWOOD KITCHENS (B) 9 Mrs E Ludlow 9-12-7 ....P Clarke (7)	40
605	330441/	MANNA REEF 639 J Edwards 11-12-7 ....C Barlow (7)	—
606	05/3213-	MILLER HILL 259 J Burbidge 13-12-7 ....C Willett (4)	65
607	113P-01	SHARP JEWEL 219 W Caudwell 8-12-7 ....—	50
608	04P56-2	SUMMONS 9 (D) J Gifford 10-12-7 ....Miss A Embiricos (7)	76
609	12U0R/P-	ARDENT WARRIOR 284 Mrs G Drury 10-12-0 ....Mrs N Ledger (7)	—
610	6FP/P3-5	AREN'T WE ALL 9 G Edwards 10-12-0 ....G Edwards (7)	44
611	156PP0-	CHEADLE GREEN 289 Steven Astaire 12-12-0 ....Miss S Belcher (7)	—
612	41DF53	DON'T SHOUT 1016 Mrs G Drury 11-12-0 ....C Gordon (7)	—
613	2F4D35/	FURTHER THOUGHT 709 (C&D) I Kennedy 14-12-0 ....C Gordon (7)	—
614	D3311/6-	KERRY JACK 311 (D) Mrs R Plummer 13-12-0 ....Mrs A H-Fairley (7	—
615		LOCH SLOY Steven Astaire 13-12-0 ....Mrs P Hill (7)	—
616	3R522/4-	MUSSEL BED 278 Mrs J Wilkinson 12-12-0 ....Mrs J Wilkinson (7)	—
617	5/0535F-	OKEYDOKE 288 P Mortimer 9-12-0 ....T Smith (7)	40
618	3U133/F-	RAGAFAN 348 (C&D) C Wood 12-12-0 ....S Claisse (7)	—
619	2FP/605-	RIBOT STAR 284 Mrs S Menzies 10-12-0 ....Miss J Draper (7)	—

Probable SP: 6-4 Half Free, 7-2 Miller Hill, Summons, 5 Fearless Imp, 7 Ragafan, 8 Amber Rambler, 10 Sharp Jewel. **FAVOURITES:** — — 2 — — 0 1.
1988: Our Fun 11-12-0 (Mr C Burnett-Wells) 11-8 fav J Gifford 14 ran.

4.00 Hunters' Chase 2m 5f (£1,198) 19 runners

23513/1 HALF FREE (13-12-7) (C P E Brooks) b g Deep Run - Broken Union by Soldado 1981-82,

2m h good (Ascot), 2m h heavy (Cheltenham), 2m h good (Ascot) 1982-83, 2½m ch good to soft (Ascot), 2m 160yds ch soft (Newbury) 1983-84, 2½m ch good (Cheltenham), 2½m ch hard (Chepstow), 2¾m ch soft (Stratford), 2m 5f ch good to firm (Wincanton) 1984-85, 2½m ch firm (Cheltenham), 2½m ch soft (Cheltenham), 2½m ch soft (Cheltenham), 2m 5f ch soft (Wincanton) 1985-86, 2½m ch good to firm (Cheltenham), 2½m ch good (Cheltenham) 1986-87, 2m 5f ch good (Wincanton), 2½m ch good (Cheltenham) 1988-89, 2½m ch good (Huntingdon). £96,665.80 (£1,142.00).

Feb 9, Huntingdon, 2½m hun chase, good, £1,142.00: 1 HALF FREE (13-11-12, Mr C Farrell,7*), **held up but in touch, led approaching two out, pushed out.** (7 to 4 fav op Evens tchd 2 to 1) 2 SUMMONS (10-12-2, Miss A Embiricos,7*), **always well placed, every chance from two out, not quicken near finish.** (4 to 1 op 2 to 1 tchd 9 to 2) 3 Mark's Methane (15-11-10,4*), B KINGSWOOD KITCHENS (9-12-2, Mr P Clarke,7*,bl), **soon behind, tailed off when brought down three out.** (50 to 1) F FEARLESS IMP (14-12-2, Mrs K Hills,7*), **well placed till fell 12th.** (10 to 1 op 20 to 1); 12 Ran. 1½l, 6l, 20l, 4l, 1½l. 5m 16.90s (a 20.90s).

April 22 1987, Cheltenham, 2½m h'cap chase, firm, £4,698.00: 1 Duke Of Milan (10-10-2, inc 2lb ow), 2 Welsh Oak (7-10-4), 3 HALF FREE (11-12-0, P Scudamore), **jumped right, backmarker till 13th, no impression on first 2 from 3 out** (11 to 8 fav op 6 to 4 tchd 5 to 4); 5 Ran. 2l, dist, 2½l. 5m 7.40s (a 3.40s). SR: 1/-/-/-.

March 19 1987, Cheltenham, 2½m chase (Listed Race), good, £12,393.00: 1 HALF FREE (11-11-12, P Scudamore), **held up, chased leader 10th, ran on to lead run-in** (5 to 4 fav op Evens tchd 11 to 8) 2 Western Sunset (11-11-8), 3 Bruges (10-11-5),; 4 Ran. 1l, 12l, nk. 5m 27.10s (a 23.10s).

3-YEAR RECORD			13Rn 5w 4p		
Yld: 4	0	1	Gd: 6	4	1	Fst: 3	1	2
2m-2m3f:	0	0	0	2m4f-2m7f:	11	5	4
3m-3m3f:	2	0	0	3m4f+ :	0	0	0

204P56-2 SUMMONS (10-12-7) (J T Gifford) ch g Rouser - Silk II by Counsel 1985-86, 2½m h good (Chepstow), 2½m h firm (Kempton) 1986-87, 2m ch good to soft (Wincanton), 2m 5f ch good to soft (Wincanton), 2½m ch good to soft (Lingfield), 2½m ch firm (Cheltenham). £23,173.00 (-).

Feb 9, Huntingdon. See HALF FREE

May 13 1988, Stratford, 2¾m h'cap chase, firm, £3,282.80: 1 Pan Arctic (9-10-4, inc 4lb ow), 2 Dudie (10-10-12), 3 The Argonaut (NZ) (10-11-10), 6 SUMMONS (9-11-10, R Rowe), **led to second, mistake fourth, in close touch, weakened two out.** (11 to 4 op 2 to 1 tchd 3 to 1); 6 Ran. 3l, 7l, ¾l, 1½l, 20l. 5m 38.80s (a 5.80s).

April 7 1988, Liverpool, 2½m h'cap chase, good, £6,700.80: 1 Worthy Knight (7-10-0), 2 Valentinos Joy (9-10-0), 3 Comeragh King (9-11-10), 5 SUMMONS (9-11-10, R Rowe), **led second to tenth, lost place, kept on onepace from two out.** (11 to 2 op 6 to 1 tchd 5 to 1); 8 Ran. 2l, 8l, 5l, sht-hd, 12l. 4m 56.20s (a 0.20s). SR: 50/48/64/33/58/37.

3-YEAR RECORD			22Rn 6w 6p		
Yld: 11	3	2	Gd: 7	1	2	Fst: 4	2	1
2m-2m3f:	2	1	1	2m4f-2m7f:	18	5	4
3m-3m3f:	2	0	0	3m4f+ :	0	0	0

Probables

(3) HALF FREE – C. Brooks 13–12.7 Mr C. Farrell (7)

F.	F.	C.	C.
Prom	(9)	—	C√
★★	★★★		D√
			G√

(8) SUMMONS – J. Gifford 10–12.7 Miss A. Embiricos (7)

F.	F.	C.	C.
Prom	(9)	—	C√
★★	★★★		D√
			G√

240

This is an example of a hunters' chase over a distance of 2m 5f. Hunters' chases are restricted to amateur riders and to horses certified as being hunted during the current season, and who have not taken part in any Flat or National Hunt races after 1 November.

The horses taking part will be horses which are graduates from point-to-point racing or horses who took part previously in National Hunt races but due to lack of ability in this sphere, or often due to loss of speed with increased age, have been sold out of professional racing stables.

Horses in hunter chases are of a wide range of ability, meeting each other on principally level weights, which is to the better horses' advantage. Occasionally top professional stables still keep a hunter or two in their yard. These invariably outshine their rivals as they are professionally trained and usually have the best amateur riders as their jockeys, as opposed to amateur-trained horses with less experienced riders.

The large field presented in Windsor's Thames Valley Hunters' Chase may at first sight seem a daunting selection proposition, but in practice resolves quite simply to the professionally trained horses. Most of the runners are well into the veteran stage (11 of the field 11 y.o. +) with their abilities well exposed, while of the younger members there is hardly one which could be considered a rising star. Analysis therefore revealed two probables, HALF FREE and SUMMONS.

They had already met once this season at Huntingdon over 2m 4f, where HALF FREE (receiving 4 lb) won, beating SUMMONS by 1½ lengths. HALF FREE, now a 13 y.o., was a dual Mackeson Gold Cup winner in its younger days, and a top-class 2m 4f horse who had never quite had the stamina to make a 3m chaser. Yet its prior race appearance had been almost 2 years earlier. SUMMONS in contrast was a highly successful novice chaser two seasons ago, winning four races, but last year had failed to graduate to handicap class. As a 10 y.o. it should be at its peak for a chaser and likely to benefit for this easing in grade. Today's meeting at level weights meant that SUMMONS was entitled to reverse the 1½ lengths beating when conceding 4 lb.

Applying the formula on star rating the pair were equal, with the conditions factor also placing them on a par. So from the subjective viewpoint, considering HALF FREE a veteran who was not the force he once was, and unlikely to be improving, SUMMONS, who was weighted to avenge previous defeat, if only marginally, was made the selection choice.

Result: 1st SUMMONS (9–2) won by 6 lengths.

241

Form Book No. 2046 *WARWICK 7 February 1989 (soft)*

4.00 — EBF STAKES (N H Flat Race) £1,200 added (£1,464.00) 2m (25)

1	DAWN BLADE 10 (D) J O'Neill 6-11-8	F Murtagh (7)
2	BATTLE BLAZE Mrs S Armytage 6-11-6	Mr M Armytage
3	NIGHT SINGER Mrs D Haine 5-11-6	L Chandler (7)
4	RED SCORPION A J Wilson 5-11-6	Gary Lyons(7)
5	SNOW ROBIN Miss G Rees 5-11-6	T Pinfield(4)
6	SUNNINGHILL CELTIC D Elsworth 5-11-6	A McCabe (7)
7	BAILEY'S PLEASE M Johnston 5-11-1	D Hood (7)
8	RICH MATILDA Mrs M Rimell 5-11-1	D Leahy (7)
9	RUM CAY 18 (D) R Curtis -4-10-12	S Mason(7)
10	BIG TIME LOUIS B Stevens 4-10-10	M Stevens (7)
11	FRIAR BUCK T Jones 4-10-10	D Skyrme (7)
12	MANDY'S TINO J Harris 4-10-10	S Turner (4)
13	MASTER MARRON D Wintle 4-10-10	—-
14	OUR MONET Mrs C Postlethwaite 4-10-10	R Fahey(4)
15	PURBECK DOVE K Bishop 4-10-10	—-
16	SWEET BEN G Gracey 4-10-10	Miss Z Davison
17	THE ILLYWHACKER Mrs J Pitman 4-10-10	J Leech (7)
18	VIRIDIAN Miss A King 4-10-10	P O'Dwyer (7)
19	AISHOLT K Bishop 4-10-5	N Hawke (7)
20	CASSCA M Pipe 4-10-5	R Macneice (7)
21	DONNA'S TOKEN R Brown 4-10-5	J Brown (7)
22	M I BABE Mrs I McKie 4-10-5	A Rolls (7)
23	QUARTOFERA R Holder 4-10-5	W Hayes (7)
24	UPHAM VIEW D Gandolfo 4-10-5	Miss E Gandolfo (7)
25	WILL DO MY BEST Mrs E Heath 4-10-5	Mr P Harding Jones(4)

Probable SP: 11-10 The Illywhacker, 3 Dawn Blade, 5 Cassca, 8 Rich Matilda, 10 Sunninghill Celtic. 16 Battle Blaze.
FAVOURITES: — — — — 13 —.

4.0 NH Flat Race 2m (£1,464) 25 runners

AISHOLT (4–10–5) (K Bishop) ch f Avocat – Bryophila (FR) by Breakspear II

BAILEY'S PLEASE (5–11–1) (M Johnston) b m Le Johnstan – Fair Victory by Double Jump

BATTLE BLAZE (6–11–6) (Mrs S Armytage) ch g Glorified – General's Daughter by Spartan General

BIG TIME LOUIS (4–10–10) (B Stevens) ch g Bulldozer – Gorgeous Gael by Atan

CASSCA (4–10–5) (M C Pipe) b f Full Of Hope – Miss Kuwait by The Brianstan

–1 DAWN BLADE (6–11–8) (J J O'Neill) b m Fine Blade (USA) – Watch The Birdie by Polyfoto **1988–89, 2m heavy (Ayr). £1,100.00 (£1,100.00).**

Jan 28, Ayr, 2m (4,5,6–y–o) nh flat, heavy, £1,100.00: 1 DAWN BLADE (6–10–12, F Murtagh,7*), **always cantering, ran on strongly to lead final furlong.** (100 to 30 op 2 to 1 tchd 7 to 2) 2 Bowlands Way (5–11–6,4*), 3 Strong Breeze (5–11–3,7*); 12 Ran. ¾l, 3l, hd, 15l, 3l, 1l, hd. 4m 17.10s.

DONNA'S TOKEN (4–10–5) (R L Brown) br f Record Token – Lyricist by Averof

FRIAR BUCK (4–10–10) (T M Jones) b g Skyliner – Really by Sovereign Gleam

M I BABE (4–10–5) (Mrs I McKie) ch f Celtic Cone – Cover Your Money by Precipice Wood

MANDY'S TINO (4–10–10) (J L Harris) b g Neltino – Mandy's Melody by Highland Melody

MASTER MARRON (4–10–10) (D J Wintle) b g Hotfoot – Sally Conkers by Roi Lear (FR)

NIGHT SINGER (5–11–6) (Mrs D Haine) b g Bonne Noel – Music Mistress by Guide

OUR MONET (4–10–10) (Mrs C Postlethwaite) b g Workboy – Mont–A–L'abbe by Military

PURBECK DOVE (4–10–10) (K Bishop) gr g Celtic Cone – Grey Dove by Grey Love

QUARTOFERA (4–10–5) (R J Holder) b f Lucky Wednesday – Avona by My Swallow

RED SCORPION (5–11–6) (A J Wilson) b g Furry Glen – Glamorous Night by Sir Herbert

RICH MATILDA (5–11–1) (Mrs M Rimell) b m Cigardee – Merlin Miss Ditton by The Ditton

–1 RUM CAY (4–10–12) (R Curtis) ch f Our Native (USA) – Oraston by Morston (FR) **1988–89, 2m good to soft (Towcester). £1,296.00 (£1,296.00).**

Jan 20, Towcester, 2m (4,5,6–y–o) nh flat, good to soft, £1,296.00: 1 RUM CAY (USA) (4–9–12, S Mason,7*), **chased leaders on wide outside, led inside final furlong, ran on.** (33 to 1) 2 Oneupmanship (4–10–3,7*), 3 Almanzora (5–11–1,7*),; 17 Ran. 1½l, 8l, 1l, sht–hd, 7l. 4m 11.70s.

SNOW ROBIN (5–11–6) (Miss G M Rees) b g Panco – Moon Glow by Right Royal V

SUNNINGHILL CELTIC (5–11–6) (D R C Elsworth) ch g Celtic Cone – Aunt Livia by Royalty

SWEET BEN (4–10–10) (G G Gracey) ch g Sweet Monday – Oolywig by Copte (FR)

THE ILLYWHACKER (4–10–10) (Mrs J Pitman) b g Dawn Review – Trucken Queen by Harwell

UPHAM VIEW (4–10–10) (D R Gandolfo) b f Oats – Real View by Royal Highway

VIRIDIAN (4–10–10) (Miss A L M King) b g Green Shoon – Cahermone Ivy by Perspex

WILL DO MY BEST (4–10–5) (Mrs E H Heath) br f Politico (USA) – The Lathkill by Clear River

Probables

(1) DAWN BLADE – J. J. O'Neil 6–11.8 F. Murtagh (7)

F.	F.	C.	C.
Prom	(10)	—	C√
★★	★★★		D√
			G√
			7 lb pen

(9) RUM CAY – R. Curtis 4–10.12 S. Mason (7)

F.	F.	C.	C.
Prom	(18)	—	C√
★★	★★		D√
			G√
			7 lb pen?

This is an example of a National Hunt Flat race over a distance of 2m. These races are often referred to as 'bumper' races and are restricted to horses which have not previously run in any Flat races, or in any hurdle or steeplechase races. In Britain no horse is allowed to contest more than three National Hunt Flat races, and the horses are to be ridden by conditional jockeys and amateur riders only. Their purpose is to serve as a training ground for both inexperienced horse and rider.

With these limitations it is usually the fittest and best-prepared horse on the day who will come out victorious. Most horses competing will be directed to a long-term National Hunt career, eventually as chasers. This aim is likely to hold preference over the mere outcome of one Flat race. In such circumstances horses with proven ability in a National Hunt Flat race are likely to hold sway over their rivals, the exception being when an unrated horse has been especially prepared for its racecourse début.

With the race in hand 23 of the large field of 25 runners are unraced, so the two experienced horses, which are both previous winners, appeared to hold a distinct advantage. Unless a dark horse had been got ready for this race the two winners should hold sway.

With no form credentials to assess the unraced horses the only way of considering their chances is from:

1. Their trainer's record in such races with débutants;
2. The engagement of a more experienced conditional jockey (i.e. one claiming 4 lb rather than the full 7 lb allowance), or an experienced amateur;
3. A close inspection of their breeding.

These factors are usually complemented by a strong market move for such a candidate.

In this instance with no strong betting developing for any of the newcomers analysis of the race suggested the two previous winners DAWN BLADE and RUM CAY as the only probables.

There was no comparable form line between the two so it was a case of educated guessing. DAWN BLADE had won, it appeared, very comfortably, 'always cantering, ran on to lead final furlong', at Ayr, while RUM CAY 'led inside final furlong, ran on' at Towcester. DAWN BLADE's run only 10 days earlier gave it a fitness advantage over RUM CAY, whose race was 18 days before. Both however were in similar class, proven over the distance and going, with the course at Warwick unlikely to cause either any inconvenience. Both were to carry 7 lb penalties offset by their riders' allowances, and both had ridden their horses to victory in the previous race. The one difference in the form was that while RUM CAY's victory at 33–1 appeared a victory unforeseen, DAWN BLADE's success held no surprise, being nicely backed at 3–1 after opening at 2–1 and touching 7–2.

Applying the formula, DAWN BLADE was made the selection choice, having the better star rating, and whose form review suggested it had achieved quite a facile previous victory.

Result: 1st DAWN BLADE (2–1 fav.) won by 1 length.

Form Book No. 3474 *STRATFORD 3 June 1989 (firm)*

5.50 — NOVICES' HANDICAP HURDLE
(£1,360) 2m 6f (15)

1	3-P3041	GENTLEMAN ANGLER (8lbex) (D) J Gifford 6-12-4 ... R Rowe
2	06-0041	LATTIN GENERAL (8lbex) C Brooks 7-11-8 ... P Scudamore
3	041431	HIGH ALOFT (B) T Casey 5-11-7 ... R Dunwoody'
4	510011	WAYWARD SINGER (CD) J Costello 6-11-5 ... G Bohane (7)
5	53-55B1	FIFTH ATTEMPT P Felgate 7-11-0 ... R Beggan
6	P22441	PROUD SOLDIER M Scudamore 6-11-0 ... D Tegg
7	PP0233	●FALWORTH (B) F Walwyn 5-10-12 ... K Mooney
8	3212	AIMEE JANE (B)(BF) M Pipe 4-10-11 R Macniece (7)
9	04015	COINAGE R Johnson Houghton 6-10-8 ... Mr G Johnson-Houghton (7)
10	23603F	KIRI'S SONG J Needham 6-10-7 ... A Gorman
11	05P6P4	WAYSIDE P Liddle 7-10-3 ... G Cook (7)
12	0P-0014	FRANK DALE G Jones 6-10-0 ... R Hyett
13	000232	SORORITY (BF) Miss S Wilton 4-10-0 ... ——
14	00-P5P	DRAW LOTS P Rodford 5-10-0 ... W Irvine (4)
15	0P0560	THORNBERRY HILL Miss S Oliver 4-10-0 ... Mr D Duggan (7)

Probable SP: 7-2 Aimee Jane, 9-2 High Aloft, 11-2 Gentleman Angler, Wayward Singer, 8 Fifth Attempt, 10 Coinage, 12 Falworth.

STRATFORD FORM

5.50 £1,360

| HurdleHcap4yo + Nov | 2m6f |

Gentleman Angler ®36

213/SP907423-P3041	**6-12-04**
J.T.GIFFORD	ch g Julio Mariner —
Starts 1st 2nd 3rd Win & Pl	San Salvador (GER)
16 2 2 3 £6,395	(Klairon)

88/9 Fontw 2m6f NovHdl HARD	.... £1,088
86/7 GowPk 2m NHF FIRM	.... £3,450
	TOTAL: £4,538

| 29 May Fontwell Park 2m6f | NovHdl £1,088 |
| 11 ran | HARD | TIME 5m12.60s (fst3.2s) |

1 GENTLEMAN ANGLER 6 11-00
.... R.Rowe 10/3
headway 7th, led 9th, easily
2 Star of Oughterard 4 11-00 . P.Corrigan 6/4F
3 FALWORTH (USA) 5 11-06b K.Mooney 7/2
*led to 7th, led 8th to 9th, ridden approaching
last, unable to quicken*
DISTANCES 15-6-15-7-dist

| 12 May Stratford 2m | NovHcpHdl £1,360 |
| 17 ran | GD-FM | TIME 3m56.1s (slw5.9s) |

1 The Howard 7 10-10 ......M.Furlong 11/1
2 Shy Hiker 6 9-13 ..... MartinJones (7) 20/1
3 Touching Star 4 10-00 ....J.Lodder (7) 7/4F
4 GENTLEMAN ANGLER 6 11-10
.... R.Rowe 16/1
*led to 2nd, led 5th to 3 out, every chance last,
one pace* [op 8/1]
DISTANCES 1½-½-1½-5-8-nk-1-2½

| 27 Apr Wincanton 2m6f | NovHcpHdl £1,478 |
| 20 ran | GOOD | TIME 5m31.7s (slw22.0s) |

1 Seven of Diamonds 4 10-02 . B.Powell 11/2J
2 Sunday For Monday 6 9-09 ...I.Lawrence
(7) 8/1
3 Democratic Boy 7 10-01 .....D.Tegg 25/1
15 GENTLEMAN ANGLER 6 11-00
.... R.Rowe 11/2J
[op 11/2 tchd 13/2]
DISTANCES 1-¾-1-2-2-2½-2

Probable

(1) GENTLEMAN ANGLER – J. Gifford 6–12.4 R. Rowe

F.	F.	C.	C.
Proven	(5)	—	C√
★★★	★★★		D√
			G√
			8 lb pen?

This is an example of a novice handicap hurdle race over a distance of 2m 6f.

Employing the approach recommended for selection in handicaps, the efficiency of this method was again positively demonstrated. Novice handicaps have an immediacy about them in that a horse's rating is most likely to be assessed on quite current form and to reflect its true current ability. These sorts of races are most appropriate for horses 'bang in form' whose ability may still put them ahead of the official handicapper.

On this basis the horses filling the top six places in the handicap came into the reckoning. Each had won its previous race, four of them within the past 7 days. However, only two of these, the top-weighted pair GENTLEMAN ANGLER and LATTIN GENERAL, due to the new 5-day entry system, escaped the handicapper's clutches for reassessment, and instead were burdened with a mandatory 8 lb penalty.

So it was upon these two that analytical attention was focused. Both horses were at the head of the handicap and therefore are proven to be the best. Had they improved further?

Both were lightly raced compared with some of the other runners. GENTLEMAN ANGLER had five previous races while LATTIN GENERAL had only four. It meant that while these two horses were fresh many of their rivals might well be jaded from their races at the end of the season.

GENTLEMAN ANGLER was top of the handicap because it had shown solid form at the end of last season, the promise of which was finally fulfilled in its previous race. It had won easily by 15 lengths and 6 lengths from its nearest rivals. What view the handicapper would take of that was anyone's guess except that it was likely to be harsher than the 8 lb penalty now set. It was also rated 10 lb superior to its nearest rival LATTIN GENERAL so unless this horse had improved by this amount it was still going to be inferior. Using the method recommended in approaching handicap form, analysis stopped with the proven best horse in the handicapper's opinion, that is, GENTLEMAN ANGLER.

Applying the formula, GENTLEMAN ANGLER drew a six-star rating with proven form, and recent fitness 5 days earlier. It was racing in similar class, was proven over the course, and over the special intermediate distance of 2m 6f (an almost unique factor), and content on the firm going. The only negative element was the 8 lb penalty which it was considered capable of overcoming.

GENTLEMAN ANGLER was made the selection choice.

Result: 1st GENTLEMAN ANGLER (9–1) won by 2½ lengths.

Form Book No. 1664 KELSO 11 January 1989 (soft)

2.45 — GRANTSHOUSE CONDITIONAL JOCKEYS HANDICAP HURDLE £1,500 added (£1,226) 2m (12)

1	2-25352	VIKING ROCKET 7 (DBF)	C Parker 5-11-10	S Turner	●78
2	3/00005	ABSONANT 7 (C&DD2)	Mrs G Reveley 7-11-7	N Smith	61
3	043	KHARIF 21	R Allan 5-11-4	Ger Lyons	68
4	505120	DANRIBO 7 (D)	J Parkes 6-11-3	I McLelland	75
5	4521-03	KIRSTY'S BOY 7 (C&D)	J S Wilson 6-11-1	J O'Gorman	77
6	3662-5P	WARDSOFF 25	T Cuthbert 12-11-0	Carol Cuthbert	—
7	0042-00	AZUSA 23	T Jeffrey 6-10-5	R Fahey	77
8	0400-33	THE FINK SISTERS 8	T Cunningham 6-10-4	S Cunningham	70
9	P000-0	PLAYJOE 23	Mrs J Pringle 6-10-2	R Hodge	—
10	034-B00	BATTLE STING 16	Mrs S Ward 5-10-2	D Byrne	73
11	640500	MAC'S MATE (13)	W Kemp 7-10-5	S McKeever	—
12	24-0005	PENDLEY GOLD 7 (D2)	M Naughton 8-10-12	P Harte	77

Probable SP: 7-2 Kirsty's Boy, 9-2 Azusa, Danriba, 5 Viking Rocket, 6 Kharif, 7 Absonant.

FAVOURITES:— 0 1 0 — — 2 . .

1988: Sunbia 7 11 12 (P Hegarty) 6-1 D Lee 15 ran.

2.45 H'cap Hurdle (0–45) 2m (£1,226) 12 runners

214142-25352 VIKING ROCKET (5-11-10) (C Parker) ch m Viking (USA) - Calcine by Roan Rocket 1987-88, 2m h soft (Perth), 2m 1f 110yds h heavy (Carlisle). £1,370.00 (-).

Jan 4, Ayr, 2m c/j h'cap hdle (0–45), soft, £1,072.00: 1 Lotus Island (5-11-6,5*,bl), 2 VIKING ROCKET (5-10-13, A Parker,5*), **always handy, led fourth till headed and hard ridden two out, one pace**. (3 to 1 jt-fav op 11 to 4 tchd 7 to 2) 3 KIRSTY'S BOY (6-10-10, T P White), **never far away, drew level two out, soon ridden and ran on one pace**. (13 to 2 op 5 to 1) 5 PENDLEY GOLD (8-10-8, P Harte), **disputed lead till driven and outpaced three out, soon beaten**. (5 to 1 op 7 to 1 tchd 8 to 1); 8 Ran. 5l, ¾l, 2l, 20l, dist, 7l. 4m 10.90s (a 31.90s). SR: 34/22/13/14/-/-.

Dec 1, Carlisle, 2½m h'cap hdle (0–55), heavy, £1,339.50: 1 Haddon Lad (5-11-1), 2 In Contention (5-10-5), 3 Big White Chief (7-11-0), 5 VIKING ROCKET (4-10-13, S Turner,4*), **tucked away, jumped ahead three out, headed and weakened after last**. (6 to 1 op 5 to 1); 13 Ran. 7l, 2½l, 2½l, 12l, 4l. 5m 34.50s (a 43.50s).

Oct 21, Carlisle, 2m 1f 110yds h'cap h'dle, soft, £1,446.60: 1 Megan's Move (5-10-12), 2 Sir Speedy (5-10-2,7*), 3 VIKING ROCKET (4-10-13, S Turner,4*), **tracked leaders, led sixth, disputed lead three out till headed and no extra approaching last**. (5 to 1 jt-fav op 9 to 2) 15 PENDLEY GOLD (7-10-8, P Harte,4*), **close up to sixth, weakened three out**. (12 to 1 op 8 to 1); 15 Ran. 1½l, 2½l, 4l, 20l, ½l, 1½l, 1½l, sht-hd, 1l, 1½l. 4m 34.80s (a 21.80s). SR: 31/26/31/11/2/17.

3-YEAR RECORD   14Rn 3w 7p

Yld: 11 2 3	Gd: 2 0 1	Fst: 1 0 1
2m-2m3f: 12 2 5	2m4f-2m7f: 2 0 0	
3m-3m3f: 0 0 0	3m4f+ : 0 0 0	

Probable

(1) VIKING ROCKET – C. Parker 5–11.10 S. Turner

F.	F.	C.	C.
Proven	(7)	—	C√
★★★	★★★		D√
			G√
			Jockey√

This is an example of a handicap hurdle for older horses, restricted to conditional riders over a distance of 2m.

Employing the method recommended in the approach to handicaps, using the ratings of the official handicapper and eliminating those without a winning chance from the head of the handicap downwards, assessment began with the top weight VIKING ROCKET. This horse had finished second in a similar race (0–45) handicap for conditional jockeys at Ayr a week earlier, and being top rated by the handicapper would seem only to have to reproduce that form to succeed here. However, it was rechallenged by another horse, KIRSTY'S BOY, who had finished third in this Ayr race and had been beaten by only ¾ length. Originally set to concede 8 lb (without the rider's allowance) in their last race the readjusted weights today were 9 lb, which meant they were re-handicapped to finish level. Two differences also occurred: VIKING ROCKET was reunited with its usual rider, leading conditional jockey Stuart Turner, while KIRSTY'S BOY had a different rider.

The question raised, with VIKING ROCKET fit, in form, and at the head of the handicap and thus superior to other rivals, was whether the slight reversal in the weights would bring a change of form with KIRSTY'S BOY. However, unless the weight turn-around is considerable, beaten horses rarely avenge defeat, especially if their ability is well exposed. Weight only slows up faster horses, carrying less weight cannot make slower horses run faster, and KIRSTY'S BOY was proven the slower. Therefore it was considered that VIKING ROCKET would again beat KIRSTY'S BOY, and being the top weight and first horse assessed was made the probable under the handicap method.

Applying the formula, VIKING ROCKET received a six-star rating on form and fitness, was racing in the same class, on the same going and distance, and on a course suited to it. Conditional jockey races (National Hunt's equivalent to apprentice races on the Flat) are invariably won by the best riders, who are usually provided with the best mounts. With VIKING ROCKET reunited with her usual pilot, Stuart Turner, leading conditional jockey during the 1988–89 season, it was made the selection choice.

Result: 1st VIKING ROCKET (5–1) won by 5 lengths.

Form Book No. 2319 *KEMPTON 25 February 1989 (soft)*

4.40 — PORTLANE HANDICAP CHASE £5,000
added (£3,460) 2m 4f (5)

601	23251U	AUGHAVOGUE 17 (D4)	J Edwards 7-11-10	T Morgan ●78
602	0-11112	FU'S LADY 50 (D2BF)	M Pipe 7-11-8	P Scudamore 77
603	004122	GEE-A 4 (D4)	G Hubbard 10-11-4	C O'Dwyer 77
604	11112F	DAVY'S WEIR 72 (D2)	J Gifford 9-10-12	Peter Hobbs 74
605	P2P21F	HERBERT UNITED 9	G Balding 10-10-7	W McFarland 76

Probable SP: 11-8 Fu's Lady, 2 Aughavogue, 7-2 Davy's Weir, 8 Gee-A, 14 Herbert United. **FAVOURITES: 2 1 0 — — 1 2.**
1988: Kelly's Boy 8-9-7 (A Adams) 3-1 N Gaselee 8 ran.

4.40 Handicap Chase 2½m (£3,460) 5 runners

242P02-36050004122 GEE-A (10-11-4) (G A Hubbard) br g Arapaho - Arctic Daisy by Arctic Slave 1986-87, 2¾m ch firm (Stratford), 2m 5f ch good (Huntingdon), 2m 5f ch soft (Huntingdon), 2½m ch good to soft (Huntingdon), 2½m ch good (Cheltenham), 2½m ch soft (Liverpool) 1988-89, 2½m ch good to soft (Huntingdon). £28,189.40 (£2,217.00).

Feb 21, Huntingdon, 2½m h'cap chase (0-55), good to soft, £2,322.00: 1 Rambling Song (9-11-2), 2 GEE-A (10-11-12, C O'Dwyer), **led until mistake fifth, ridden along eleventh, every chance 14th, mistake and one pace from two out.** (9 to 4 op 7 to 4) 3 Beau Derek (9-12-0),: 4 Ran. 8l, 25l. 5m 12.80s (a 16.80s). SR: 50/52/29.

Feb 9, Huntingdon, 3m h'cap chase (0-55), good, £2,385.00: 1 Rambling Song (9-10-12), 2 GEE-A (10-11-7, U Smyth,4*), **pressed leaders, ridden three out, rallied last, stayed on same pace.** (6 to 1 op 4 to 1) 3 General Chryson (9-10-12),: 8 Ran. 2½l, 1l, 1½l, dist. 6m 14.10s (a 25.10s).

Jan 26, Huntingdon, 2½m h'cap chase (0-55), good to soft, £2,217.00: 1 GEE-A (10-12-0, U Smyth), **made virtually all, ridden and drew clear after last.** (2 to 1 op 4 to 1 tchd 9 to 2) 2 Solar Cloud (7-10-12), 3 The Fruit (10-10-0),: 5 Ran. 3l, 15l, 12l. 5m 16.60s (a 20.60s).

3-YEAR RECORD			47Rn 7w 15p		
Yld: 18	4	6	Gd: 19	2	5	Fst: 10	1	3
2m-2m3f:	1	0	1	2m4f-2m7f:	34	7	11
3m-3m3f:	10	0	2	3m4f+ :	2	0	0

Probable

(3) GEE-A G. Hubbard 10–11.4 C. O'Dwyer

F.	F.	C.	C.
Prom	(4)	—	C√
★★	★★★		D√
			G√

This is an example of a handicap chase over a distance of 2½m. With the withdrawal of the top weight AUGHAVOGUE the field was reduced to only four runners. Applying the elimination method appropriate to handicaps we begin with the now top-weighed FU'S LADY. Trained by record-breaking Martin Pipe, FU'S LADY had made considerable progress during the season, winning four of her five races, but had been raised 26 lb by the handicapper since her second win. It would be a remarkable feat for her trainer to be able to continue her improvement and it appeared that having been defeated in her previous race (although not a handicap) the handicapper had at last got her measure.

The next horse in the handicap was GEE-A, a tough horse now competing in its twelfth race of the season. Its last three races, all at Huntingdon, showed admirable consistency, winning once and finishing second twice, the last of these only four days previously against the improved RAMBLING SONG, who had just completed a hat-trick of wins. GEE-A's consistency meant the handicapper would not relent his hold, but a reproduction of its recent form suggested GEE-A was still weighted to go close today. In accordance with the elimination method applied to handicaps, analysis could now stop with the remaining runners further down the handicap obviously inferior. Quickly scanning their form credentials this was confirmed. DAVY'S WEIR was a faller in its previous race 72 days earlier, and HERBERT UNITED, a former useful hurdler, was still only a novice at chasing and had also fallen in its previous race 9 days ago. Applying the formula, GEE-A was made the selection.

Result: 1st GEE-A (9–2) won by a distance.

It can be seen from the foregoing examples that although the selection formula provides an objective view of the factors upon which to make a judgement, throughout the selection process and form analysis there are vital stages where the selector has to bring personal subjective experience of racing to bear.

This is why successful selection of winners is an art as much as a science, and besides showing the fascination and skill of the horse-racing game, also demonstrates that no mechanical 'system' can ever be successful. This is shown also by the fact that bookmakers show no fear of systems and are indeed more than willing to work any system on behalf of a 'systems' backer.

There is no substitute for experience and observation, disciplined by logical principles.

13 CONCLUSION

The ultimate conclusion to selection is the race result. This is the moment of truth, the actual outcome of the race gives rise to the post-race questions: 'how' and 'why' did the horse win the race?

The question 'how' may be quickly answered; it is because on the day, at the time of the race the horse was the first to reach the winning-post! The question 'why', however, requires further examination, especially when selection is made on the understanding that all events are the subject of rational cause and effect.

The reasons can vary from the almost inexplicable to the incomprehensible but extremely rare. In the majority of instances, however, the reasons rest within the bounds of reasoned probability.

The elements identified in the selection formula are the most important factors affecting race results.

Reasoning probabilities therefore play a major role in successful prediction. By using the selection formula the backer is able to assess the issues objectively.

Only by the use of a truly objective method can the backer hope to remain detached in the act of betting. It is essential to the understanding of success for the backer to retain an unemotional detachment which will allow the selection process to be carried out in an attitude of balance and calm.

Intuitive powers and inspiration undoubtedly play a part in selection and betting, but should never replace reasoning. The intuitive insight can quickly become clouded in an emotional chase for financial reward.

Successful betting demands a cool calculated approach, best achieved by the objective method provided in the Selection Formula.

Although the formula is analysed and presented in this book to display only the abstract facts of the situation, imagination and experience translates this to an appreciation of the living events – the flesh and blood issues behind the names, numbers and symbols.

SUMMARY

Here are 10 commandments for the backer to obey:

1. NEVER BET WITH MONEY YOU CANNOT AFFORD TO LOSE.
2. NEVER BELIEVE BETTING IS SOMETHING FOR NOTHING.
3. NEVER RETAIN AN OPINION WHEN NEW EVIDENCE DEMANDS YOU CHANGE IT.
4. ALWAYS BET ON THE BEST – the best horses, jockeys and trainers.
5. ALWAYS BET WINNERS – winners win again.
6. ALWAYS BET ON RECENT FORM – this has the greatest bearing on results.
7. NEVER GET GREEDY WHEN YOU WIN – playing up winnings usually loses them.
8. NEVER CHASE LOSSES WHEN YOU LOSE – bookmakers depend upon punters trying to get their money back and losing more in the process.
9. NEVER LOSE YOUR CONFIDENCE – whatever else you might lose.
10. ALWAYS HAVE THE COURAGE TO BACK YOUR CONVICTIONS – yet if in doubt – don't bet.

    REMEMBER THERE'S ALWAYS ANOTHER RACE TOMORROW

You might break these rules some of the time and remain unscathed, but once you make a habit of doing so it can be guaranteed you will quickly end up wearing no shoes or socks.

REFERENCES

Computer Racing Form. (Racing Research, 21 Upper Green Lane, Hove Edge, Brighouse, West Yorkshire HD6 2NZ. Tel. 0484 710979.)

Daily Mail: daily – national newspaper recommended by the author for racing coverage. (Associated Newspapers Group, Northcliffe House, 2 Derry Street, Kensington, London W8 5TT. Tel. 071 938 6000.)

Directory of the Turf: annual – biographical backgrounds of trainers, jockeys, owners, etc. (Pacemaker Publication, Douglas Lodge, 9 Chevely Road, Newmarket, Suffolk. Tel. 0638 662745.)

Raceform Up-to-Date: weekly – official form book; Flat-racing edition and National Hunt edition. (Raceform Limited, Compton Newbury, Berks RG16 0NL. Tel. 0635 578 080.)

Raceform Up-to-Date Flat and National Hunt Annual: annually. (Published by Raceform Limited – see above.)

Racing Post: daily – national daily racing paper. (Cannon House, 120 Coombe Lane, Raynes Park, London SW20 0BA. Tel. 081 879 3377.)

The Racing Post Record: annually – record of every runner, trainers and jockeys plus other features, Flat and National Hunt edition. (Published by *Racing Post*.)

The Sporting Life: daily – national daily racing paper. (Mirror Group Newspapers Limited, Alexander House, 81/89 Farringdon Road, London EC1M 3LH. Tel. 071 831 1969.)

The Sporting Life Annual Form Books: Flat Results in Full 19—, National Hunt Results in Full 19—. (Published by Macdonald/Queen Anne Press, Maxwell House, 74 Worship Street, London EC2A 2EB.)

Timeform ('Black book'): weekly. (Timeform Publications, Timeform House, Northgate, Halifax, West Yorks HX1 1XE. Tel. 0422 63322.)

Timeform Racecards (Flat and National Hunt meetings): daily. (Published by Timeform Limited – see above.)

Racehorses of 19— (Flat): annually, March. (Published by Timeform Limited – see above.)

Chasers and Hurdlers (National Hunt): annually, October. (Published by Timeform Limited – see above.)

FURTHER READING

Aesculus Press: annuals in Flat and National Hunt-Course Form, Trainer Form, Directory of Racehorses, Pocket Companion. (P.O. Box 10, Oswestry, Shropshire SY 10 7QR. Tel. 0691 70426.)

Pacemaker: Update International, weekly racing magazine. (Haymarket Publications Ltd, Lancaster Gate, London W2 3LP. Tel. 071 402 4200.)

Racing Calendar: weekly – official Jockey Club record of entries; Stewards report; horses' official handicap rating, etc. (Weatherbys, Sanders Road, Wellingborough, Northants NN8 4BX. Tel. 0933 440077.)

Statistical Record: annual – details of sires' and dams' performances. (Published by Weatherbys – see above.)

Turf Newspapers: all racing publications. (18 Clarges Street, London W1Y 7PG. Tel. 071 499 4391.)

Superform: (weekly form book) Flat racing and National Hunt editions – results and interpretation of form. (Furlong Press, High Street, Shoreham, West Sussex BN4 5LH.)

Superform – Races and Racehorses: Form book Annual, Flat and National Hunt edition. See above.

INDEX

The numerals in **bold** type refer to the illustrations

Betting   50–63
  accumulative staking   62
  ante-post   71–2
  bookmaker's percentage   55–8
  odds   54–5, 58–9, 62–3
  on course market   66–7, 68–9
  prices (*see odds*)
  single selection   53
  stakes   61–3
  staking systems   53
  summary   61–2
  technique   50–2
  Tote odds   60–1
  value hints   60
Blinkers   4, 159–61, **160**
Bookmakers   64–72
  off-course   70–1
    cash   70
    credit   70–1
  on-course   64–8
    rails   64–8
    Silver Ring   68
    Tatts   68
Breeding   161–4

Class   2–3, 114–17, 200
Conditions   3–4, 118–58, 200–1
  courses   4, 129–34
  Distance   3, 118–20, 200
  draw   4, 137–9, 201

fences   135–7
Going   3
Weight   3
Courses   4, 129–34, 138–9
  Flat racing   131–3, 138–9
  National Hunt   134

Distance   3
Draw   4, 137–9, 201

Fitness   2, 101–13, 199
  by looks   108–9, **102–3**
  date of last run tables   109–13
  seven-day   104–8
Flat-Race horse   6–7
  all-age   16
  amateur   33
  apprentice   32–3
  auction   30–1
  claiming   31–2
  Classic race trials   29
  Classics   28–9
  level weight   11–14
  nursery handicaps   25–6
  selling   30
  three-year-old   13–16
  two-year-old   12–13
Flat Racing Season   5–6
Form   2, 73–100, 198

changing   78–9, 85–6
collateral   95
commentaries   86–9
date of   75–7
favourites   99
for age   90–1
grades of   73–4
handicap   94–5
National Hunt   91–4
Proof of   74–5
ratings   98–9
speed   97–8
summary   99–100
time   95–7
winning   77
Form Book   45–7, **46**
Form Sheets   47

Going   3, 200–1

Handicaps   22–7, 92, 93–4, 94,
        127–9
chases   26, 93–4
form   94–5
hurdler   26, 92–3
nursery   25–6
principles   22–5
summary   27
weightscale   127–9

Jockeyship   4, 139–58, 201
Flat-race jockeys   143–53
    W. Carson   144, **145**
    S. Cauthen   144–8, **145**
    R. Cochrane   149–50, **146**
    P. Eddery   148–9, **146**
    W. Newnes   151
    J. Reid   151–2
    M. Roberts   150, **147**
    B. Rouse   152
    W. Swinburn   150–1, **147**
National Hunt jockeys   153–8
    H. Davies   156–7, **155**
    R. Dunwoody   153–6, **154**
    M. Dwyer   156
    B. Powell   157, **155**
    P. Scudamore   153, **154**
    S. Smith-Eccles   157–8, **158**

National Hunt horses   8–10
National Hunt races   11–12, 17–21,
        30, 32–5
amateur   33
apprentice   32–3
condition chases   19–20
condition hurdles   19
flat   34–5
handicap chases   20–2, 26
handicap hurdles   26–7
hunter chases   33–4
level weight   11–12
novice chases   20–1
novice hurdles   17–19
selling   30
National Hunt Season   7–8
Newspapers   37–45
Daily   37–40, **38–9**
Daily racing   40–5, **41–4**

Owners   190–5
K. Abdullah   191
H.H. Aga Khan   191
Al Maktoum family   192
Lady Beaverbrook   193
H.M. Queen Elizabeth II   192–3
Lord Howard de Walden   193
R. Sangster   193
C. St. George   194

Selection Formula using   197–249
examples   204–49
keynote   198
modalities   199–201
race selection   196
star ratings summary   203

Flat Race Season 1989   205–27
  Winners
    Rock City (7–4)   205–7
    Intimidate (5–2)   207–8
    Allasdale (2–1)   209–11
    Old Vic (6–4)   211–13
    Piquant (9–4)   213–15
    Zawahir (9–4)   216–18
    A Little Precious
      (Evens)   218–19
    Kabcast (Evens)   219–21
    Top Dream (14–1)   222–5
    Winning Gallery (10–3)
      225–7
National Hunt Season   228–49
  Winners
    Dominion Treasure (5–2)
      228–9
    King's Harvest (7–2)   230–1
    Waterloo Boy (6–4)   232–3
    Slalom (9–4)   234–5
    Yahoo (5–1)   236–9
    Summons (9–2)   239–41
    Dawn Blade (2–1)   242–4
    Gentleman Angler (9–1)
      244–6
    Viking Rocket (5–1)   246–8
    Gee-A (9–2)   248–9

Timeform   47–9, **48**
Trainers   165–90
  Flat Race   167–74
    H. Cecil   167, **170**
    L. Cumani   167–8, **170**

J. Dunlop   168, **171**
  G. Harwood   168–9, **171**
  D. Hern   169, **172**
  B. Hills   169–74, **172**
  M. Stoute   174, **173**
  A. Stewart   174, **173**
National Hunt   175–87
  G. B. Balding   175, **177**
  M. H. Easterby   175, **177**
  D. Elsworth   175–6, **178**
  J. Fitzgerald   176, **178**
  T. Forster   176–83, **179**
  J. Gifford   183, **179**
  N. Henderson   183–4, **180**
  D. Nicholson   184, **180**
  M. Pipe   184–5, **181**
  Mrs. J. Pitman   185, **181**
  G. Richards   185–6, **182**
  W. A. Stephenson   186, **182**
  F. Walwyn   186–7, **183**
Records   187–90
  jockey engagement   190
  meetings   188–9
  racecourse   187
  significant travelling   189–90
  time of season   188
  Visors   4, 159–61, **160**

Weight   3, 122–9
  allowances   129
  for age   124–6
  penalties   124–7
  scale   127–9
  sex allowance   123–4